Cognitive Bases of Second Language Fluency

Exploring fluency from multiple vantage points that together constitute a cognitive science perspective, this book examines research in second language acquisition and bilingualism that points to promising avenues for understanding and promoting second language fluency. *Cognitive Bases of Second Language Fluency* covers essential topics such as units of analysis for measuring fluency, the relation of second language fluency to general cognitive fluidity, social and motivational contributors to fluency, and neural correlates of fluency. The author provides clear and accessible summaries of foundational empirical work on speech production, automaticity, lexical access, and other issues of relevance to second language acquisition theory. *Cognitive Bases of Second Language Fluency* is a valuable reference for scholars in SLA, cognitive psychology, and language teaching, and it can also serve as an ideal textbook for advanced courses in these fields.

Norman Segalowitz is Professor of Psychology at Concordia University in Montreal, Canada, and the Associate Director of the Centre for the Study of Learning and Performance. He has published widely on cognitive psychological issues in second language acquisition and functioning in adults.

Cognitive Science and Second Language Acquisition Series
Peter Robinson, Editor

Cognitive Bases of Second Language Fluency

Norman Segalowitz

Routledge
Taylor & Francis Group

NEW YORK AND LONDON

First published 2010
by Routledge
270 Madison Avenue, New York, NY 10016

Simultaneously published in the UK
by Routledge
2 Park Square, Milton Park, Abingdon, Oxon OX14 4RN

*Routledge is an imprint of the Taylor & Francis Group
an informa business*

© 2010 Taylor & Francis

Typeset in Sabon by Glyph International
Printed and bound in the United States of America on acid-free
paper by Walsworth Publishing Company, Marceline, MO

Library of Congress Cataloging in Publication Data
Segalowitz, Norman.
Cognitive bases of second language fluency/Norman Segalowitz.
p. cm. – (Cognitive science and second language acquisition)
Includes bibliographical references.
1. Second language acquisition. 2. Language and languages–Study
and teaching. I. Title.
P118.2.S455 2010
418.001′9–dc22   2009048689

ISBN 13: 978-0-8058-5661-3 (hbk)
ISBN 13: 978-0-8058-5662-0 (pbk)
ISBN 13: 978-0-203-85135-7 (ebk)

Dedicated to the memory of
Wallace E. Lambert (1922–2009)
and
Alexandr Romanovich Luria (1902–1977)

Contents

Illustrations

Figures

Tables

Series Editor's Preface

The Cognitive Science and Second Language Acquisition (CS&SLA) series is designed to provide accessible and comprehensive coverage of the links between basic concepts, and findings, in cognitive science (CS) and second language acquisition (SLA) in a systematic way. Taken together, books in the series should combine to provide a comprehensive overview of the conceptual and methodological intersects between these two fields. This means the books in the series can be read alone, or (more profitably) in combination. The field of SLA is related to, but distinct from, linguistics, applied linguistics, cognitive psychology, and education. However, while a great many published book series address the link between SLA and educational concerns, SLA and linguistics, and SLA and applied linguistics, currently no series exists which explores the relationship between SLA and cognitive science. Research findings and theoretical constructs from cognitive science have become increasingly influential upon SLA research in recent years. Consequently there is great reason to think that future SLA research, and research into its educational applications, will be increasingly influenced by concerns addressed in CS and its subdisciplines. The books in the CS&SLA series are intended to facilitate this interdisciplinary understanding, and are grouped into four domains: (1) knowledge representation; (2) cognitive processing; (3) language development; and (4) individual differences.

Norman Segalowitz addresses the goals of the CS&SLA series admirably well in the present book, *Cognitive Bases of Second Language Fluency*, by putting the study of fluency in a broad cognitive science perspective. While centrally concerned with the second of the domains of cognitive science just described, *cognitive processing*, the implications of research into second language fluency for our understanding of *knowledge representation, language development*, and *individual differences* is made very clear. Beginning with his stated goal, "to locate the idea of fluency in a context that is much broader than what people usually think about when considering fluency in a language other than their native tongue," in the first chapter Norman Segalowitz describes the multidimensional nature of the construct of fluency, its place at the intersect of different subdisciplines of cognitive science, and describes a dynamic framework for "thinking systematically about fluency" that locates it at this intersect. Throughout the book, as each chapter focuses on a particular aspect of fluency, such as units of analysis for measuring fluency, its relation to general cognitive fluidity, social and motivational contributors to fluency, and neural correlates of fluency, the initially presented framework is elaborated. Stimulating connections are made between each of these areas as the book builds impressively to the concluding chapter and agenda for research presented there.

While elaborating his framework for conceptualizing, operationalizing, and researching fluency, Norman Segalowitz presents many clear and accessible summaries of foundational empirical work on speech production, automaticity, lexical access, and other issues of relevance to second language acquisition theory, and theory-based proposals for language pedagogy. This will be a very important contribution to the study of second language fluency, placing it in full cognitive science perspective, and it goes well beyond anything previously published on this topic.

Peter Robinson
Series Editor

Dedication and Acknowledgments

This book is dedicated to the memory of two special people, both pioneers in the field of language research, whom I had the very good fortune to have as mentors while still an undergraduate student—social psychologist and psycholinguist, Wallace E. Lambert, and neuropsychologist and aphasiologist, Alexandr Romanovich Luria.

Lambert (1922–2009), who passed away just weeks before completion of the final draft of this book, was my undergraduate thesis supervisor (along with G. Richard Tucker) at McGill University. Lambert was a founding father of the social psychology of bilingualism and second language acquisition. In addition to his many ground-breaking contributions, he was an inspiration to all his students in a way that was perhaps best captured by Anwar Dil in his summary of the impact Lambert had on all who worked with him:

> The overall meaning of Lambert's work can perhaps be grasped best in terms of his aspiration to help create a climate of human life in which people are no longer restricted and bound by barriers of language and culture. In particular, he has sought to bring the benefits of bilingual and bicultural life within easy reach of common people and large sectors of populations rather than letting them remain the exclusive monopoly of the privileged few. In this sense Lambert is a crusader for the greater freedom of human beings to move freely and without discrimination across language and culture boundaries. Among the major theoretical generalizations that have emerged from his psycholinguistic experiments to date, the following can be identified as the broad outlines of his credo: that language barriers are not difficult to circumvent; that bilingualism does not imply various types of handicaps, but rather offers assets and enrichments of all sorts; that a person can comfortably become bilingual and bicultural; that one's attitudes toward the other group whose language is being learnt play an important role in language acquisition and that such attitudes both affect and are affected by one's motivation to learn the other language; that the study of language

through an analysis of bilingualism is one of the most instructive ways of determining the cybernetic and neurophysiological functions of the human brain; that since styles of using language often engender social prejudice and unfair discrimination, safeguards against such discrimination must be built into educational, social, and political systems; and that the study of bilingualism as a person and societal phenomenon, especially in situations of conflict, is a critical area of psycholinguistic and sociolinguistic inquiry.

(1972, pp. xiii–xiv)

Luria (1902–1977) was my mentor during a year I spent in Moscow as an exchange student, while I was still an undergraduate. Luria, a major pioneering figure in twentieth-century aphasiology, was also an inspiration to all who worked with him, imparting to students and colleagues a spirit of interdisciplinarity, an appreciation of the need to be adaptive and inventive in order to conduct good research, and above all always showing deep respect and compassion for the individual who is the focus of study. One gets a measure of the man from this passage in his autobiography:

If one wants to understand the brain foundations for psychological activity, one must be prepared to study both the brain and the system of activity in as great detail as contemporary science allows. In many cases important clues can be gotten from specialists in related fields. This was true in our studies of neurolinguistics. It was true as well in our studies of the disturbance of memory and problem solving. But in each of these cases, we found that we must use the work of specialists as a starting point, modifying tasks and theories as we want, because the conditions of clinical work do not permit the well-controlled application of many experimental methods. And in dealing with patients, we must never forget that an individual human life is at stake, not a statistical abstraction which, on the average, supports a theory.

(Luria, 1979, p. 173)

Many people contributed directly and indirectly to the writing of this book. First and foremost, I would like to thank Elizabeth Gatbonton, my wife and closest colleague, for her unwavering support, patience, encouragement, and especially for her ability to listen and give sage advice (and to do so ever so tactfully!) on all drafts throughout the whole process. Many of the ideas in this book have grown out of discussions I have had with her over the years based on her own insights and original theoretical and research-based ideas regarding L2 pedagogy and L2 acquisition. Without her support and input, this book simply would not have been possible. I would also like to thank our two daughters. Nina provided encouragement and support in many ways for which I am grateful. Miri also provided stimulating and challenging input during our many discussions about interdisciplinarity, as we explored how some of the ideas in this book might apply to areas outside second language acquisition.

I especially want to thank Pavel Trofimovich, my colleague and close friend, who provided thorough and constructive feedback on a full, earlier draft of this book. His encouragement and support throughout were invaluable. I also want to thank Sid Segalowitz, who, in addition to reading sections of this manuscript, has for decades been a close colleague, sounding board, and research collaborator on many of the topics discussed in this book. Several other people also provided feedback on specific sections of the manuscript and I am happy for the opportunity to acknowledge their input. These include Nivja de Jong, Paul Meara, Yu Miao, and Natalie Phillips. I thank all these people for their constructive feedback. Of course, I take full responsibility for any errors that remain.

Over the years, my professional life has been enriched by friendships, research collaborations, and conversations with students and with many scholars in SLA and other research areas—people whose ideas have helped to shape my own thinking and intellectual development in various ways and to whom I owe a debt of gratitude. The list is too long to present here in full, but I would especially like to mention the following: Jeanette Altarriba, Phil Cohen, Roberto de Almeida, Zoltán Dörnyei, Dan Dewey, Jane Dywan, Nick Ellis, Barbara Freed, Elizabeth Gatbonton, Jan Hulstijn, Judith Kroll, Gary Libben, Patsy Lightbown, Paul Meara, Renata Meuter, Michel Paradis, Aneta Pavelenko, Natalie Phillips, Diane Poulin-Dubois, Andrew Ryder, Sid Segalowitz, Carolyn Turner, Pavel Trofimovich, Dick Tucker, and Alison Wray.

I also wish to thank Peter Robinson for his support, encouragement, and helpful suggestions in his role as editor of this series. I also thank Ivy Ip of Routledge/Taylor & Francis Group for her invaluable help and her patience.

Finally, I would also like to thank my colleagues and the students in Concordia University's Applied Linguistics Research Group and in the Centre for the Study of Learning and Performance. I especially thank Randall Halter, our Research Associate in the CSLP, and Maia Yarymowich, Research Coordinator for our language and health projects; both provided invaluable help during the process of writing this book.

1 Fluency, Second Language Acquisition, and Cognitive Science

For euen as a hauke flieth not hie with one wing;
euen so a man reacheth not to excellency with one tong.
(Roger Ascham, 1571/1967, p. 151)

This book is about second language fluency. Its goal is to locate the idea of fluency in a context that is much broader than what people usually think about when considering fluency in a language other than their native tongue. This book examines fluency from multiple vantage points that together constitute a cognitive science perspective. In doing so, it examines research in second language acquisition and bilingualism that point to promising avenues for understanding—and ultimately helping to promote—fluent second language skills. This introductory chapter provides an overview of the volume as a whole. It presents five anchor questions that the volume will address, and then summarizes the main take-home message about fluency.

Why Study Fluency?

Roger Ascham (1515–1568), cited above, was tutor to Queen Elizabeth I. He recognized that knowledge of languages beyond one's mother tongue was important for gaining access to the intellectual and artistic wealth of Europe, and indeed the rest of the world. Ascham emphasized the need for high-level mastery of these languages and wrote at length on how to achieve it. Many of his suggestions would be regarded as outdated and inappropriate nowadays, but the need to be proficient in more than one language remains, if anything, greater today than it was in Ascham's time, even if the reasons for it have changed. Today, for example, there is an unprecedented mobility of populations, a global scope in communications, and an ever-widening economic integration across the planet, all driving the need for bilingualism (and multilingualism). Indeed, it is believed that nowadays most people in the world *do* know more than one language (Tucker, 1997). Dewaele, Housen, and Wei (2003), for example, point out that there are in the order of 6,000 languages in the world but only about 200 countries, most with different national languages, and therefore most people likely have to function in more than one language. Often, people use one local language for their daily business, another regional or national language for economic and political participation at a wider level, and a world language (English, French, Chinese, etc.) for communicating on yet a larger plane. And therein lies an interesting challenge.

Although most people may have some knowledge of at least one second language (as is customary in the literature, any language beyond the first, including third, fourth, etc. languages, will also be referred to here as L2), they nevertheless are rarely able to use it with the same—or even close to the same—level of skill as their first language (L1). Not only is knowledge of the L2 weaker, but typically people are markedly less fluent using what L2 knowledge they do have. There is a fluency gap. This fluency gap is often a source of frustration and regret; most people would like to be more skilled in their weaker language(s). Unfortunately, most only ever achieve limited fluency, although there are, of course, many notable exceptions. Ultimately, if something is to be done about improving fluency, there will need to be a greater understanding of what underlies such fluency gaps, why the gaps are so difficult to overcome, and what conditions are best for reducing them.

These questions need to be addressed at two levels. First, we need to find out why *within-individual* fluency gaps exist. That is, if people are fluent in their L1, why is it often so difficult for them to become fluent in another language? After all, it would appear that they bring the same basic intelligence, emotional, and personality traits as well as the same basic cognitive and perceptual abilities to the learning situation, whether it be for the L1 or L2. Second, we need to understand why *between-individual* differences exist in the magnitude of such fluency gaps. Some people appear to be much more successful than others in using their L2, whereas the range of individual differences in the L1 is much narrower, nearly everyone seeming to have little difficulty becoming relatively fluent. How can we explain such within and between individual differences? Answering these questions surely will help in the long run in identifying practical steps to reduce unwanted fluency gaps. There is, however, a more basic, deceptively simple yet pressing question that must be addressed first—What do we actually mean by the term *fluency*?

On this point, the literature is at times confusing and disappointing. There are a multitude of meanings for *fluency* as the term is used in English. Anyone reading the scientific literature will quickly find that researchers provide many different ways of operationalizing what they mean by the term fluency, as will be seen shortly. Moreover, there is no generally accepted model or framework to allow one to think about fluency in a systematic way, although there are some proposals that provide promising elements for such a framework. It is the aim of this volume to offer a perspective on fluency and a framework for thinking about it that will, it is hoped, lead to new insights about why fluency in an L2 is often so difficult to achieve and why there exist such large individual differences in fluency achievement. Accomplishing this will require bringing together several literatures. By doing so, it will be possible to define and operationalize fluency for research purposes, to bring a cognitive science perspective to bear on fluency, and to elaborate a framework for conducting research on it. In the sections that follow, these three goals are discussed briefly. This is followed by a presentation of five anchor questions that will shape the rest of the volume.

What is L2 Fluency?

Answering the question *What is L2 fluency?* will involve examining qualitative definitions of fluency that correspond to intuitive and subjective perceptions of a speaker's L2 performance. It will also involve looking at how researchers and language performance evaluators have more precisely operationally and quantitatively defined fluency. In the discussion that follows, L2 speakers are assumed to exhibit normal fluency in their L1, and that any L2 dysfluencies relative to L1 fluency reflect the normal challenges of using an L2, not neurophysiological challenges of a clinical nature (see chapters in Ardila & Ramos, 2007, for discussion of clinical dysfluencies in bilinguals).

Qualitative Issues in Defining Fluency

To begin with, consider the following basic question: *What does it mean, in ordinary language, to say that someone is fluent in an L2?* This question is more complex than might appear at first glance. Kaponen and Riggenbach (2000) discuss some of the historical origins of the word *fluency* in English and its equivalents in other languages. For example, they report (p. 6) that for the English word *fluently*, Germans tend to use *fliessent* and *flüssig* (runningly and flowingly, respectively), Russians use *beglo* (runningly), and Finnish speakers use *sujuvasti* (in a flowing or liquid manner). As a noun, French uses *aisance* (ease), and Swedish uses *flyt* (flow). Kaponen and Riggenbach point out that in these and other languages, including English, there is a conceptual metaphor underlying the meaning of fluency, namely that "language is motion" (p. 7). As will become evident in the rest of this volume, this metaphor also underlies much of the scientific research on fluency. Additional discussions of the meanings of the word *fluency* can also be found in Chambers (1997), Hieke (1985), Kormos and Dénes (2004), R. Schmidt (1992), and Wood (2001), and in the edited volume by Riggenbach (2000).

This focus on the movement-like or fluidity aspects of speech seems to correspond to how most laypeople use the term *fluency*. Of course, in everyday speech, and in some research studies too, people sometimes intend something entirely different by the term *fluency*. For example, *fluency* is sometimes used to refer to the ability to express any idea in the L2 that one can also express in the L1, or to the ability to speak with little or no accent in the L2, or to be able to use a large vocabulary, or to speak with few grammatical errors. Indeed, at times one even hears *fluency* used with respect to the ability to read novels, to give extemporaneous speeches, to appreciate poetry or other difficult material in the target language, to use the language to counsel someone on a sensitive topic or to provide accurate translations to and from the language. In short, there are a very large number of behaviors that people might have in mind when thinking about fluency. Clearly, the natural language term *fluency* is not well defined. Indeed, the various behaviors associated with fluency may actually belong to different categories that, for research purposes, will need to be carefully distinguished from each other.

As mentioned above, a theme underlying the meaning of the word *fluency* is the conceptual metaphor *language is motion*. This metaphor focuses on those aspects of speech having to do with its fluidity or flow-ing quality. There is evidence that people do think about fluency in this way. For example, Freed (2000) asked six native speakers of French, three of whom were French teachers, to evaluate the fluency of student learners of French, to explain the basis for their observations, and to rank the importance of potential features of fluency listed for them by the researcher. More than half of the judges selected "rate of speech," "smoother speech with fewer false starts," "fewer pauses/hesitancies," and "better grammar and vocabulary" (p. 254) as critical to their idea of fluency. As can be seen, three of the four refer to the fluidity of the speech. Freed also found, of course, that individual judges sometimes departed from using fluidity as the basis for their fluency judgments, but overall she did find that fluidity was the predominant underlying idea.

Fillmore (1979), in a classic paper on the topic, identified four kinds of fluency that people may be thinking about when making judgments about fluency. One is the ability to talk at length with a minimum of pauses. The second is the ability to package the message easily into "semantically dense" sentences without recourse to lots of filler material (for example, "you know," "the thing is that," etc.). The third is the ability to speak appropriately in different kinds of social contexts and situations, meeting the special communicative demands each may have. The fourth is the ability to use the language creatively and imaginatively by expressing ideas in new ways, to use humor, to make puns, to use metaphors, and so on. Although each of these four types of fluency may seem to belong to a different category, one can argue that they also reflect the feature of fluidity or flow. All of them lose their force as examples of fluent language use if not delivered with appropriate timing within the ever-evolving communicative situation; in this sense all four, as examples of kinds of fluency, are based on a temporal flow in the use of language.

Quantitative Issues in Defining Fluency

Researchers have had to find practical ways to define fluency so that it can be precisely measured. As will be discussed in Chapter 2, researchers have proposed many quantitative measures for fluency. These include speech features such as speech rate, hesitation and pause phenomena, density of clause usage, and combinations of these, among others. While many of these seem like obvious candidate features to use for measuring fluency, there can be problems. For example, regarding pauses and hesitations, Luoma (2004) makes an important observation about a problem often encountered in the search for quantitative measures of fluency. It is natural to want to think about fluency as being characterized by an absence of undue hesitations or excessive pauses, etc. However, whereas hesitations and pauses are amenable to quantitative, physical measurements of the speaker's speech, the notions of "undue" and "excessive" are more qualitative and subjective, and they tell us more perhaps about the listener than about the speaker (Luoma, 2004, p. 88).

Kormos (2006), in her review, provided a table summarizing 10 measures of fluency that have been proposed in the literature (see Table 1.1; see also R. Ellis & Barkhuizen, 2005, especially Chapter 7). Examination of Kormos' list reveals that fluidity is *the* predominant feature of fluency in the minds of researchers, but even here we see that there are many different ways of conceptualizing what that means exactly. Fluidity, it would seem, is itself a multidimensional construct and so pinning down precisely what *fluency* means is clearly going to be a challenge! One goal of this volume is to suggest that, in order to meet this challenge, it might be useful to think about fluency in a way that grounds it in a larger context extending beyond the audible aspects language.

So far, we have been looking at fluency in a relatively atheoretical manner, focusing on intuitive and practical approaches to its definition. If work on fluency is to become the object of focused scientific inquiry, then fluency phenomena need to be seen through a lens that links them to the wider context of scientific inquiry into the nature of language. This brings us to the cognitive science perspective.

A Cognitive Science Approach to Fluency

As the title of this book suggests, the focus here is the *cognitive bases* of fluency, in keeping with the cognitive science perspective of the series in which this volume appears. It is natural to ask then, what would be a cognitive science perspective on fluency? How would such a perspective differ from other perspectives, and what is the particular advantage of a cognitive science approach? We turn briefly to these questions now.

Stainton (2006, p. xiii), writing in a volume that addressed major issues in contemporary cognitive science, defines cognitive science as

Table 1.1 Overview of Measures of Fluency, Based on Kormos (2006, p. 163, Table 8.2)

Measure (units)	Definition
(1) Speech rate (syllables/minute)	60 sec./min. times the total number of syllables divided by total time (including pauses) in seconds
(2) Articulation rate (syllables/minute)	60 sec./min. times the total number of syllables divided by total time (excluding pauses) in seconds
(3) Phonation-time ratio (percentage ratio)	Percentage ratio of time speaking to time to take the whole speech sample
(4) Mean length of runs (number of syllables)	Average number of syllables between pauses (period of silence ≥ 250 ms)
(5) Silent pauses per minute (number of silent pauses/minute)	60 sec./min. times total number of pauses (periods of silence > 200 ms) divided by the total time speaking in seconds
(6) Mean length of pauses (seconds)	Mean length of all pauses (periods of silence > 200 ms)
(7) Filled pauses per minute (filled pauses/minute)	60 sec./min. times total number of filled pauses (pauses filled with uhm, mm, er, etc.) divided by the total time speaking in seconds
(8) Dysfluencies per minute (dysfluencies/minute)	60 sec./min. times total number of dysfluencies (repetitions, restarts, repairs) divided by the total time speaking in seconds
(9) Pace (stressed words/minute)	Number of stressed words per minute
(10) Space (ratio of stressed words/total words)	Proportion of stressed words to total number of words

"the interdisciplinary attempt to understand the mind" involving four branches or groups of disciplines: (a) behavioral and brain sciences—including psycholinguistics, neuroscience, and cognitive psychology; (b) social sciences—including anthropology, sociology, and sociolinguistics; (c) formal disciplines—including logic, computer science, linguistics, and artificial intelligence; and finally (d) philosophy of mind. For Stainton, the "hallmark of cognitive science, in brief, is that it draws on the methods and results of all these branches" (2006, p. xiii). A cognitive science perspective on L2 fluency, then, would be one that looks at fluency from the vantage point of all the disciplines mentioned above.

A skeptical reader may well ask how such a multidisciplinary approach could yield a coherent account of L2 fluency, one that would be more than an unrelated hodgepodge of different points of view. The long answer to this question might go something like this.

Fluency in a second language is an observable characteristic of real-time speech behavior. This behavior reflects the execution of the neurological and muscular mechanisms that a speaker has developed over an extended period of time through socially contextualized, communicative activities. The operation of these mechanisms reflects the cognitive and emotional states of the speaker at the time of speaking. Fluency thus reflects the developmental history and the current state of the speaker. Because of this, fluency in communication matters. Fluency conveys information that may be important to the listener over and above the primary message encoded in the semantics and syntax of the speaker's utterances. Only by taking a cognitive science approach, capitalizing on the variety and richness of its many component disciplines, can one hope to capture in a coherent perspective all the relevant factors that jointly determine fluency at any given moment.

The short answer is this.

> Because fluency is a multidimensional construct, the multidisciplinarity afforded by a cognitive science perspective is indispensable. The intersection of the contributing disciplines will be the locus of a cognitive science perspective on fluency.

From this perspective, one way to think about the goal of this book is that it aims to find and explore that area of intersection (see Figure 1.1).

A cognitive science approach to fluency will differ from most single-discipline treatments of the topic in two important ways. First, a cognitive science approach will be broader, encompassing phenomena usually not covered by any single-discipline approach. Second, a cognitive science approach will (ideally) be more integrative than a single-discipline approach insofar as it aims to bring together the insights of its various component disciplines, in order to reveal a more global view that cannot be achieved by any one discipline alone. Of course, at this time a fully developed cognitive science approach to L2 fluency does not exist. It is hoped that this volume will provide a framework for developing such an approach. This brings us to the next topic—the search for a framework for thinking about fluency.

A Framework for Thinking about L2 Fluency

There does not yet exist a fully developed framework—cognitive science based or otherwise—for thinking systematically about fluency. This is disappointing. Frameworks for thinking about issues can be most useful. A framework helps to integrate results, at least to clarify connections in what otherwise might appear to be disparate research findings. A good framework for fluency would prompt new questions in a systematic way and stimulate thinking that goes beyond simply looking for practical answers to questions about language training; it would guide the search

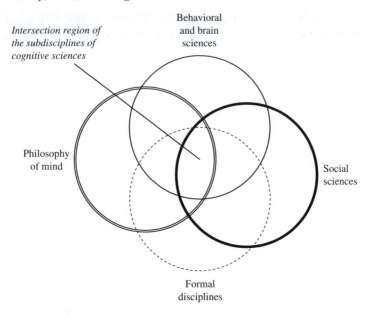

Figure 1.1 The primary questions and phenomena that define a cognitive science approach to L2 fluency are located in the overlap region, where each circle can be thought of as representing the range of fluency-relevant questions and phenomena that are the focus of the individual subdisciplines of cognitive science.

for answers grounded in theory. Finally, a good framework holds the seeds of its own destruction insofar as it is able to raise questions that will eventually make clear its own limitations and point in the direction of a new framework that will replace it. Although such a framework is still lacking, there does exist, nevertheless, a promising starting point for one, and this will be described now.

Blueprint of the L2 Speaker

One very well-known model for thinking about speaking provides a good starting point for thinking about L2 fluency. This is De Bot's (1992) bilingual adaptation of Levelt's (1989, updated in 1999) "blueprint" of the unilingual speaker, which has been widely cited by many authors writing on L2 speech issues. Levelt's "blueprint" is important because it provides, in graphical form, a summary of what could reasonably be called the consensus view of the linguistic, psycholinguistic, and cognitive issues underlying the act of speaking. In his paper, De Bot (1992) discussed the implications of Levelt's (1989) blueprint of the unilingual speaker for understanding the L2 speaker. De Bot accepted the main tenets of Levelt's blueprint and advanced the discussion by pointing out where in the blueprint one can locate points of specific relevance to L2 use.

Many papers in the literature on L2 speech performance cite the 1989 version of Levelt's blueprint and De Bot's (1992) adaptation of it. The following discussion is based on Levelt's 1999 update of the blueprint, integrating De Bot's observations of L2 speech issues into it (see also Kormos, 2006, Chapter 9). Figure 1.2 below presents this updated and integrated blueprint. In addition, the figure shows specifically where L2 fluency issues of special interest might arise.

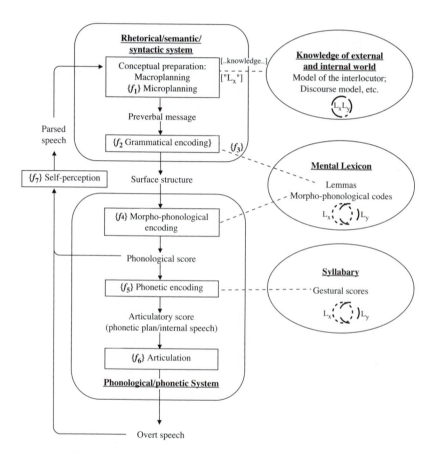

Figure 1.2 Model of the L2 speaker, adapted from Levelt's (1999, Figure 4.1) "blueprint" of the monolingual speaker and incorporating De Bot's (1992) points regarding the bilingual speaker. The dotted and dashed L_x and L_y circles refer to how information pertinent to languages (or registers) x and y are thought to be related to each other, where partially overlapping and fully overlapping circles indicate partially distinct and undifferentiated systems, respectively. ["L_x"] refers to information that tags language-specific identity (i.e., this piece of knowledge is linked in some way to language $_x$). The $\{f\}$ symbols (for *f*luency vulnerability points) refer to potentially critical points where underlying processing difficulties could be associated with L2 speech dysfluencies (see text).

The blueprint shown in Figure 1.2 starts with the speaker generating something to say, based on his or her encyclopedic knowledge of the external world and, importantly, knowledge about the interlocutor's internal state of mind (the *Theory of Mind* that people have about other people; Gallagher & Frith, 2003; Wimmer & Perner, 1983), plus knowledge about discourse conventions, etc. This first step—planning what to say—is referred to by Levelt (1999, p. 90) as *macroplanning*. The encyclopedic knowledge source supporting macroplanning is represented as an ellipse (as are all knowledge sources in the blueprint), located at the top right of the figure. Levelt allows here for the monolingual's knowledge about different speech registers to enter into the act of message creation, for example, about whether the message to be created will be located in the context of formal or casual discourse. De Bot suggests, consistent with Paradis (2004), that selecting which language to use is similar to choosing a speech register (e.g., formal versus casual speech) to use, and this choice will be determined by knowledge about the sociopragmatic aspects of the situation. Thus, information about language choice becomes part of the information package, along with all other encyclopedic information, that is used in the macroplanning stage.

Even though the encyclopedic knowledge source provides information about the choice of language or register choice (as shown in the figure, L_x versus L_y), both Levelt (1989, 1999) and De Bot (1992) nevertheless assume that the information in the encyclopedic and social knowledge source is not organized in language specific terms. For example, the knowledge that London is the capital of England is not held in a specifically English or French knowledge store but retrieval of this knowledge may be accompanied by information that the conversation happens to be taking place in French, so that at some point in the creation of the message, London will be expressed as *Londres* rather than as *London*. The choice of *Londres* over *London* would reflect a microplanning event that is realized at a later stage when the surface form of the utterance is constructed. The idea that encyclopedic information is not differentiated by language is represented in the figure by two fully overlapping dashed circles, one each for L_x and one for L_y but appearing as one circle only because of the complete overlap. No L2-specific fluency issues arise at this macroplanning level because the processes involved are presumed to be non-language specific and, for this reason, language mastery level cannot impact on how well macroplanning processes are carried out.

The implications of macroplanning and microplanning for fluency have begun to be explored. In the L1 literature on this topic, researchers have attempted to identify temporal cycles in the speech production that reflect macroplanning and that can be distinguished from the effects of microplanning. For example, Roberts and Kirsner (2000) examined the spontaneous speech of nine native speakers of English speaking about themselves for about five minutes. The speech was analyzed in terms of two measures of fluency—the proportion of successive 200 ms windows that was speech, and a measure based on pause-speech units. The researchers also identified topic shifts in the participants' speech as a measure of topic structure of the discourse. With these measures, they were able to conduct a time series analysis of fluency to determine whether there were periodic cycles of fluency in the speech, and whether such patterns were related to the topic structure of the discourse. The results indicated that fluency decreased during topic shifts. This was consistent with the idea that macroplanning takes place at the time of a topic shift (planning what to say for the next topic segment), and this activity takes resources away from the microplanning required to actually turn thoughts into speech. Roberts and Kirsner concluded that speech "does not become fluent until the macroplanning process is complete and the system's resources are available solely to speech preparation and production processes" (p. 153). Clearly, this can have implications for L2 fluency. The more macroplanning a communicative situation requires, the more vulnerable the L2 speech will be to dysfluencies because of the diversion of processing resources. This means that L2 users who have difficulty carrying out microplanning (speech preparation and execution) in an automatic fashion will need the extra time to make sure that macroplanning has been adequately completed before attempting to speak. It appears that temporal cycles in L2 speech production have not yet been studied using the techniques described in Roberts and Kirsner (2000). However, research discussed in Chapter 2 by Tavakoli and Skehan (2005) provides support for this conclusion.

As mentioned above, however, information about language choice is part of the package of information that guides the actual formulation of the message. Acting on the choice happens at a subsequent *microplanning* stage, a process that ends with the formulation of a preverbal message. Microplanning, like macroplanning, is conceptual in nature and is not simply a lexical process (putting thoughts into words). However, microplanning is far narrower than macroplanning insofar as the content of microplanning output includes only concepts that can be put into words appropriate for the preverbal message, as illustrated by an example that Levelt gives. Levelt (1999, p. 88) points out that not all concepts a speaker might want to express are necessarily lexical and therefore not all the concepts will enter the message creation process. For example, Levelt (1999, pp. 91–92) considers a message aimed at conveying a visual scene involving a house with a tree to its left. This message has to be formulated as a proposition because there is no single word for such a scene. There are many possibilities for how this may be done, including propositions equivalent to "There is a house with a tree to the left of it" and "There is a tree with a house to the right of it."

For microplanning purposes, the speaker has to decide which perspective to take so that the preverbal message will properly reflect how the speaker construes the event. This may involve, in the present example, more than simply figuring out which object is to the right or the left of the other. The preverbal message will need to convey information that takes into account the position of the speaker, or of the listener, or of the house which has a front to it, or of the emphasis the speaker wishes to convey (this is a message about the house, not about the tree), etc.

In the case of speaking in the L2, De Bot (1992) suggests that sometimes a speaker may not know the lexical items needed for microplanning (that is, not know how to convey the intended construal). Moreover, he or she may also be aware of this shortcoming. The speaker may, under these circumstances, take this shortcoming into account when formulating the preverbal message. The speaker can do this by strategically formulating the preverbal message in a way that helps to get around his or her linguistic limitations. The action of figuring out how to build correct construal information into the message, given one's limitations, might have a negative impact on fluency, for example, by slowing down the formulation of the preverbal message. This point of possible vulnerability to dysfluency is represented in the figure by $\{f_1\}$ at the microplanning level.

The output of microplanning is a *preverbal message*. This preverbal message can be thought of as a conceptual structure that can be implemented in words but which has not yet been formulated in words. That is, it is not yet a *surface structure* that contains lexical items and a grammatical shape. For the preverbal message to become represented as a surface structure, it must first be encoded into a grammatical structure into which elements from another knowledge source—the mental lexicon—can be inserted. Grammatical encoding gives linguistic shape to the preverbal message by specifying what words are to be used and how they are to be related to each other in order to convey the speaker's intentions (that is, the speaker's perspective or construal of the world that is the content of the message). At this point, something akin to Slobin's (1996, 1997) idea of "thinking for speaking" comes into play. For example, English speakers tend to use *relative* spatial locations (e.g., *left* or *right*) for describing object positions whereas Arrernte speakers, an Aboriginal language of central Australia, tend to use *absolute* spatial locations (*east* or *west*) (Wilkins, 2006). Or, to take another example, consider how one would express the thought "the girl found her book" in English versus French. In English, the selection of the possessive determiner *her* (feminine form versus masculine form) is governed by the grammatical gender of the possessor (girl), whereas in French the possessive determiner has to agree with the grammatical gender of the object that is possessed. Here, that would be the masculine form *son* and not the feminine form *sa*, as in

La	fille	a	trouvé	son	livre.
The	girl	aux (past)	found	3rd person possessive pronoun (masc.)	book (masc.)

Strictly speaking, without further context, the listener cannot tell from this sentence whether the girl found her own book or somebody else's. In each of the above examples, the speaker has to think about the message—by focusing, for example, on spatial locations in a relative or absolute way or on the grammatical gender of the nouns involved—in a way that is appropriate for formulating the sentence (thinking for speaking) (more on this topic later in Chapter 4). An L2 speaker might experience processing difficulties in engaging in the appropriate "thinking for speaking." He or she might find it difficult to retrieve and make use of the appropriate linguistic resources required for creating the correct grammatical foundation for the surface structure. This point of possible vulnerability to dysfluency is identified in the figure by $\{f_2\}$ at the grammatical encoding level.

To complete the conversion of the preverbal message into a surface structure (for subsequent conversion into spoken form), the speaker must recruit information from the mental lexicon, the knowledge source represented as the middle ellipse on the right side of Figure 1.2. This knowledge source encompasses all the lemmas (families of related words, including idioms and fixed expressions) in each language, and so to some extent it must be language specific. This does not necessarily mean, of course, that brain representation involves separate neural regions for the lemmas of each language. Just as synonyms, near synonyms, and related words within one language (e.g., English *chair* and *bench*) are presumed to be represented in neurally related regions, so it may be assumed that translation equivalents and near equivalents (e.g., English *chair* and French *chaise*) would similarly be neurally represented. That is, there is no need to postulate that a speaker's repertoire of different language lemmas must be segregated in the brain in distinct, neural regions (see Paradis, 2004). This idea is represented in Figure 1.2 by the partially overlapping circles for L_x and L_y.

Not represented in Figure 1.2, however, is an important distinction between lexicon and vocabulary that Paradis (2009) reminds us about. The *lexicon* is the repository of the speaker's implicit knowledge about the meanings and uses of words, including knowledge about the interactions between lexical items and their syntactic properties. This is procedural knowledge, about which the speaker has no awareness or formal understanding. Most of the L1 is represented in this way because the language is not learned through formal instruction but through communicative experience. This knowledge is implicit, not declarative (able to be spoken about). For example, L1 speakers know implicitly the difference between mass nouns like *news* and count nouns like *reports* and can use them correctly with singular or plural verbs, etc., even though they might not be able to explain the difference. *Vocabulary*, on the other hand, is the repository of the speaker's explicit knowledge of word meanings that have been taught. This knowledge involves declarative memory. Typically, L2 users acquire an L2 vocabulary through explicit instruction while all the time possessing an L1 lexicon acquired implicitly through experience. Of course, it is possible—even in the L1—to learn something about items that are in the lexicon, for example by having the mass/count noun distinction explained. But this new explicit knowledge will still be different from the implicit knowledge in the lexicon. Likewise, L2 vocabulary could in principle become so practiced that an L2 lexicon reflecting implicit knowledge emerges (Paradis, 2009, suggests that normally this does not happen for an L2 learned later than the L1). The overlapping circles in Figure 1.2 miss this distinction between lexicon and vocabulary, but separate circles would wrongly convey the idea of neurally separate stores for the L1 and L2, as opposed to a distinction between declarative and nondeclarative memory. This oversimplification in the figure needs to be acknowledged but will have to stand for now.

The selected lemmas are realized in the surface form as individual words and fixed multiword expressions. There are a number of important theoretical questions that arise here about how this is accomplished in the L1 (Levelt, Roelofs, & Meyer, 1999) and, especially, in the L2. For example, there is the question of how the L2 is linked to the L1 (Kroll & Stewart, 1994; Kroll & Tokowicz, 2005). Are L2 lemmas accessed via the L1 (e.g., the English speaker intending to speak in L2 French first thinks of the concept BOY and then retrieves the lemma *boy* in English in order to access the lemma *garçon* in French), or directly (e.g., thinks of the concept BOY, then retrieves the lemma *garçon* in French), or in some other way? Does the answer to this question depend on the level of proficiency in the L2? Are all lemmas accessed in the same manner for a given L2 user or are some lemmas handled one way and other lemmas in other ways? The important point here is that we have a possible source of dysfluency—difficulty in accessing lemmas during the creation of the surface structure. As made explicit by De Bot (1992, p. 14), "[o]ne of the most salient characteristics of a non-balanced bilingual is the occurrence of lexical retrieval problems," a topic taken up in more detail later in Chapter 4 in relation to L2 cognitive fluency. This point of possible vulnerability to dysfluency is represented in Figure 1.2 by $\{f_3\}$, where the grammatical encoding level is linked to the lemmas in the mental lexicon.

Once the intended message has been formulated as a surface structure, it has to be converted into a form that can be realized as overt speech.

In Levelt's (1999) model, this formulation takes place in the second major component shown in the blueprint—the phonological/phonetic system. Stored with each lemma in the mental lexicon are the morpho-phonological codes associated with it, making it possible to generate a *phonological score* needed for the generation of overt speech. Levelt describes the generation of phonological words in the L1 that will make up this phonological score as involving a three-step morpho-phonological encoding process. This process is based on syllable programs rather than individual phonemes. The details of this process can vary from one language to another depending, for example, on whether the language in question is stress timed (e.g., English) or syllable timed (e.g., French) (Martin, 1972). Also, languages can differ in terms of the number of syllable programs they involve (e.g., English has a larger syllable repertoire than does Chinese or Japanese; Levelt, 1989). Levelt (1989) points out that normally this whole process proceeds in a highly automatic way and that (L1) fluency involves being able to look ahead appropriately (that is, not too far ahead) to build the phonological model of the word incrementally, as opposed to working in a strictly serial fashion, one element at a time. Levelt (1989, p. 24) gives the example of saying *sixteen dollars*, where the upcoming word *dollars* changes the stress within the word *sixteen* (thus, *SIXteen [DOllars]*, and not *sixTEEN*). As De Bot (1992) suggests, L2 fluency issues can arise here. If the L2 speaker does not have automatic access to syllable programs, then one can expect reduced fluidity in how the process is carried out, manifesting itself in hesitations. Thus, we can identify another potentially critical point for L2 fluency at the level of morpho-phonological encoding, leading to the generation of a phonological score that underlies the rest of the process of formulating overt speech. This point of possible vulnerability is shown in Figure 1.2 as $\{f_4\}$.

The phonological score contains information at a relatively abstract, phonological level (although see Port [2007] for a view challenging the abstract nature of phonological representations). It is necessary to convert this phonological score into an articulatory score to guide the speech apparatus in producing the required phonetic events. Levelt (1999) posits a *syllabary*, a knowledge source that contains the gestural scores for turning phonological score information into motor plans for producing speech. This knowledge source is shown as the bottom ellipse in Figure 1.2. The information contained in the syllabary is assumed to include various parameters that have to be set for realizing the phonological score as a phonetic event, including such local parameters as duration, amplitude, and pitch movement, and more global parameters such as key (range of movement in a phonological phrase) and register (pitch level of the baseline intonation) (Levelt, 1999, pp. 110–111).

The process of using gestural scores to convert a phonological score into an articulatory score is called *phonetic encoding* by Levelt (1999).

The output of the phonetic encoding process is an articulatory score or phonetic plan for setting into motion the motor activity for articulating the message and creating the overt speech. Different languages will make use of different repertoires of gestural scores, some highly similar across languages and others quite different. De Bot (1992) makes the point that, because most speakers have accents in their L2, it must be that they are using one articulatory system in which the gestural scores are not strongly segregated by language (shown in Figure 1.2 by partially over-lapping dashed circles). Fluency issues can arise here if the speaker effort-fully, as opposed to being able to automatically, attempts to select the appropriate gestural score ($\{f_5\}$ in Figure 1.2) and attempts to execute that score ($\{f_6\}$).

Other fluency considerations need to be mentioned at this point. These concern more global issues regarding the operation of the processes iden-tified in the blueprint. One is the role of self-perception. Speakers are almost always monitoring their own speech, at the many different levels shown in Figure 1.2, whether they are using their L1 or L2 (see Kormos, 2006, Chapter 6, for an extended discussion of L2 monitoring). This allows them to catch errors and reformulate the message when they do make a planning error. Indeed, sometimes slips of the tongue can reveal the operation of self-monitoring. For example, Seyfeddinipur, Kita, and Indefrey (2008) reported a study that found evidence of L1 speakers interrupting themselves upon detection of an error in their spontaneous speech. The pattern of interruption supported the view that speakers preferred to optimize fluency (the flow) of their speech over immediately stopping to repair inaccuracies. That is, speakers appeared to interrupt themselves when they were ready to make a correction (i.e., they planned the correction while continuing to talk until ready to deliver it), thereby minimizing any hesitation time that would be needed for re-planning after an interruption had been made. This contrasts with the possibility of interrupting speech immediately upon error detection, which would entail longer hesitation time while the speaker engages in the re-planning needed for the correction.

Thus, we see that in self-monitoring there can be a tradeoff between maintaining accuracy versus fluency in speech, and that L1 speakers appear to generally favor fluency. In any event, it is clear that self-mon-itoring does lead speakers to interrupt the fluidity of their speech, thereby reducing its flow. Clearly, such self-monitoring might occur more frequently and/or be more cognitively demanding in the L2 than in the L1, depending on the speaker's level of proficiency and the circumstances under which one is speaking. For example, in some circumstances it may be especially important to display optimal proficiency in the L2 and hence maximal self-monitoring may be called for. Speech rate in the L2 may also be reduced relative to the L1, perhaps to make it easier to self-monitor, or when self-monitoring reveals that more time is required to allow various encoding processes to operate accurately. Self-monitoring is thus another potential locus of dysfluency (shown in Figure 1.2 as $\{f_7\}$).

In summary, the blueprint of the L2 speaker that emerges from consideration of Levelt (1989, 1999) and De Bot (1992), as represented in Figure 1.2, suggests that there are at least seven critical points in the architecture of the speaking system. These are "fluency vulnerability" points where processing difficulties might be expected to give rise to L2 dysfluencies. This discussion about the nature of the L2 speaker is useful, as far as it goes, but it does have some important limitations. Both Levelt (1989, 1999) and De Bot (1992) point out that this blueprint approach to understanding the L1 and the L2 speaker, and by implication to understanding fluency issues, is limited in that it provides only a snapshot of the speaker at one moment in time. What is missing is an indication of how proficiency skills develop over time, and how speaker-environment interactions impact on the act of speaking and on the nature of the underlying processes themselves (see also the issues raised in Chapter 4 on automatic and attention-based processing and in Chapter 6 on the neurocognitive underpinnings of fluency). De Bot, Lowie, and Verspoor (2007) and others, notably Herdina and Jessner (2002) and Larsen-Freeman and Cameron (2008), have addressed this missing element by proposing a *dynamical* (or *complex*) *systems theory* approach to L2 development and proficiency. It is to this approach that we now turn.

Dynamical Systems Theory Approach

The idea of dynamical systems, also often referred to as complex systems, dynamic systems, complex adaptive systems, and other combinations of these terms, is not entirely new in applied linguistics (see the historical review in Larsen-Freeman & Cameron, 2008; see also Dörnyei, 2009a, pp. 99–112) and it certainly has a respected place in many branches of psychology (Port & Van Gelder, 1995; Van Gelder, 1998; Ward, 2002). Moreover, many of the main tenets of a dynamical systems approach to applied linguistics are compatible with ideas in cognitive linguistics (P. Robinson & Ellis, 2008), with the competition model (MacWhinney, 1997, 2008), with emergentism (N. Ellis, 1998; O'Grady, 2003), and other approaches to L2 acquisition. Nevertheless, a dynamical systems approach is still relatively new in second language acquisition theorizing and, to my knowledge, such an approach has never been explicitly discussed with respect to L2 fluency issues. It is worthwhile to explore the case made by Larsen-Freeman and Cameron (2008) for adopting a dynamical systems approach to applied linguistics in general and to see what promise this may have for addressing issues in L2 fluency.

Larsen-Freeman and Cameron (2008) point out that language needs to be seen as dynamic ("there is nothing static about language"; p. 6), in which learners assemble "their language resources in order to respond in an intentional way to the communicative pressures at hand" (pp. 6–7). Under this view, they argue, it makes little sense to sharply distinguish competence from performance. This is because what normally would be assigned to "competence" is constructed or assembled in the course of "performing," and thus reflects performance considerations in an integral way. In addition, the context in which this assembling takes place is itself not stable and fully independent of the learner as an individual. Rather, the individual and context are coupled (p. 7), and the context changes or adapts to the individual just as the individual adapts to the context. An important point here is that this coupling is not simply a passive interaction between individual and environment; rather, the individual can be seen to be *shaping* his or her own context (p. 7).

In order to make the above points more specific, Larsen-Freeman and Cameron (2008) focus on the following five features of dynamical systems as being especially relevant. The first is that, in dynamical as opposed to non-dynamical systems, there exists *heterogeneity of elements and agents*, that is, a variety of elements (objects, actors, processes) that are interconnected to form a whole system, and these elements interact with each other. Here one can include, among others, the individual learner, the social context (with its physical, cultural, technological, political, demographic, and other characteristics) in which that individual is embedded, plus the cognitive and perceptual processes, beliefs, motivations, emotions, knowledge, aptitudes, and attitudes the individual brings to the situation. The second feature is that there exist *system dynamics*, that is, the connections and interactions between elements change over time. For example, the scope of social interactions involving L2 communication can be expected to change over time (perhaps becoming larger or more constrained, or changing qualitatively), resulting in changes in the way the social environment impacts on the individual. The third feature is the *non-linearity* of the system, that is, not only are there changes in the way elements connect and interact, there are changes in the change itself. A well-known example of this in first language development is vocabulary learning, the rate of which at first increases rapidly, then plateaus and then decreases. The fourth feature is the *openness* of the system, that is, a dynamic system is susceptible to influences that are external to it and these influences play a crucial role in stabilizing the system by making possible a dynamic equilibrium as opposed to a steady-state equilibrium. Larsen-Freeman and Cameron (2008, p. 33) give, as a language example, the case of the English language itself, which is continually changing yet remains identifiable as the same language over many centuries. The final feature is *adaptation*, in which a change in one part of the system leads to a change in the way the system functions as a whole. In language acquisition an example of such adaptation might be how increased exposure to particular expressions might lead to greater automatic processing and this in turn might have a global impact on how language is processed (see Chapter 6).

These five characteristics—heterogeneity of elements and agents, system dynamics, non-linearity, openness, and adaptation—all reflect a fundamental underlying feature of dynamical systems, namely the interconnectedness of all its components. In particular, even "the context is not separate from the system but part of it and of its complexity" (Larsen-Freeman & Cameron, 2008, p. 34). This, of course, poses a challenge for researchers, because this interconnectedness may render it very difficult, perhaps impossible in some cases, to predict the behavior of the system as a whole, rendering some hypotheses about the system unfalsifiable. Larsen-Freeman and Cameron (2008) point out additional risks and challenges posed by this way of thinking. One is the risk of adopting dynamical systems thinking only as a metaphor for approaching questions in applied linguistics, with all the limitations that come with metaphorical thinking (Boyd, 1993; see also Wilks & Meara, 2002), without addressing seriously and rigorously the research implications of the perspective shaped by the metaphor.

Another problem is one pointed out by N. Ellis (2007), in a commentary on the dynamical systems approach to L2 acquisition proposed by De Bot et al. (2007). This is the problem of overestimating the flexibility of the system and thereby failing to recognize the existence of its significant regularities (e.g., aspects of morpheme acquisition order in L2 English; Goldschneider & DeKeyser, 2001). That is, on the one hand, dynamical systems may at times behave in ways that are difficult to predict due to the complex nature of the interconnectedness of their components yet, on the other hand, they are not infinitely open-ended and flexible. Moreover, as Meara (personal communication, 2009) has pointed out, sometimes behavior seems to be complex, yet the apparent complexity may, in fact, be understood in terms of the operation of simple elements, removing the need to appeal to an underlying complex system (see discussion of Meara's demonstrations of this with respect to vocabulary development in Chapter 6).

Larsen-Freeman and Cameron (2008, p. 41) suggest that by following certain guidelines researchers can benefit from a dynamical systems perspective without either overestimating its flexibility or rejecting some of its crucial premises. Larsen-Freeman and Cameron's guidelines are sensible and, indeed, they inform good research strategies in general, not just in a dynamical systems approach where they are particularly important. They include—based on Larsen-Freeman and Cameron (2008, p. 41, slightly reworded and regrouped here)—the following four points:

- identifying the components of the system (agents, processes, subsystems), including the timescales and levels of social organization on which components operate
- describing relations among components

- describing system dynamics (how components change over time, and how relations among components change over time)
- describing how system and context adapt to one another to achieve dynamic equilibrium.

It is appropriate now to ask whether the five features of dynamical systems described earlier, as identified by Larsen-Freeman and Cameron (2008), apply specifically to L2 fluency, as opposed to applied linguistics and L2 acquisition in general. A starting point for addressing this question is provided by Figure 1.3. This figure presents a *framework* for thinking about L2 fluency in terms of a dynamic systems approach. At this time, the framework is provisional but it will be elaborated upon later in this volume (see Figures 5.3 and 7.1). The goal of this framework is to identify major sources of influence on L2 fluency acquisition and the broad patterns of interaction among these influences.

When considering the framework depicted in Figure 1.3, it is important to keep in mind the explanatory level that it addresses. The framework is formulated at a fairly high level of abstraction and generality in order to focus on "big picture" issues; it is *not* intended to be a model of how L2 speech processing unfolds in real time. In this sense, it contrasts with the Socio-Pragmatic Psycho-Linguistic (SPPL) interface model presented by Walters (2005)—a model that addresses the interaction between social and cognitive factors in L2 speech production. However, unlike the proposed framework, the SPPL model aims to describe the flow of information in L2 communication (Walters, 2005, p. 14). Ward (2002) presents other examples of dynamical systems approaches to language and cognition that seem, in principle, to be applicable to L2 processing phenomena. These approaches lend themselves to testing and falsification insofar as they specify expected patterns of, say, response times or of evoked potentials that can be observed in real time. Again, this contrasts with the framework proposed in this book, which does not directly address real time processing. Dörnyei (2009a, p. 104) also noted that at present the contribution of dynamic systems theory to L2 acquisition theory seems to be more conceptual than methodological.

Heterogeneity of Elements and Agents

Consider first the system components that might be implicated in L2 fluency. Figure 1.3 shows four broadly defined components that in one way or another contribute to a speaker's L2 fluency. Of course, each component itself could be considered a collection of elements and subsystems that could be further broken down and analyzed. One of these components is the individual and his or her cognitive and perceptual (sub)systems and processes, many details of which have been

Figure 1.3 A provisional framework for thinking about the dynamic relationships among sources of influence on L2 fluency.

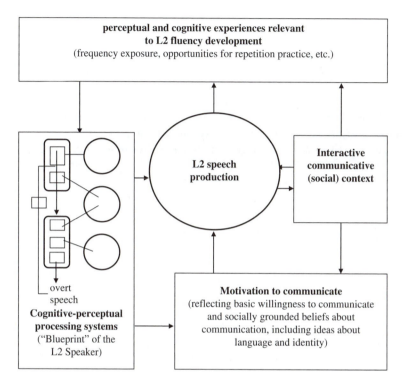

This figure is somewhat revised in Chapter 5. *L2 speech production* (central ellipse) is subject to at least four broadly defined influences that interact with one another, creating a system that is continuously changing and adapting over time, and that has the features of a dynamical system (see text). System components include: the way the speaker's *cognitive/perceptual systems* operate (see the "blueprint of the speaker"), the speaker's *motivation to communicate*, the nature of the *interactive communicative* or *social context* that is produced by the act of communicating and which in turn shapes the act of communicating itself, and the *perceptual and cognitive experiences* resulting from communicating and from the social context. These perceptual and cognitive experiences affect speech production fluency by shaping the way the speaker's processing systems operate.

addressed by Levelt (1989, 1999) and De Bot (1992) in their blueprint of the speaker and summarized here in Figure 1.2. As discussed earlier, the efficiency of these systems may be expected to have an impact on the fluency of speech delivery. This is the component that has received by far the largest attention in the literature on L2 fluency (see Chapters 4 and 6).

A second broadly defined component underlying fluency includes the individual's motivational and belief system (not part of the "blueprint" description of the speaker). Motivation can be expected to play a role in "energizing" and shaping the speaker's commitment to communicate with optimal fluency at a given moment, and to decide whether to enter into a social context requiring L2 use (see Chapter 5).

A third component is the larger social context in which the communication is embedded. This social context may be expected to shape certain aspects of the speaker's output, for example, by defining the sociolinguistic demand characteristics of the communication and thereby affect the observed fluency in a particular way (see Chapter 5).

The fourth component shown in Figure 1.3 is the set of perceptual and cognitive experiences that result from the very act of engaging in L2 communication and from the social context that is created by that communication. These are the experiences that have direct relevance to the operation of the speaker's cognitive and perceptual systems and which, in turn, directly affect fluency. For example, such experiences might include opportunities or lack thereof to hear and produce certain target words or expressions under conditions that promote the development of automatic word retrieval (this theme is addressed throughout this volume).

These elements can be seen to form a system by the fact that they are related to and interact with one another. For example, it seems reasonable to hypothesize that the efficiency of a person's cognitive and perceptual processing skills will influence motivation to engage in communication. That is, if it seems to an L2 speaker that a particular communication task will be difficult, then that speaker may be less willing to engage in it (Song & Schwarz, 2008) and, conversely, if the communication seems to be easy to engage in, then the speaker may be more willing to participate in it. There may also be an interactive relation between the communicative act and the social context component. That is, the way in which the L2 speaker engages in the communicative act might shape the nature of the social context in which that communication continues to take place. For example, if the interlocutor has to make major adjustments to accommodate to the L2 speaker's low level of fluency (Ferguson, 1975; Gass, 1997) or if the L2 speaker is unable to use a socially appropriate register to communicate (Segalowitz, 1976), then this might impact on the relationship between the L2 speaker and the interlocutor, affecting the manner in which both communicate. It might also impact, in turn, on the L2 speaker's judgments about the interlocutor (Segalowitz, 1976) and thereby affect motivation.

Also, there may be a relation between the social context component and the cognitive/perceptual systems of the individual (Segalowitz, Gatbonton, & Trofimovich, 2009). For example, a social context is created by the very fact that the L2 speaker is communicating at some level of fluency with another person. This event will inevitably generate a series of experiences for the L2 speaker, including—but not limited to—various forms of linguistic feedback from the interlocutor and from others in the social environment. These experiences can serve as input to the L2 speaker and thereby have an impact on the speaker's cognitive and perceptual systems. Such input might, for example, facilitate or prevent the development of automatic word recognition skills, the tuning of phonetic and articulatory processing abilities, the acquisition of attention-focusing skills relevant to grammatical processing, etc. In this way the social environment and cognitive/perceptual systems might mutually impact on each other in ways that ultimately affect fluency development.

System Dynamics

The system components depicted in Figure 1.3 are all known to be susceptible to change over time, and this can come about in a large number of different ways. For example, with increased instruction and/ or exposure to L2 environments, over time L2 speakers normally develop more and more efficient cognitive and perceptual processing systems. Conversely, with disuse over long periods of time there can be a loss of cognitive and perceptual processing efficiency with respect to the L2. Because these changes in experience can occur in a graded fashion (that is, not simply all or none) and in qualitatively different ways (e.g., disusing L2 academic discourse while increasing L2 casual social discourse, or vice versa), there can be great variation in the way dynamic changes occur in this component. The motivation component can change over time too, rising and falling as a function of changes in the need to communicate with the target group, in beliefs about the importance of doing so and about the impact doing so has one's own social standing within different groups, and so on. The interactive communicative (social) component—the contexts in which communication takes place— can also vary both quantitatively and qualitatively over time in many different ways. This can come about as a function of changing social relationships, such as marrying into the community of the target language speakers, becoming a refugee in a different language community, changing employment, and so on. Each of these different social contexts carries with it different communicative demand characteristics and so these changes could, in principle, have a significant impact on the speaker's fluency in the L2. Finally, the cognitive and perceptual experiences that arise from the communicative interaction can be expected to change over time as a function of how the communicative context changes over time.

Non-linearity

The system of interacting components will operate in a non-linear fashion. This is because the elements in the system are modified over time by the direct and indirect feedback links between them. For example, as mentioned earlier and as will be discussed later, certain social environments become accessible to speakers as a function of their current level of fluency. Such environments might create input experiences that promote increased automatic word retrieval skills, thereby ratcheting up fluency in ways that open up qualitatively newer possibilities for social interaction and facilitating even newer achievements in fluency. The possibilities for such non-linear effects are understated in Figure 1.3 because the component factors shown there are really categories that subsume many sub-factors, each of which might impact on fluency and which might interact with other sub-factors. For example, beliefs about language and identity that are associated with L2 proficiency are themselves multidimensional (Gatbonton & Trofimovich, 2008; Gatbonton, Trofimovich, & Magid, 2005), and different beliefs can have a different impact on fluency as a function of the social context in which the speaker is communicating. It would be incorrect, therefore, to expect that a particular change in one component would lead invariably to a simple proportional change in some aspect of fluency for all speakers in all circumstances; the operation of the whole system has to be taken into account.

Openness

As a feature of dynamical systems, openness refers to the idea that the system is continually open to (subject to) external influences and these influences normally help, rather than hinder, the system to achieve equilibrium. In the case of the system underlying L2 communicative fluency, equilibrium would mean maintenance or growth in fluency in the face of external forces instead of fluency loss or language attrition. The system underlying L2 fluency will normally be open for the following reasons. L2 users typically engage in communication that involves the exchange of information in which the speaker is genuinely committed to the exchange and which takes place in an environment that is changing in unpredictable ways. This means that the speaker will harness all his or her resources to try to ensure the success of the communication, including dealing with the unexpected. For example, the speaker cannot predict everything the interlocutor is likely to say (otherwise there would be no need to communicate), nor can the speaker predict the direction the conversation will take (including the emotional reactions of the interlocutor, sudden changes in topic, shifts in speech register, etc.).

Long (1983) proposed that the process of dealing with an interlocutor under such circumstances is critical for further language development. Long focused on the acquisition of new L2 knowledge, and he called the process *the negotiation for meaning*. The idea is that L2 speakers, especially those not yet highly fluent, do not just passively receive messages from their interlocutors and respond in set ways. Rather, when they do not sufficiently understand the input, they explicitly seek clarification or engage in stratagems to obtain more information by trying to elicit repetitions, by paraphrasing, etc. All this involves active engagement on the part of the L2 speaker. In the process of negotiating meaning, the speaker benefits by expanding his or her knowledge of the language and improving fluency through practice in implementing that knowledge. Long's proposal was intended as an improvement to Krashen's (1985) comprehensible input hypothesis, which held that language is learned simply through exposure to input that is just a little above the speaker's current level of attainment. There is considerable evidence supporting the negotiation for meaning hypothesis (see Gass, 1997). The psychological significance of the idea of negotiation for meaning will be presented in Chapters 5 and 7. What is important for the present discussion is that, by engaging in genuine (authentic) communication (that is, by having a real stake in the success of the message exchange; Gatbonton & Segalowitz, 2005), the speaker is exposed on a continuous basis to the variability and unpredictability inherent in normal communication. These unpredictable conversational events, which always occur in genuine communication, are the source of the external influences that could potentially destabilize the system. However, if the speaker is able to handle the unpredictability, then the acts of attempting to communicate fluently will stabilize, and fluency skills will benefit from the experience. It is in this sense that the system is open.

There is a second important way in which openness is relevant to the manifestation of fluency, an idea captured by Swain's (2005) output hypothesis (see also Muranoi, 2007, for further discussion). According to this idea, it is crucial for speakers to generate output that they can monitor, both in terms of matching what they say to what they intend and in terms of the responses elicited from the interlocutor. This monitoring allows them to notice aspects of their own speech that can be further developed. Without this output, the speaker will be unable to fine-tune his or her speaking skills beyond a certain point and will thus fail to reinforce and further develop fluency (and other aspects) of L2 speech. Speakers generate this valuable output when engaged in genuine communication. The role of external influences here is to involve the speaker in activities resulting in the generation of this output which, as Swain argues, helps to promote the acquisition of knowledge and of fluency.

Adaptation

In the context of dynamical systems theory, adaptation refers to the idea that a change in one part of the system affects how the whole system works. This feature of the system underlying L2 fluency can be seen in Figure 1.3.

The figure shows that there are multiple linkages between components with feedback from one to another, ensuring that changes in one part of the system will cascade throughout. For this reason, a change in any one part will affect the whole system. It is not difficult to imagine how certain adaptations will come about. For example, speakers may slow their speech to allow more time for monitoring or for re-planning of utterances, or even as a way to induce the interlocutor to slow his or her input. Or the speaker may limit or expand exposure to certain L2 environments. For example, the speaker might avoid (or seek out) certain kinds of opportunities to use the L2, such as communication about sensitive topics (e.g., where ethnolinguistic identity issues are salient).

Perhaps, then, one of the hallmarks of L2 fluency is the degree to which the speaker has become an autonomous L2 user (Oxford, 2003), able to navigate through all sorts of communicative environments regardless of the challenges they present and, in the process of doing so, continues to hone the skills necessary to remain a successful linguistic navigator. This idea is discussed further in the final chapter.

Overall, one can see that the system of processes, subprocesses, mechanisms, and information stores depicted in Figure 1.3 has the five features of a dynamical system cited by Larsen-Freeman and Cameron (2008). Future research will need to determine the ways these features manifest themselves and the limits in how they do so. For example, it will be important to establish what categories of external influences the system is open to, what the details are regarding how a dynamic equilibrium supporting fluency is achieved, and so on. The important conclusion at this point is that it is possible to view the behavior of a speaker attempting to communicate fluently in the L2 as behavior supported by a complex, dynamical system. This conclusion may lead one to ask questions about fluency and pursue links between what people normally think about regarding fluency (e.g., oral fluency) and other factors (e.g., beliefs) that might not otherwise have been considered. The dynamical system framework will be retained throughout this book as the chief perspective for identifying and integrating issues. In the final chapter the framework will be re-examined in relation to its usefulness for identifying topics for future research and for understanding pedagogical issues in L2 fluency.

The Plan of the Book

The chapters that follow discuss fluency with reference to the following five anchor questions regarding a *cognitive science* perspective on L2 fluency.

- *Fluency in the L2: What features of L2 oral performance are reliable indicators of fluency?* For most people, this is *the* basic question about fluency. Chapter 2 discusses the various characteristics of

L2 oral performance that fluency researchers have examined. The main directions of this research are identified, along with some of the challenges that have to be addressed in L2 oral fluency research. An important reformulation of this anchor question is then proposed.

- *Fluency in general cognitive processing and other skill domains: Can studies of general cognitive processing fluency and of skill acquisition outside bilingualism contribute to an understanding of L2 fluency?* For many years, fluency—considered as an aspect of cognitive processing quite apart from anything related to L2 fluency—has been an important idea in a number of areas within cognitive psychology. In particular, research on cognitive fluency has examined issues regarding memory, perception, and judgment. Fluency issues have also been investigated in areas such as music performance, reading, and motor skills. Chapter 3 explores in what ways such considerations about fluency outside the area of bilingualism can make a useful contribution to understanding L2 fluency.

- *Cognitive aspects of L2 fluency: Are there elements of cognitive fluency (cognitive fluidity) specific to L2 performance that underlie L2 fluency?* Chapter 4 follows up the previous discussions regarding fluency or fluidity in general cognitive processing by asking whether there are cognitive underpinnings specific to L2 fluency. The principal focuses of this chapter are the roles of automatic and attention-based processing.

- *Social factors underlying fluency: To what extent and in what way do social, motivational, attitudinal, and other factors serve as sources of influence on L2 fluency?* Up to this point, the discussion will have focused primarily on the operation of perceptual and cognitive processing systems in fluency. Chapter 5 looks at how the idea of an underlying cognitive fluency provides a useful explanatory framework for linking together other aspects of L2 acquisition that are usually discussed in isolation (including linguistic, sociolinguistic, social psychological, and individual differences in learning style).

- *Other cognitive science approaches to L2 fluency: What insights concerning L2 fluency do other branches of the cognitive sciences offer?* Chapter 6 provides a review of important studies relevant to L2 fluency from the perspectives of neurolinguistics and neurocognition, computational modeling, and philosophical approaches to understanding the mind.

Chapter 7 rounds out these discussions with a concluding discussion that summarizes and integrates the main points of the cognitive science perspective presented throughout the book. The guiding perspective is that of a dynamical systems framework as shown in Figure 1.3, but this framework will also be critically evaluated in the final chapter.

The chapter also examines the implications of a cognitive science perspective for L2 pedagogy and fluency acquisition.

Chapter Summary

This chapter presented an overview of the volume, identifying five anchor questions that are addressed, and it presented the outline of a dynamical systems framework for thinking about L2 fluency. The main conclusions that emerged and that will be carried forward to the final chapter are the following:

- *Fluency can be thought of as a property of L2 use that emerges from the complex interplay of many factors interlinked in a dynamical system.*
- *The components of this dynamical system include the neurocognitive machinery for speech production, a motivational system that supports engagement in L2 communication, the social context in which L2 communication is embedded, and an environment of communicative experiences that shape the development and processing capacities of the neurocognitive processing system.*

We now turn to the first anchor question.

2　Measuring L2 Oral Fluency

> The complete speech act is a dynamic process, demanding the mobilization
> in proper sequence of a series of complex procedures and is the temporal
> integration of serial phenomena.
>
> Goldman-Eisler (1968, p. 6)

This chapter addresses the first anchor question guiding this book, *What features of L2 oral performance are reliable indicators of fluency?* As currently formulated, this question provides a good place to begin an inquiry into L2 fluency. However, as we will see, it is based on some widely accepted assumptions that turn out to be problematic, and so it will be reformulated later in the chapter. Now, over the past several decades many applied linguists have been concerned with identifying a set of critical features of oral production that might be diagnostic of L2 fluency. They have tried to identify aspects of L2 speech that could reliably be associated with fluency, such as speech rate or the way pauses and hesitations are distributed in speech. It was hoped that the availability of such objective indicators would reduce reliance on what some might consider to be less objective methods, such as listener judgments of fluency. The search for measurable features of fluency has also been motivated to a large extent by their potential usefulness in evaluating approaches to L2 training aimed at promoting fluency. This chapter reviews some of the main studies in this area, with the goal of identifying the most promising approaches to finding indicators of fluency. The chapter ends by listing critical points to bring forward to the final chapter.

The Search for Potential Markers of L2 Oral Fluency

The principal strategy behind applied linguistic research on L2 fluency has been to examine speech samples for features that reliably differentiate more fluent from less fluent speakers. Typically, one starts by differentiating more from less fluent speech on some basis independent of the speech features to be measured, for example, by listener ratings. Another approach has been to use speech samples from speakers' L1 (which are presumably more fluent) as baseline measures against which to contrast their L2 speech (presumably less fluent). Still other ways include taking samples from the same speakers at different times during L2 development (e.g., before and after experiences expected to enhance fluency). A closely related but different strategy is to define fluency *a priori* in some way (e.g., defining fluency by educational level attained) and then to investigate which features most influence the way listeners judge fluency.

The systematic study of fluency began with the pioneering work of Frieda Goldman-Eisler (1951, 1961, 1968, 1972; Henderson, Goldman-Eisler, & Skarbek, 1966). Her work focused on L1 speech, and was soon followed up in the 1970s and 1980s by others looking at L2 speech. Important works on L2 fluency are reported in papers by Dechert (1980) and Grosjean (1980a, 1980b), and those found in volumes edited by Dechert, Möhle, and Raupach (1984; see especially the chapters by Dechert, Lennon, and Möhle) and by Dechert and Raupach (1987; see especially the chapters by Clahsen, Rehbein, and Sajavaara). In the 1990s and afterward, studies of L2 fluency grew dramatically. The language testing literature (e.g., Bachman, 1990; Bachman & Palmer, 1996; Fulcher, 1996, 2003; Luoma, 2004; McNamara, 1996) addresses a number of important technical issues regarding how to operationalize measures of fluency for assessment purposes.

The widely cited study by Lennon (1990) provides a good place to begin the present review of more recent research on L2 fluency. Lennon pointed out that fluency is a purely performance phenomenon; there is no fluency "store" in the way there might be for other aspects of proficiency, such as a knowledge store for idiomatic expressions, vocabulary, syntactic complexity, etc. He argued, instead, that "fluency is an impression on the listener's part that the psycholinguistic processes of speech planning and speech production are functioning easily and efficiently" (p. 391). Note the idea here that the speaker's observable performance reflects an underlying "cognitive fluency," and that what Lennon is calling fluency is the listener's inference about that underlying "cognitive fluency" made from hearing the speech. The focus of his research, therefore, was to examine features of performance that could objectively indicate the ease and efficiency with which the underlying planning and production processes function. Lennon explicitly avoided making any claims about the actual processes or mechanisms responsible for particular aspects of fluency or about their functions (p. 398). Rather, his goal was simply to identify the critical overt manifestations of fluency. Even though it may be possible to relate the phenomena Lennon studied to fluency vulnerability points in the cognitive system underlying production, such as those shown in Figure 1.2 in Chapter 1 and marked as f_1 through f_4, Lennon nevertheless did not directly address the links that might exist between cognition and oral fluency. His goals appear to be much more pragmatic, namely, to identify a set of quantifiable indicators that could be useful in assessing how learners improve their fluency over time. Such indicators would make it possible to systematically explore the basis of teachers' and others' subjective assessments of fluency. It would also make it possible to study how some speakers use fluent delivery to direct listeners' attention away from weaknesses in other aspects of their speech (p. 391), including accent, grammatical accuracy, and aspects of their discourse (see also Kormos, 2006, Chapter 7, for a more extensive review of this topic).

Lennon's (1990) study involved only four participants—female German-speaking students who spoke English as a foreign language and who were in England for the purpose of improving their L2 skills. They were tested near the beginning and the end of their six-month residency. The learners were already considered to be advanced speakers of English at the beginning of their stay, but nevertheless a panel of native speakers subjectively judged them all to have improved in fluency by the end of their stay. This judged improvement provided the basis for deciding whether a particular aspect of oral performance could be considered an indicator of fluency.

Lennon examined the following 12 quantifiable features of oral performance as potential indicators of fluency:

- two measures of *speech rate* (words per minute; *unpruned*—i.e., with all self-corrections, asides, etc. included; and *pruned*—i.e., with such words excluded)
- three measures of interruptions—repetitions, self-corrections, filled pauses (ums, ers, etc.), where pauses were defined by a minimum duration of 0.2 seconds of silence, computed as a function of T-units, defined as "one main clause and all its attendant subordinate clauses and nonclausal units" (1990, p. 406) (see Foster, Tonkyn, & Wigglesworth, 2000, for alternatives to T-units and comments on related units of speech analysis)
- percentage of repeated and self-corrected words as a function of unpruned words
- two pause measures—filled and unfilled pauses, as a function of total speaking time
- mean length of speech runs (number of words) between pauses
- three measures relating T-units and the combination of filled and unfilled pauses (percent of T-units followed by a pause; percent of total pause time at all T-unit boundaries; mean pause time at T-unit boundaries).

The main findings were as follows: All participants improved over time in terms of increased speech rate (based on pruned words per minute) and decreased number of filled pauses per T-unit. In addition, three of the four participants also decreased their number of T-units followed by a pause. Lennon (1990) concluded that speech rate differences were more a reflection of pause time differences, especially in position, length, and frequency of pauses, than they were of articulation speed (i.e., they exhibited fewer silences rather than faster talking). He also reported that repetition and filled pauses appeared to be closely related to each other and might reflect planning functions (this is as near as Lennon came to addressing mechanisms). In contrast, self-corrections appeared not to be a good fluency indicator and he suggested that possibly even the contrary is true, namely, that an important aspect of fluency development is to *increase* one's ability to self-correct in real time. In other words, as L2 users' fluency and proficiency develop generally, so does their tendency to interrupt themselves to self-correct. Lennon's (1990) results suggest that simple speech rate and pausing phenomena by themselves were not critical indicators of fluency. Rather, it was these features in combination with the complexity of the speech being delivered that did so. These findings are consistent with the idea that oral fluency indicators reflect the operation of higher level processes, as opposed to lower level articulation.

Towell, Hawkins, and Bazergui (1996) reported research that took the study of temporal factors in L2 oral fluency one step further. These authors attempted to explicitly address processes and mechanisms underlying oral fluency, as revealed in speech performance. They proceeded from the perspective of Anderson's (1983) ACT theory that skilled—and, in our terms, one could say fluent—performance involves the conversion of declarative knowledge into procedural knowledge. Declarative knowledge is usually conscious, and often describable in words (e.g., explicit knowledge about the application of grammatical rules), whereas procedural knowledge is usually unconscious, automatic, and not describable (e.g., the ability to apply grammatical rules without thinking explicitly about what one is doing). Towell et al. (1996) aimed to determine how that conversion process takes place and what exactly becomes proceduralized. (In passing, it should be noted that they based their theoretical approach, in part, on a Universal Grammar position regarding the development of parameter setting in L2 acquisition [Baker, 2003; Towell & Hawkins, 1994; White, 1990, 2003]. This aspect of their theoretical analysis, however, is not central to the findings or interpretation of the data presented here and so will not be further focused upon here.)

Towell et al. (1996) tested 12 English-speaking university students learning French, aged 18–19 years at the beginning of the study. The participants' task was to retell a short, wordless film story. Each participant was recorded in French at the beginning and at the end of a year abroad in a French-speaking country, and a year later in English, using the same task each time.

The oral performance variables examined were the following:

- speech rate (syllables per minute)
- phonation/time ratio (percentage of time speaking/total time, i.e., with pauses included)
- articulation rate (syllables per second without pause times included)
- mean length of runs (mean number of syllables between pauses of .28 seconds or longer; see the discussion in Towell et al., 1996, p. 91, for the rationale for the .28 seconds criterion).

Towell et al. (1996) reported that there were significant increases in performance on three of these four measures, from Time 1 before the period of study abroad to Time 2 after study abroad. They found faster articulation rate and longer runs between pauses. There was no significant change in the phonation/time ratio (i.e., not greater speaking time in relation to total time when pauses are included). They also found that mean pause length did not change over time. From these results they concluded that the improvement in speech rate was due primarily to increases in the mean length of runs, rather than in a decrease in pausing. They concluded that observed gains in fluency reflected gains in "the way linguistic knowledge is stored as procedural knowledge rather than as changes in the way subjects either have learnt to conceptualize the knowledge in the L2 or to articulate speech in the L2" (p. 103).

The authors also reported in considerable detail interesting qualitative analyses of the performance of two of the subjects, one much more fluent and the other less fluent at the outset. The qualitative analyses were conducted in order to understand which aspects of speech might have become proceduralized (more automatic) through learning. In their analyses, they focused on the use of fixed expressions and formulaic language (Nattinger & Decarrico, 1992; Wray, 2002), such as syntactic phrases (e.g., NP + Aux + VP), collocations, generalized productive frames (e.g., "a N [+time] ago"], fillers, and lexical phrases. The last category included polywords such as "by the way," institutionalized expressions such as "How do you do?," phrasal constraints such as "as far as I know," and sentence builders such as "not only X but also Y." They observed that the less fluent subject seemed to be "laboriously putting together sentences very much under the control of interpretive mechanisms" (Towell et al., 1996, p. 109), making relatively little use of formulaic and fixed expressions that weren't interrupted by pauses. In contrast, the more fluent speaker made more effective use of formulaic and fixed expressions, with longer uninterrupted runs, especially at Time 2, when new forms of sentence and phrase units were used. This subject seemed to demonstrate gains reflecting more effective use at Time 2 of resources already present in her speech at Time 1, thus speaking faster and with less hesitation. Towell et al. interpreted this as evidence for increased proceduralization, allowing the student to package longer and longer strings of words as whole and unalterable chunks. Thus, the qualitative analyses revealed that, while both these subjects made use of formulaic language and fixed expressions, one achieved a high degree of proceduralization whereas the other did not.

The work of Towell et al. (1996) further reinforces the idea that increases in fluency reflect complex underlying changes (e.g., the proceduralization) in how the speech output is generated. The gains that people observe are not just gains in the smoothness of the articulatory aspects of speech as such, but gains in smoothness resulting from restructuring of the underlying processes (see Chapter 4). Their work also underscores the value of qualitative analyses for revealing interesting individual differences and for pointing to possible mechanisms.

More recently, Iwashita, Brown, McNamara, and O'Hagan (2008) also found associations between oral production measures and fluency level. They analyzed 200 recorded samples from L2 speakers of English, selected from a larger study where the speakers had been classified by trained raters as being in one of five different ability levels. The speech samples had been collected through the use of five oral elicitation tasks, ranging in nature from giving an opinion, recounting an event in a context without dialogue, to explaining with dialogue. The tasks involved a variety of preparation times and speaking times ranging from 30 to 90 seconds. The samples were analyzed on a number of dimensions, including grammatical accuracy, grammatical complexity, vocabulary, phonology, and fluency. The fluency measures taken were speech rate (syllables per second, after pruning the speech of repairs and removing pauses longer than 3 seconds), filled pauses/minute (ums and ers), silent pauses/minute (pauses defined as 1 second or more of silence), repairs/minute (repetitions of exact words, syllables or phrases, replacements, reformulations, false starts, partial repetitions of words or utterance), total pausing time (sum of all silent pause time), and mean length of run (syllables between pauses greater than 1 second). Three of these measures—speech rate, silent pause rate, and total pause time—showed clear relationships with proficiency level, with speech rate showing the strongest effect. Filled pauses, repairs, and mean length of run yielded no significant associations with proficiency level.

Other researchers have also investigated the relationship between L2 fluency and measurable features of speech performance. Of particular interest here are the studies by researchers using computer-based, automated techniques for detecting silences and syllable stress in speech samples, allowing one to automatically compute various measures of speech rate and silent pauses without the need to transcribe the speech samples first. The use of technology in this way has enhanced the feasibility of analyzing data from very large samples and of doing so faster, and in a more reliable and objective way (e.g., Cucchiarini, Strik, &

Boves, 2000, 2002; De Jong, Schoonen, & Hulstijn, 2009; De Jong, Steinel, Florijn, Schoonen, & Hulstijn, 2007; De Jong & Wempe, 2009). Cucchiarini et al. (2000), for example, used such automated techniques to analyze samples of read L2 speech. They found strong correlations between expert ratings of fluency and five objective measures which factor analysis later reduced to two factors—articulation rate (i.e., speech rate with pauses excluded) and number of pauses. In a follow-up study, Cucchiarini et al. (2002) compared beginner and intermediate L2 learners, and read versus spontaneous speech. They found results consistent with the previous findings. In addition, they found that speech rate and phonation time ratio were important correlates of fluency for beginners, whereas mean length of runs was an important correlate of fluency in spontaneous speech in intermediate learners.

De Jong et al. (2009) used different software (De Jong & Wempe, 2009) that also enabled them to obtain automated measures of oral fluency (speech rate, measures of silence) in the L2 Dutch of Turkish and English native speakers. They used eight speaking tasks employing pictures depicting short scenarios (e.g., a cyclist having an accident) to elicit speech samples from the participants in both the L1 and L2. Their analyses yielded speed fluency measures based on words per second including filled pauses, words per second excluding filled pauses (filled pauses within and between utterances were determined from manual transcriptions of the spoken samples), and length of silent pauses between and within utterances.

The first important results from their analyses were significant relationships between L1 and L2 performance (apparently the first study to demonstrate this using automated analyses of narrative speech samples), L1-L2 correlations of $r = .27$ and $r = .64$ for syllables per second and phonation time, respectively. They reported further analyses of the English data (n = 27), based on measures taken from manual transcripts (similar analyses on the Turkish speakers were not yet available in this preliminary report). The authors reported significant L1-L2 correlations in the range of .52 to .76 for length of pauses both between and within utterances, for number of filled pauses (use of "uh") by the English sample, and for words per second both including and excluding filled pauses. Only the number of silent pauses per word did not yield a significant L1-L2 correlation. These high L1-L2 correlations provided strong evidence that a great deal of fluency-related phenomena (hesitations, speech rate) may be characteristic of the way individuals speak in general and not just characteristic of their L2 speech. This finding is particularly important in that it underscores the need for obtaining fluency data in the L1 to use as baseline measures when investigating the nature of L2 fluency. To date, most researchers have not done this, perhaps with the consequence that individual speech differences unrelated to the L2 have provided an unwanted source of noise that may have masked important L2 fluency phenomena.

A second result De Jong et al. (2009) reported were findings pointing to the need to distinguish between L1-L2 correlations versus L1-L2 difference scores in the analysis of individual differences in fluency. L1-L2 *correlations* reflect individual differences in overall fluency, regardless of the language spoken. That is, the association between L1 and L2 reveals something about what is common to both languages and hence is not specific to the L2. The magnitude of the association between L1 and L2 performance is reflected in the shared variance as given by the square of the L1-L2 correlation, r^2. In contrast, L1-L2 *difference scores* reflect differences in proficiency in the L2 versus in the L1. That is, difference scores indicate something about how much more difficult the L2 is for the speaker, compared to the L1. The magnitude of the *difference* between L1 and L2 is reflected in the effect size (how many standard deviation units by which the performance in the L2 differs from baseline performance in the L1). De Jong et al. (2009) used Cohen's d (Cohen, 1988) to gauge effect sizes for the differences, and converted Cohen's d to r using Cohen's (1988, p. 23) formula to calculate r^2. They reported that when effect sizes were examined, only words per second (speed fluency)—with and without filled pauses included; stronger results when filled pauses were not included—revealed meaningful effect sizes (r^2 values were about .5). They also found an effect size ($r^2 = .24$) for percentage of silent pauses per word. De Jong et al. (2009) suggested that it is particularly interesting to identify features of speech that show meaningful effect size results for L1-L2 differences while at the same time showing little or no L1-L2 correlation. This was offered as one way of identifying language differences that are not attributable to general, non-L2-specific effects.

A third result that De Jong et al. (2009) reported concerned *repair* fluency—that is, repetitions and/or corrections made by the speaker. They reported, not surprisingly, only weak L1-L2 correlations on measures of word repetitions and corrections ($r^2 < .35$). However, when L1-L2 *differences* on repairs were computed, there was an effect size of $r^2 = .5$ for percentage of words corrected, whereas the effect size for word repetitions approached zero.

Taking all their results together, De Jong et al. (2009) suggested that the oral variables best reflecting L2 fluency, using the L1 as a baseline—at least for the English-Dutch L1-L2 language pair—are effect sizes for L1-L2 differences on three measures—percent of silent pauses per word (but not length of silent pauses); words per second speech rate, especially excluding filled pauses; and percentage of corrections or self-repairs per word. Future research will have to explore the generalizability of these results to other L1/L2 language pairs.

Many other researchers have also investigated the relationship between fluency and the temporal and hesitation features of L2 speech (e.g., Derwing, Rossiter, Munro, & Thomson, 2004; Freed; 1995; Freed,

Segalowitz, & Dewey, 2004; Iwashita, McNamara, & Elder, 2001; Kormos & Dénes, 2004; Mehnert, 1998; O'Brien, Segalowitz, Freed, & Collentine, 2007; Ortega, 1999; Riggenbach, 1991; Segalowitz & Freed, 2004). Of particular interest is the work of Derwing and Munro and their colleagues. They have been examining the role of oral production features—such as speech rate—in the perception of fluency by untrained listeners. Derwing et al. (2004), for example, using a variety of speech elicitation tasks, examined the perceived fluency of Mandarin speakers in their L2 English. Derwing et al. computed the speakers' speech rate in terms of pruned syllables per second (i.e., with self-corrections, self-repetitions, false starts, filled pauses, and asides removed), number of silent pauses (longer than 400 ms), and mean length of run between silent pauses. They also obtained fluency ratings of the L2 speakers from untrained native speakers of English. The relevant findings here are that there was a significant relation between people's perception of fluency and aspects of speech rate and pausing phenomena. They found, for example, that the number of pauses and pruned syllable speech rate together accounted for 65 percent or more of the variance in the fluency ratings, whereas frequency of silent pauses did not significantly account for any variance in fluency ratings. They also found that fluency ratings varied across different elicitation tasks (e.g., picture description versus conversation). The authors concluded that judgments about fluency are selectively based on some aspects of oral production and not others.

As can be seen from this brief review of their work, a major focus of Derwing and Munro and their colleagues has been to understand on what basis people make fluency and proficiency judgments of the L2 speech they hear. They have also been interested in whether these judgments vary as a function of the circumstances under which they are made (see also Derwing, Thomson, & Munro, 2006; Derwing et al., 2004). They have found that sometimes the relationship is not simple and direct. For example, Munro and Derwing (2001) found a non-linear relationship between speech rate and listeners' judgments about a speaker's accentedness and comprehensibility. They obtained U-shaped curves indicating that accent and comprehensibility were judged to be optimal at speech rates that were neither too slow nor too fast. Together, the results of their program of research suggest that, when using raters to judge L2 speech, researchers need to be mindful of the impact speech rate can have on listener judgments.

There is a subtle but important difference in focus between the studies of Derwing and Munro and most of the others mentioned earlier. Most studies have approached the question of fluency characteristics by asking what the oral production features are that correlate with independently determined levels of fluency (based, for example, on listeners' judgments about fluency level). In this case, fluency level is the independent variable and oral production features are the dependent variables. In contrast,

Derwing and Munro and their colleagues have approached the question by asking how perceptions and judgments of fluency correlate with the objectively determined features of oral production. In this case, oral features are the independent variable and judged fluency is the dependent variable. Each approach is valid, of course, when considered separately, and each makes a valuable contribution. However, when studies of the two types are considered together, there can be confusion as to which is the dependent and the independent variable and, at worst, a risk of a form of circular argumentation as we try to answer the anchor question. To help see this more clearly, consider the following example. Suppose a set of speech samples is claimed to exemplify highly fluent speech because listeners judge it to be fluent, and their judgments turn out to be based on the presence of a particular feature of the speech (say, fast speech rate). Then, a new set of speech samples is examined and it is claimed that they exemplify fluent speech because of the presence of that particular feature, providing a basis for studying how listeners judge fluency (demonstrating, say, that listeners use speech rate when making such judgments). All one can really say from this is that there is a connection between particular features of speech (e.g., speech rate) and listeners' ratings of the fluency. What really needs to be decided is whether fluency should be considered first and foremost something that resides in the ear of the beholder (Freed, 2000) and in the mind of the listener ("an impression on the listener's part"; Lennon, 1990, p. 391) or, on the contrary, whether fluency refers first and foremost to particular characteristics of oral production, regardless of how that production is actually perceived and judged by listeners. Fluency cannot be considered both a psychological impression residing in the listener and a physical property of the speech at the same time, without risking circular reasoning (similar in some respects to the conundrum created by the claim that intelligence is what intelligence tests measure).

To break out of the potential circularity, it will first be necessary to make finer-grained distinctions between different categories of fluency as it relates to speech features. Skehan (2003), for example, has called for just this. He proposed focusing on at least three categories: *speed fluency* (related to speech rate), *breakdown fluency* (related to hesitation phenomena), and *repair fluency* (related to self-corrections, repetitions, reformulations, etc.). Separate from these is what is being called here *perceived fluency*, which is related to the fact that characteristics of a speech sample can cause listeners to have impressions about the fluency of that speech sample. In the light of these distinctions, Derwing and Munro's work can be seen as showing that perceived fluency depends in complex ways on various aspects of oral production. Moreover, speed, breakdown, and repair fluencies themselves can vary as a function of the speech elicitation tasks used and of the level of task difficulty (see, especially, Tavakoli & Skehan, 2005). Thus, while there are statistically significant relationships between measures of fluency based directly on oral productions and other ways of evaluating fluency, the situation is complex. The research reveals that it is not possible to globally characterize a person's L2 speech as "fluent" in some unidimensional, absolute fashion. All that one can say at this point is that under such and such circumstances a person's L2 speech has certain objectively measurable characteristics and that these can be interpreted by listeners to be fluent or dysfluent in particular ways. We can see here that an important assumption implicit in the original anchor question has been put into doubt, namely that there is a straightforward relation between speech and some entity that can be called fluency.

It is evident now that, despite several decades of work, researchers have not discovered universally applicable, objective measures of oral fluency. It is true that speech rate and silent pause phenomena seem to be emerging as significantly associated with proficiency more often than some of the other measures. However, even here close examination of the studies reveals lack of agreement on the fine details; compare, for example, some of the results reported earlier in this chapter. The problem, as Kormos (2006, p. 162) pointed out, is that researchers have not been consistent in the way they have operationalized oral performance variables. For example, silent pauses have been defined with different minimum durations by different authors (ranging from 200 ms to 1 sec.) and the methods for measuring silent pauses have not always been clear from the published articles. Some investigators have measured speech rate in syllables per second or minute, others in words per second or minute, some with pruning and some not. Moreover, as research on L2 oral fluency grows to encompass second languages other than English, theoretical and technical challenges will undoubtedly arise (e.g., are there universal, cross-language definitions for *word* and *syllable*?). Some studies have used very small sample sizes, making it difficult to perform satisfactory tests of reliability. As well, speech elicitation techniques have varied from study to study, where some involve the retelling of a picture or film story while others use interviews, and reading a fixed text. As mentioned earlier, studies have even differed as to whether *fluency* is regarded as a separately defined criterion variable (e.g., judged by listeners) to be predicted by oral performance indicators versus defined in terms of a particular oral performance indicator (e.g., speech rate) to be used as a predictor of perceived fluency or of some other aspect of L2 proficiency such as increased communicative competence. Clearly, all these sources of variability across studies have contributed to variability in outcomes and conclusions.

An additional part of the reason for lack of convergence on oral indicators of fluency is that particular oral performance measures can sometimes reflect more than one function. For example, Grosjean (1980a), in a study of pause distributions, concluded that "[p]erformance pause structures can ... be characterized as the product of two (sometimes conflicting) demands on the speaker: the need to respect the linguistic structure of the sentence [e.g., reflecting NP and VP constituency breaks] and the need to balance the length of the constituents in the output [e.g., breaking up very long VPs to keep pauses more evenly distributed]" (p. 99). These different needs can vary in a given study depending on the speech elicitation procedures and conditions used, as Towell et al. (1996, p. 92) have pointed out. Towell et al. went on to say that "Change in such [pause] measurements may be caused by the demands of a particular task, it may be a characteristic of an individual, it may be a sign of individuals having difficulty knowing what to say ... [or] how to verbalize what is already in the mind" (p. 93).

As mentioned earlier, and as Towell et al. also indicated in the quote above, yet another part of the problem may be that individual differences unrelated to L2 performance—revealed in significant L1-L2 correlations—contribute noise to the data and obscure interesting patterns in the L2 (e.g., Cucchiarini et al., 2000, 2002; De Jong et al, 2009; Freed et al., 2004; Segalowitz & Freed, 2004; Towell et al., 1996). One way of resolving the problem is to use L1 measures wherever possible to partial out sources of variability that are not related specifically to the dysfluencies in L2 but that characterize a person's general performance in the given testing conditions. For example, some of the features that researchers routinely interpret as signs of dysfluency—pauses filled with ums, uhs, etc.—may actually serve important communicative functions. Fox Tree (2001, 2002; Clark & Fox Tree, 2002) reported that English speakers make deliberate use of filled pauses to draw the attention of the interlocutor to something about their speech—an upcoming delay, rephrasings, errors, repairs, an intention to speak, etc. Their conclusion that filled pauses impact on the listener's attention has received support from recent neuroimaging evidence reported by Collard, Corley, MacGregor, and Donaldson (2008). That study found that neural event-related potentials (ERPs) reflecting attention to an unexpected target (mismatch negativity and P300) were absent when a target in a speech stream was preceded by a natural-sounding filled pause (the dysfluent speech condition). This result indicates that attention had already been forewarned about the target. In contrast, the ERP signal was present when the target was not preceded by a filled pause (the fluent condition). It is possible that there exist general individual differences in the use of pauses, and so without L1 data as baseline it is difficult to assess the appearance of pauses in the L2. Moreover, these findings about the function of L1 pauses pose another challenge for research on L2 dysfluency. If filled pauses can sometimes fulfill communicative functions rather than being straightforward symptoms of dysfluency, how does one distinguish between the two? Again, including L1 performance baseline measures would be appropriate, on the assumption that the L1 is generally more fluent than the L2. Obviously, to optimize the benefit of doing this, the speech elicitation technique used for the L1 measures should resemble as closely as possible that used for the L2.

In summary, the research to date has not revealed compelling, consistent patterns of oral production features that may be considered reliable markers of fluency. To some extent, this may be due to variability in the way studies have been conducted. There is certainly a need to standardize data collection and analysis procedures, to increase sample sizes, and to take greater account of general individual differences in oral performance as revealed in the L1 speech. It may turn out, however, that even after meeting all these conditions, fluency remains such a complex phenomenon that no simple set of highly consistent measures will be found. This is a concern that we will return to in the final chapter, where an integrated view of fluency is discussed.

In addition to concerns about the different ways researchers have gone about taking measurements and about the infrequent use of L1 baseline data, there are other concerns. One of these is that speakers can employ various strategies to compensate for what might otherwise be manifestations of dysfluencies in their speech. Unless this phenomenon is taken into account, it can compromise research on fluency. Another concern is that different speech elicitation tasks can yield different fluency outcomes, another potential source of variability across studies. These two issues are discussed briefly next.

Communication Strategies

One normal consequence of communicating with others, whether in the L1 or L2, is that speakers will sooner or later encounter some difficulty that can threaten to disrupt the smooth flow of speech. For example, speakers may have difficulty in recalling a particular word, or they may not be able to complete an obligatory grammatical construction correctly simply because of the way they have begun their utterance. When this happens, speakers can engage in a variety of problem-solving strategies to get around the difficulty and to maintain the flow of speech to ensure successful communication. They can, for example, slow down their speech to buy time while they search for the word or grammatical construction that has temporarily eluded them. They may substitute other words or simpler expressions or, if the problem occurs in the L2, they may "foreignize" an L1 word to make it sound like a word in the L2. Dörnyei and Kormos (1998) list over a dozen such strategies that people use to help maintain the integrity and comprehensibility of their messages (see also Dörnyei & Scott, 1997; Kormos, 2006, especially Chapter 7, for extended discussion of this topic).

From the point of view of L2 fluency research, speakers' use of such strategies provides both an opportunity and a problem. The opportunity comes from the fact that strategy use reveals a need to cope with a potential fluency vulnerability and, at the same time, indicates an ability to compensate for this vulnerability. For example, as mentioned earlier, Towell et al. (1996) found that nonfluent L2 speakers can resort to the use of prefabricated chunks of speech to create the impression of fluency. If the L2 speaker uses prefabricated chunks in a way that departs from normal L1 patterns, then it might point to a compensatory strategy by the L2 speaker. The problem comes from the fact that speakers can often mask their dysfluencies by means of such strategies, making themselves appear to be more fluent than they would under different circumstances. Such masking could create difficulties for researchers attempting to find relationships between features of oral-production aspects of underlying cognitive fluency thought to be central in oral production.

For our purposes here, the most relevant ideas regarding communication strategies have to do with the ways speakers might handle problems arising from dealing with time pressure. This is probably the most common circumstance to disrupt the smooth flow of L2 speech. Dörnyei and Kormos (1998) provide a useful list of the problem-solving mechanisms that L2 speakers might engage in when dealing with time pressure. These include lexicalized pauses, non-lexicalized pauses, and repetitions. Lexicalized pauses are stretches between elements of the main message where the speaker uses filler words, self-repetitions, and repetitions of what the interlocutor said, all as strategies to buy time. Filler expressions can include phrases such as *you know, actually, this is rather difficult to explain* (see Kormos, 2006, p. 151). Non-lexicalized pauses include silent pauses, pauses filled with *um, er, uh,* etc., and sound lengthening (e.g., drawing out a sound, as in *I'mmmmm ...,* in order to gain time). Excessive use of such stalling tactics, compared to the speaker's L1 speech where such tactics will also appear (Kormos, 2006), would indicate that the speaker is susceptible to certain fluency vulnerabilities. Presumably, evidence that speakers have resorted to these strategies will appear when time pressures are great enough to create the need for them to avoid the emergence of dysfluencies but not so great as to preclude the planning necessary to engage in compensatory strategies in the first place.

Speech Elicitation Tasks

A quick scan of the literature on L2 fluency reveals that researchers have used a wide variety of speech elicitation tasks. However, none of them has been standardized in any systematic way. Because the specific nature of the task can have an impact on the fluency of a speaker's output, this lack of standardization makes it difficult to resolve discrepant findings. The tasks most researchers have used fall into four distinct categories. In the first category are reading tasks, where participants are given a short text to read into a computer. Reading tasks are perhaps the most widely used because they are the easiest to administer. More importantly, reading tasks have another advantage not found in other tasks, namely, they do not require participants to conceptualize what to say. In reading tasks, the need for macroplanning (see Figure 1.2; same as Levelt's 1989 Conceptualizer) is greatly reduced. Second, to a large extent speakers don't even have to formulate their conceptualizations into language—that is, there is reduced need for microplanning (see Figure 1.2; same as Levelt's 1989 Formulator); the text does this for the speaker. Thus, assuming that the speaker is able to fluently read the orthography, reading tests can be seen as primarily addressing basic articulation issues.

In the second category are picture description tasks where photos, cartoons without words or silent films are used as stimuli. Speakers are required to describe the depicted stories while looking at the stimuli. A wide range of such tasks has been used. Among the more commonly used are the wordless Frog stories by Mayer (1969) and picture stories designed to stimulate conversation in learners (Heaton, 1966/1995). Some researchers have used wordless cartoons consisting of one or several frames (Tavakoli & Foster, 2008; Tavakoli & Skehan, 2005). Other researchers have also used films, such as the wordless Mr. Bean or Chaplin films. The advantage of tasks in this category is that they allow the researcher to constrain what the speakers will talk about while not putting specific words or sentence constructions into their mouths, and without making demands on memory for story events encountered before. Unfortunately, there have been few attempts to articulate clear criteria for selecting visual stimuli to use in speech elicitation tasks. This lack of criteria can pose problems for making comparisons across studies. One exception is Rossiter, Derwing, and Jones (2008), who list 33 criteria to consider when selecting picture stimuli for eliciting speech. The criteria touch on the storyline (e.g., avoid flashbacks or flashforwards), cultural content (e.g., avoid culture-specific body language) and picture format (e.g., ensure actions are clear, such as picking something up versus putting something down). Tavakoli and Skehan (2005) and others have also pointed out that the structure of storylines can affect oral production, making it easier or harder for speakers to respond fluently. Eventually, picture story criteria will have to be explicit about the different ways the internal structure of stories can be fluency-relevant.

In the third category are story-retelling tasks, where the participants read or hear a story in the L1 and then retell it in the L2. All the advantages and concerns about picture description tasks apply here as well. A major additional issue here is that the information is not in front of the speaker at the time of the retelling and so individual differences in working memory can play a role in the quality of the oral productions. For this reason, it is useful when using story-retelling studies to obtain working memory measures from participants to allow taking this source of individual differences into account (for discussion of measures of L2 working memory and its role in individual differences in L2 proficiency, see Michael & Gollan, 2005, and Miyake & Friedman, 1998).

Finally, there are spontaneous speech samples. Often these are obtained by asking participants to describe some experience they have had, such as their most frightening experience (Labov, 1970) or their opinion about some issue. The advantage of eliciting spontaneous speech is that it has greater ecological validity. Speaking spontaneously is what people do most of the time. The general disadvantage, of course, is that researchers have minimum control over what speakers attempt to say and this can introduce unwanted sources of variability into the data. A more controlled technique for obtaining spontaneous speech samples is to use a standardized interview technique with a trained interviewer. Freed et al. (2004) and Segalowitz and Freed (2004), for example, used procedures based on the Oral Proficiency Interview (OPI; Breiner-Sanders, Lowe, Miles, & Swender, 2000) with trained interviewers in studies of L2 learning in study-abroad contexts. The advantage of this approach is that the evaluation of proficiency is based on the fluency judgments of an interviewer trained to elicit samples and to make judgments according to standardized criteria. Results are, in principle, comparable across interviewers, settings, and studies. The OPI procedure requires the speaker to engage in both the conceptualization (macroplanning) and formulation (microplanning) phases of speaking. Here, the OPI more realistically imitates life than do picture tasks. A disadvantage of the OPI, however, is encountered when it is used for obtaining speech samples that are subsequently analyzed acoustically for temporal and hesitation phenomena. The disadvantage arises when one tries to extract speech samples from the longer interview. The OPI interview can take different directions with different speakers, depending on that person's level of proficiency. This is because the trained interviewer is supposed to adjust the interview according to the speaker's capabilities. In addition, the OPI procedure is divided into different segments with different goals (e.g., sometimes pushing the speaker's limits of expression, sometimes not). This means that an individual may display different fluency levels at different times within the 20- to 30-minute interview. Extracting comparable 2- or 4-minute slices of interview for acoustical analysis can thus become a challenge. Also, see Bachman (1988) and Johnson and Tyler (1998) for other concerns about the OPI.

To summarize thus far, the study of L2 fluency has suffered from a lack of standardization in the speech elicitation procedures used. Probably, however, no one task (reading, picture description, story retelling, spontaneous speech, etc.) will ever satisfy all the needs of the fluency researcher. Nevertheless, a feasible goal for the field might be to develop minimal criteria that can serve researchers working in different L1 and L2 contexts, thereby helping to make data across studies more comparable.

Related to the matter of speech elicitation tasks is the issue of the structure and difficulty of the task itself. A study by Tavakoli and Skehan (2005) is especially relevant in this regard. They tested 80 participants of different levels of English L2 proficiency, using picture description tasks to obtain L2 speech samples, where the picture stories varied in structure and the testing conditions varied in the time allowed for strategic planning before speaking. Tavakoli and Skehan analyzed the impact of these factors on oral production by looking at L2 speech variables. Factor analysis revealed clear distinctions among the oral production variables. The analysis revealed six items loading onto the first factor, namely length of run (mean number of syllables between pauses > .28 seconds), speech rate, total amount of silence, total time spent speaking, number of pauses, and length of pauses, especially the speech rate and silent pause measures. Taken together, these items reflect what the authors called a "breakdown fluency/rate of speech/unit size" factor (p. 266), which they described as reflecting "a capacity to organize speech in real time" (p. 266). This factor can be referred to as *temporal fluency* because of its emphasis on timing issues (p. 258), and it combines what Skehan (2003) had called speed fluency and breakdown fluency. Reformulation, false starts, replacements, and repetitions loaded onto the second factor and reflected what the authors (see also Skehan, 2003) called *repair fluency*, and which they described as reflecting "a concern to modify utterances on-line" (Tavakoli & Skehan, 2005, p. 266). A third factor emerging from the analysis included two variables—accuracy and complexity, reflecting aspects of form, related to meaning.

The findings of Tavakoli and Skehan (2005) are generally consistent with the results others have reported, in particular those showing that when speakers have more time available for strategic planning, and when storylines are inherently structured, then speakers show evidence of better temporal and repair fluency (e.g., R. Ellis & Yuan, 2005; Mehnert, 1998; Ortega, 1999, 2005; and others in R. Ellis, 2005). Skehan (1996) and P. Robinson (2001a), in fact, have proposed placing central emphasis on the impact on oral production of task structure, complexity, load, and difficulty. Skehan focuses on the way tasks draw on the speaker's attentional capacity. This has the potential of affecting fluency because fluency "consists of the capacity to mobilize one's linguistic resources in the service of real-time communication, i.e., to produce (and comprehend) speech at relatively normal rates, approaching (but not necessarily identical to) one's own native-language speech rates" (p. 48). He goes on to identify rate, pausing, reformulation, and hesitation among the elements of fluency that would be relevant to consider. Skehan's goal is to understand how task complexity impacts on learning and fluency development so that one might harness its effects in learning contexts in order to promote fluency. Robinson similarly proposed a framework for thinking about task complexity, learners' perceptions of task difficulty, and the impact these have on the course of learning and performance. His framework distinguishes among task complexity, task conditions, and task difficulty. Task complexity involves cognitive factors that are resource directing or resource depleting. Task conditions involve interactional factors that address participation variables (kind of interaction implicated) and participant variables (personal characteristics). Task difficulty involves learner factors, which include affective and ability variables. Robinson's framework postulates, for example, that task complexity will be a more important consideration for determining appropriate sequencing criteria for tasks than will be either task conditions or difficulty. Such systematic approaches to understanding how task structure affects production are extremely important because, beyond their potential pedagogical value for L2 training, they can guide the way tasks are selected for testing purposes and they can help researchers understand how to interpret the results of fluency studies (Skehan, 1998) where different tasks have been used.

In light of the issues just reviewed, and the difficulty encountered in answering the anchor question, it is now appropriate to consider reformulating that question in a way that makes it more amenable to research within a cognitive science perspective.

Cognitive Fluency, Utterance Fluency, and Perceived Fluency

In its original version, the first anchor question was: *What features of L2 oral performance are reliable indicators of fluency?* The review of the literature just presented suggests that this question, in its present form, is not likely to be answered satisfactorily. It needs reformulation. To begin this recasting of the question, consider the following definitions of fluency:

1   "Fluency" means that the activities of planning and uttering can be executed nearly simultaneously by the speaker of the language (Rehbein, 1987, p. 104).
2   Fluency equals the communicative acceptability of the speech act, or "communicative fit," and expectations concerning this fit vary according to the situation (Meisel, 1987, p. 86).

To these two ideas we can add the observation from Goldman-Eisler, quoted at the very beginning of this chapter:

3   The complete speech act is a dynamic process, demanding the mobilization in proper sequence of a series of complex procedures and is the temporal integration of serial phenomena (Goldman-Eisler, 1968, p. 6).

By combining and integrating the ideas contained in these three points, it becomes possible to recast the anchor question in a constructive way. The new version of the question reads as follows:

New version of Anchor Question #1:

What features of L2 oral performance serve as reliable indicators of how efficiently the speaker is able to mobilize and temporally integrate, in a nearly simultaneous way, the underlying processes of planning and assembling an utterance in order to perform a communicatively acceptable speech act?

This formulation of the question differs in emphasis from the original. The original question asked about the mapping of speech characteristics onto fluency, where fluency was left relatively undefined. The new version focuses on the relationship between the operation of underlying cognitive processes producing the utterance and certain characteristics of that utterance. Shifting the focus in this way has important consequences for how the terms *fluency* and *fluent* are to be used. These consequences are discussed next.

The new anchor question requires one to make a distinction among three different meanings of fluency where before one word was used more or less imprecisely to cover all three. To illustrate these different meanings, consider the following statement: *Noriko speaks Inuktitut quite fluently for a Japanese.* This sentence can be said to have (at the very least) a three-way ambiguity in meaning:

- The sentence could mean that Noriko has the ability to mobilize her cognitive system for speaking Inuktitut in a highly effective and efficient manner, similar to what happens with native speakers of Inuktitut.
- The sentence may also mean that the utterances Noriko produces in Inuktitut have, objectively speaking, certain characteristics of speech flow in terms of rate, pauses, hesitations, and repair features that render the speech quite fluid.
- Finally, the sentence could also mean that people who hear Noriko speak Inuktitut will infer, based on their perceptions of her speech, that she has highly efficient cognitive skills for speaking the language, i.e., that she sounds like she is a "fluent" speaker.

Normally, all three meanings will more or less coincide and be mutually supportive or, at least, people will normally assume this to be the case. Of course, this assumption may not always be true and, in any case, the three senses of fluency address rather different issues. It is important, therefore, to keep these three senses of fluency apart, and we will do so here by labeling them *cognitive fluency, utterance fluency,* and *perceived fluency* respectively.

Cognitive fluency has to do with the speaker's ability to efficiently mobilize and integrate the underlying cognitive processes responsible for producing utterances with the characteristics that they have. The mobilization referred to here is the mobilization Goldman-Eisler was talking about in the quotation cited earlier. Producing an utterance involves coordinating the activity of many different, interacting cognitive processes, as illustrated in Figure 1.2 in Chapter 1. This coordination must be carried out quickly and efficiently, in a manner that ensures that the utterance is produced as intended, in good time, and in a manner that keeps the flow of speech moving. This process involves mobilizing mechanisms for planning the utterance, for lexical search, for packaging the information into a grammatically appropriate form, for generating an articulatory script for speaking the utterance, etc. It also involves integrating all of these processes in a way that minimizes inefficient processing, reduces or eliminates internal sources of interference and crosstalk that could disrupt the fluidity and evenness of production over time. In this sense, the cognitive system itself exhibits fluency in how efficiently and fluidly it is able to carry out this mobilization and integration of processes. Thus, cognitive fluency is the fluency that a speaker possesses.

Utterance fluency has to do with the features of an utterance. It refers to the temporal, pausing, hesitation, and repair characteristics, examples of which were discussed earlier. These characteristics are actual properties of the utterance, not just impressions a listener might have. There are, of course, many possible candidate features for utterance fluency, and sometimes there are several ways to operationalize a given feature (e.g., speech rate as syllables per second, syllables per pause; stressed words per minute). In theory, the number of possible fluency-relevant properties one might imagine investigating could be very large indeed. One hopes, however, that research will narrow down the list of potential features to a small set of critical items. This gives rise to the important question of how to decide which features to keep and which to reject as important for utterance fluency. This question will be addressed more fully in the final chapter. What is important for the moment is to recognize that utterance fluency needs to be distinguished from cognitive fluency. Utterance fluency refers to the fluency characteristics that a speech sample can possess.

Perceived fluency has to do with the inferences listeners make about a speaker's cognitive fluency based on their perception of utterance fluency. In other words, perceived fluency is a judgment made about speakers based on impressions drawn from their speech samples. Sometimes, of course, listeners may be asked to judge a particular speech sample for its fluency, without reference to the speaker as such. More often, however, listeners are asked—or it is implied by the task given to them—to say how fluent they believe the *speaker* who produced the sample to be, based on their impressions of the speech sample. In this regard, listeners do not normally treat every pause and hesitation as evidence of dysfluency, a fact sometimes recognized in definitions of fluency that refer to the absence of *undue* pauses and hesitations, implying that a certain amount of pausing and hesitation is acceptable and even expected in so-called fluent speech. Although perceived fluency was not explicitly mentioned in the revised anchor question, it is nevertheless necessary to distinguish it from cognitive and utterance fluency. Perceived fluency is the fluency that is ascribed by a listener to a speaker, based on impressions drawn from hearing speech samples produced by the speaker.

Figure 2.1 presents in graphical form these various distinctions underlying the new version of the anchor question. The figure shows that there are at least two functions carried out by underlying processes in the cognitive/perceptual system—the planning and the assembling of an utterance. These functions need to be integrated temporally for utterances to be executed with the desired characteristics of timing, pausing and hesitation, and repair features. The domain of *cognitive* fluency is the operation—in particular, the efficiency of the operation—of these planning and assembling functions and of their integration and execution. The domain of *utterance* fluency is the set of objectively determined timing, pausing/hesitation, and repair features of the utterance, reflecting the impact of the cognitive fluency on the underlying speech production processes. Finally, the domain of *perceived* fluency is the inference that listeners make about the connection between utterance and cognitive fluency (i.e., it is inferred that the speaker has such and such a level of cognitive fluency given the apparent utterance fluency of the person's speech sample).

Posing the question this way calls for a different way of looking for the answer. First, it calls for a focus on the mobilization and temporal integration of underlying processes. Such a focus makes it necessary to define what the relevant elements of cognitive and perceptual processing might be and to operationally define ways of assessing their efficiency of operation. These topics are presented in this chapter and Chapter 4, and to some extent in Chapter 6.

Second, the reformulation of the question directs the focus on the features of oral performance that might directly reflect cognitive fluency. To do this it is necessary to explore a range of potential oral production features in order to find just those that have an important relationship to the relevant elements of cognitive fluency. Moreover, because this exploration concerns questions about L2 fluency, it is important to ensure that they focus on L2-*specific* aspects of cognitive and utterance fluency, as distinguished from aspects having to do with general cognitive abilities. As suggested earlier, it should possible to accomplish this by using L1

Figure 2.1 Graphical representation showing the domains of cognitive fluency, utterance fluency, and perceived fluency, and their relationships.

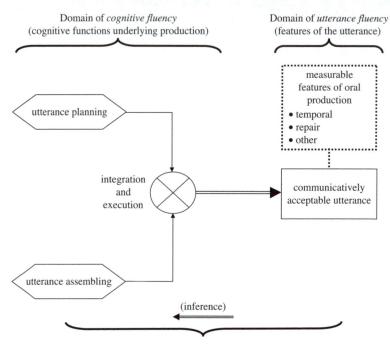

Cognitive fluency refers to the efficiency of the speaker's underlying processes responsible for fluency-relevant features of utterances, *utterance fluency* refers to the oral features of utterances that reflect the operation of underlying cognitive processes, and *perceived fluency* refers to the inferences that listeners make about a speaker's cognitive fluency based on perception of the utterance fluency features of the speaker's speech output.

data to control for such general cognitive processing skills. (Note, however, that using the L1 for such control purposes might be inappropriate where L2 acquisition has resulted in significant L1 attrition; Schmid, Köpke, Keijzer, & Weilemar, 2004; Seliger & Vago, 1991.)

Finally, the anchor question focuses on the communicative acceptability of the speech act. This focus requires understanding of the different ways in which oral communication can succeed or fail to be communicatively acceptable. There are two aspects of this focus on communicative acceptability that need to be kept in mind. One is that speakers may find it cognitively challenging to meet certain norms of communication (e.g., to use a certain speech register; to speak at a certain rate). These challenges may tax the cognitive system, compromising its efficiency and hence the speaker's cognitive fluency, with the result that utterance fluency suffers. Another is that listeners may pick up on aspects of the utterance that they feel are not communicatively acceptable and this noticing of communicatively unacceptable elements in the speaker's speech may influence perceived fluency. To address all of these issues, one must consider the context in which communication takes place, and this in turn makes it necessary to understand how in general the social dimensions of communication are realized through language. This topic is covered in Chapter 5.

By focusing on these three aspects of fluency—the efficiency of underlying cognitive processes, the temporal and repair features of utterances, and the communicative acceptability of utterances—one obtains a richer and more nuanced way of thinking about fluency compared to the lay view of fluency as simply a performance characteristic that lies on a single continuum stretching from low to high fluency. The process of investigating these three aspects of fluency will require, of course, considerable trial and error. Theoretical considerations may at first suggest that particular aspects of cognitive fluency ought to be key to utterance fluency. To demonstrate this, however, requires identifying the right underlying processes as the candidate aspects of cognitive fluency, and also selecting the right features of utterance fluency. One must also select appropriate tasks for the data collection, tasks that do not mask or prevent the expected relationships from revealing themselves. All this will be challenging. Ultimately, however, it is hoped that it will be possible to identify a reasonably small set of cognitive processes that can be reliably associated with an equally reasonably small set of utterance fluency phenomena. Success in doing so will provide an answer to this first anchor question.

By way of concluding this chapter, another comment from Frieda Goldman-Eisler is especially germane. Writing about the temporal aspects of fluency in the L1, she observed that

> Hesitation is thus shown to be an indicator of the internal act of generating information rather than of the statistical predictability of the linguistic expression. In line with the expectation, as soon as this becomes habituated, the link between hesitation and information disappears.
>
> (1968, p. 57)

In other words, the crucial factor in fluency, according to her, is the efficiency (the level of habituation) with which speakers are able to execute the cognitions underlying speech production. One would expect that in the L2 this efficiency factor would be all the more critical for oral fluency. Goldman-Eisler is also saying here that only when the underlying cognitive activity has become sufficiently habituated (automatic) can the speech itself be executed in a fluent manner. This brings us to the second anchor question guiding this book—the first of two questions addressing cognitive fluency: *Can studies of general cognitive processing fluency and of skill acquisition outside bilingualism contribute to an understanding of L2 fluency?*

Chapter Summary

This chapter reviewed studies relevant to the first anchor question concerned with features of oral production that might serve as indicators of fluency. In the course of this discussion the following three conclusions were drawn that will be brought forward to the final chapter for the concluding integrative discussion:

- *The search for oral correlates of fluency needs to focus on features of L2 performance that are reliable indicators of how efficiently a speaker is able to mobilize and temporally integrate, in a nearly simultaneous way, the underlying processes of planning and assembling an utterance in order to perform a communicatively acceptable speech act.*
- *One needs to distinguish among (a) cognitive fluency—the efficiency of operation of the underlying processes responsible for the production of utterances; (b) utterance fluency—the features of utterances that reflect the speaker's cognitive fluency; and (c) perceived fluency— the inferences listeners make about speakers' cognitive fluency based on their perceptions of their utterance fluency.*
- *The study of the relation between cognitive and utterance fluency requires controlling for individual differences in processing that are not specific to the L2, and taking into account task-specific effects related to the speech elicitation methods used and to the testing conditions under which they are administered.*

3   Fluency in General Cognitive Processing

Children learn language from their language experiences—there is no other way ... They bring to this learning general cognitive and interactive skills ... Language development can be explained in terms of species-specific learning and intentional communication.

(Lieven and Tomasello, 2008, p. 168)

In the last two decades or so, a number of authors have advocated a usage-based approach to L1 language acquisition, an approach that runs counter in many ways to theoretical positions based on Universal Grammar in linguistics (e.g., Langacker, 1987; Tomasello, 2000, 2003; authors in the edited volume by Barlow & Kemmer, 2000). A strong commitment to the usage-based approach underlies the quote above from Lieven and Tomasello (2008). Their statement provides a good starting point for this chapter, which addresses the second anchor question guiding this book—*Can studies of general cognitive processing fluency and of skill acquisition outside bilingualism contribute to an understanding of L2 fluency?*

Barlow and Kemmer (2000, pp. viii–xxii) identify some of the main assumptions underlying usage-based approaches that are shared by most of its adherents. These assumptions are the following:

- There is an intimate relationship between linguistic structures and instances of use of language.
- Frequency of exposure plays an important role in acquisition.
- Comprehension and production are integral, rather than peripheral, to the linguistic system.
- Learning and experience play a central role in language acquisition.
- Linguistic representations are emergent, rather than stored as fixed entities.
- There is an intimate relation between usage, synchronic variation, and diachronic change.

- The linguistic system is interconnected with non-linguistic cognitive systems.
- Context plays a crucial role in the operation of the linguistic system.

Whether or not one agrees with a usage-based approach for L1 acquisition, or even L2 acquisition, a usage-based approach is probably the appropriate way to address questions about L2 *fluency*. Indeed, the Lieven and Tomasello quotation at the head of this chapter could easily be paraphrased in relation to L2 fluency—with very little change to the wording—as follows:

> L2 users develop language fluency from their language experiences— there is no other way. They bring to this development general cognitive and interactive skills. L2 fluency development can be explained in terms of general processes of human learning and intentional communication.
>
> (paraphrase of Lieven & Tomasello, 2008, p. 168)

This chapter explores what some of these general cognitive and interactive processes might be. The goal is to propose aspects of general cognitive processing with potential promise for application to L2 fluency issues because they are grounded in empirical work.

The general literature on skills not related to L2 acquisition has been growing very rapidly in recent years and to review it comprehensively here would require us to stray from the main topic of L2 fluency. It is interesting to note, though, that in this literature the term *fluency* has not been restricted to language (e.g., speaking, reading, writing, second language, etc.) or to motor skills (e.g., general locomotion, sport, dance). In fact, for decades now cognitive psychologists have been interested in various aspects of general cognitive processing fluency—as seen in studies of perceptual fluency, fluency heuristics, fluency illusions, and more, none having to do with language or motor fluency per se. One can ask, therefore, whether the study of these more general forms of *cognitive* processing fluency can yield findings and insights relevant to L2 fluency. If so, then it may be possible to situate L2 fluency issues within a richer and broader context than has been done so far. As will become evident below, there are indeed a number of relevant processing fluency phenomena that have captured the attention of cognitive psychologists, although one does not typically read about them in the L2 acquisition literature.

Three aspects of general cognitive processing fluency are addressed here, all of which are based on a substantial psychological literature from outside the area of L2 acquisition, proficiency, and fluency. These are *fluency heuristics*, *transfer appropriate processing*, and *processing flexibility*. The phenomena associated with these three shed light on aspects of memory, perception, judgment, evaluation, and cognitive control, and therefore they are relevant to L2 fluency. A fourth aspect of cognitive fluency—*automaticity*—also has a substantial literature behind it, with obvious relevance to L2 fluency. However, treatment of this topic has been reserved for the next chapter.

Fluency Heuristics

An important and obvious fact about the way humans process information is that some kinds of information are processed faster than others, and that more quickly processed information is subjectively experienced as being easier to handle cognitively. For example, one's own name spoken in a noisy room is usually recognized sooner than a less familiar name. This indicates greater processing fluency for one's own name compared to the processing of other stimuli. Other examples of processing fluency include faster recollection of a particular word or fact, and speedier judgments about an object's properties such as its familiarity, frequency, distance, or aesthetic quality. Consider Figure 3.1, which shows sets of stimulus pairs, based on examples described in the research literature. The first member of each pair is typically processed more fluently than the second member. Set A shows two pairs of sentences, the ones on the left being easier to read than the other because of the font used. In Pair B (this illustration only roughly approximates the original), the left item is visually less occluded (20 percent overlay of random dots in the original study) and hence easier to see than the right item (40 percent overlay of random dots). In Pair C the structurally simpler and shorter word is more readily understood than the more complex, longer synonym. In Pair D the rhyming character of the left-hand expression makes it easier to process than the right-hand expression. In Pair E, when the target is a repetition of a previously, rapidly presented prime, it is easier to process than when it is not. In all such cases, one can talk about stimulus processing fluency, where processing fluency refers to the speed and ease of processing the stimulus.

Of course, it is not surprising that the second member of each pair in Figure 3.1 is processed less fluently than its first member counterpart. It is intuitively obvious that words can be made relatively easier to process by providing prior experience with them or by presenting them under better viewing conditions. There is, however, a more interesting fact about processing fluency. When people are able to process a stimulus fluently, they often have a subjective experience of the ease of that processing, even if they are not aware of the source of that processing fluency. This subjective awareness of one's own ease of processing can itself become information about the world that people use in various ways. If they are not able to identify the true reason for the fluency, they may misattribute the experienced fluency to the wrong source.

Set	Stimulus pair		Critical feature	Source
	First member: **Stimulus processed with greater fluency**	**Second member:** **Stimulus processed with less fluency**		
A	Instructions were shown in this font.	*Instructions were shown in this font.*	Font	Song & Schwarz (2008)
	Instructions were shown in this font.	**Instructions were shown in this font.**		Alter & Oppenheimer (2008)
B	target	target	Visual clarity	Whittlesea, Jacoby, & Girard (1990)
C	"use"	"utilize"	Length/ complexity	Oppenheimer (2006)
D	"What sobriety conceals, alcohol reveals."	"What sobriety conceals, alcohol unmasks."	Rhyme	McGlone & Tofighbakhsh (2000)
E	Target also appears in an immediately preceding, rapidly presented prime	Target does *not* appear in an immediately preceding, rapidly presented prime	Repetition	Whittlesea, Jacoby, & Girard (1990)

Figure 3.1 Examples of stimulus pairs that differ in relation to one another in terms of the processing fluency associated with them.

When people do make an attribution, correct or incorrect, they engage in what is called a *fluency heuristic* for making other judgments about the stimulus. This judgment is based on the (possibly incorrect) assumption that if this stimulus feels easy to process then it must have such and such properties (e.g., it is more frequent in the language; it was seen before). It turns out that people do indeed use such fluency heuristics in a number of ways (e.g., see the studies cited in Figure 3.1). This phenomenon may be relevant to L2 fluency insofar as it tells us something about when and how people might monitor and draw conclusions about their own ongoing L2 language experiences as a function of the processing fluency they experience in that language.

One of the earliest demonstrations that people do in fact use the subjective experience of their own processing fluency to make judgments of various kinds comes from a series of studies reported by Tversky and

Kahneman (1973). In their Study 8, Tversky and Kahneman had participants listen to a list of 39 names presented at a rate of 2 seconds per name. Nineteen of the names were clearly male names and 20 were clearly female names (or vice versa). Participants had to report afterward whether there were more male or female names. The lists were constructed so that the smaller set (e.g., the 19 male names) always consisted of the names of famous people (e.g., Albert Einstein) and the larger set consisted of the names of non-famous people. It was expected that the names of famous people would generally be easier to recall, because the many past encounters with those names would result in them being processed more fluently at the time of presentation and hence be more available during later recall. It was hypothesized that participants would use this enhanced availability of famous names to make decisions about the predominance of male or female names. That is, as participants tried to recall the names they had heard, they would more readily recollect the famous names and treat them as representative of the full sample of names. The results strongly supported the hypothesis. Over 80 percent of the participants reported—wrongly—the gender of the famous names in the list as the predominating gender. This is an example of how fluency (here, the ease of recalling famous names) was used by people to make a judgment about something else, namely, the relative frequency of male versus female names in a list.

Since the 1970s there have been many studies demonstrating the interesting ways people use fluency heuristics (for reviews and other examples of heuristics people are known to use, see Alter & Oppenheimer, 2009; Pohl, 2006; and Whittlesea & Leboe, 2003). For example, Alter and Oppenheimer (2008) found that when people were instructed to describe the characteristics of a city, they responded more abstractly (e.g., New York is a civilized jungle) and reported the city as being farther away when the written instructions were presented in a font that reduced processing fluency. In contrast, they responded more concretely (e.g., New York is a large city) and as being closer when given instructions in a format that permitted greater processing fluency (see examples in Figure 3.1, Row A).

Whittlesea, Jacoby, and Girard (1990) reported a set of experiments investigating the role of perceptual fluency on the memory illusion known as "feeling of familiarity." In their Experiment 1, participants saw a rapidly presented series of seven words followed by an eighth test word that had to be pronounced aloud as quickly as possible and then judged as "old" or "new" depending on whether or not it had appeared in the immediately preceding group of seven words. The test word always appeared with a visual noise dot pattern mask that manipulated the perceptual clarity of the word, and it did so in such a way that participants were not consciously aware of the differences between light and heavy visual noise conditions. The results were that participants generally pronounced the test word more quickly when the visual noise was light, indicating that there was greater perceptual fluency for these words. More importantly, participants reported significantly more often that the test word was a repeated word—that is, it felt familiar—when that word was presented under conditions favoring perceptual fluency (light visual noise), whether or not it truly was a repeated word. Their Experiment 2 demonstrated a similar effect using a font case manipulation, where the font case of the test word had to be judged as same or different as its earlier presentation in the word list. In their Experiment 4, they asked participants to judge whether the visual noise on a test word was greater than or less than the visual noise presented on one of the words in an immediately preceding prime list, where half the time the test word also appeared in the prime list. They found that when the test word was a repetition of the masked prime list word, participants reported the test word to be more visually clear than when it was not a repeated word. That is, perceptual fluency induced by repetition affected judgments about the word by producing an illusion of visual clarity. Overall, Whittlesea et al. (1990) demonstrated that perceptual fluency, manipulated by visual clarity and by repetition, could influence people's judgments about stimuli in an illusory way (see also Whittlesea & Williams, 1998, 2000).

Reber, Winkielman, and Schwarz (1998) reported a study showing that perceptual fluency could also influence liking for and aesthetic judgments about a stimulus. It had already been well established that frequent exposure to a stimulus increases positive regard for that stimulus—known as the "mere exposure effect," probably through increased processing fluency due to the increased viewing from repetition (Bornstein, 1989). Unlike cases of the mere exposure effect, however, Reber et al. demonstrated a fluency effect on stimuli in the absence of increased viewing experience. They asked participants to judge visually degraded drawings of affectively neutral objects (e.g., horse, plane) shown for 2 seconds. Prior to each presentation participants saw a prime stimulus, also a degraded picture shown for only 25 ms, which was either a contour of the figure (matching prime) or the contour of a different figure (mismatching prime). Participants reported no awareness of the primes. The series of pictures was presented twice. On one round, the task was to rate the pictures in terms of prettiness on a nine-point scale. On the other round, the task was to press a key as soon as the picture was recognized. Results were that pictures preceded by a matching prime were judged to be significantly prettier and they were also recognized significantly faster, suggesting that perceptual fluency (as evidenced by faster recognition) was responsible for the preference effects. Thus, Reber et al. showed that a preference effect can be obtained from increased processing fluency without repetition.

The larger relevance of these examples to L2 fluency will be taken up later in this section. For the moment two points about processing fluency are worth emphasizing. First, these studies show that stimuli can be processed with different degrees of ease or fluency, depending on a number of well-defined presentation conditions (e.g., prior exposure, viewing clarity), and this processing fluency can be subjectively felt. Second, people use these subjective feelings when making judgments about stimulus properties and when making preference judgments. Processing fluency is thus an heuristic that serves decision-making. As will be discussed later, the use of a fluency heuristic may be relevant to L2 fluency acquisition.

The cases presented so far have been drawn from examples of *conceptual* and *perceptual* fluency. There is also an emerging literature on how *motor skill* fluency can produce effects similar to the ones just described. Typing skills provide an interesting case in point and it is not hard to imagine that the results could generalize to other areas of motor skill. In an early study, Van den Bergh, Vrana, and Eelen (1990) asked skilled typists and non-typists to make affective judgments (subjective liking) about pairs of letter dyads and triads (e.g., OL—IG; XZS—QLB). The task required no typing and participants were unaware that typing skill was a variable in the study. In each pair, one member—if typed using standard professional typing techniques—would have required using the same finger for all its letters (e.g., OL), whereas the other member of the pair would have required different fingers (e.g., IG). Different-finger sequences are normally typed more fluently than same-finger sequences because movements for the different fingers can be programmed simultaneously, thereby allowing movements to be executed with a shorter interval between letters. The study revealed that skilled typists preferred (reported subjectively liking) the different-finger members of the pairs— that is, those letter sequences that were easier to type fluently—and they preferred same-finger members less than did non-typists. Non-typists had no preferences. Moreover, when asked about the stimuli and the basis for their preferences, neither the typists nor non-typists had any awareness of the reasons for their choices, nor what principle differentiated the two members of each pair. The authors concluded that, for the typists, the stimuli automatically activated motor information in memory and that, despite not having any specific intentions of thinking about the stimuli in terms of how they would be typed, they nevertheless were influenced by these motor-based memories. These results are an example of how motor fluency can have an automatic (i.e., activated without conscious intention) impact on evaluative judgments.

Yang, Gallo, and Beilock (2009) reported a study that looked at the impact of motor fluency on memory judgments. Participants were "expert" and "novice" typists. Participants were not aware that typing skill was an aspect of the study or that the stimuli had been constructed according to the same-finger/different-finger criteria as in the Van den Bergh et al. (1990) study. In the study phase, all the participants typed eight same-finger dyads and eight different-finger dyads, presented in random order. Next, they were given a surprise recognition memory test in which they had to report if a given dyad had appeared in the study phase or not. Both groups of typists scored equally well on hits in the recognition task. However, the expert typists had more false alarms for different-finger dyads—that is, for those letter combinations that if typed would have been typed more fluently—than for same-finger dyads. Moreover, in their Experiment 2, Yang et al. added a finger-pressing secondary task during the recognition phase. One version of the secondary task required using the same fingers that would be associated with the motor memory of the letters involved in the dyad, thereby interfering with motor memory. In another condition the secondary task was set up so as not to interfere with those fingers. The result was that only the expert typists were affected differentially by the interfering versus non-interfering versions of the secondary task. For them, in the non-interference condition there was a greater false alarm effect for different-finger dyads compared to the same-finger dyads (that is, a greater tendency to wrongly think that a more fluently typed dyad had occurred during the study phase), whereas in the interference condition this effect disappeared. The secondary tasks did not have any effect on the false alarms of novices. These results indicate that the expert typists, but not the novice typists, had "embodied" representations of the letter dyads that were automatically activated when they saw the dyad and that the motor production fluency associated with these representations influenced memory recognition.

Together, the results of all the studies reviewed above indicate that there exists cognitive fluency outside the domain of L2 production. This cognitive fluency appears to "have considerable impact on high-level processes, such as memory judgments" (Yang et al., 2009, p. 1365) as well as on perception, preferences, and other judgment categories. What relevance might this have for L2 fluency? There are no studies to my knowledge that have looked directly at L2 cognitive fluency issues in terms similar to the studies just reported. However, it is possible to speculate on how the association between L2 cognitive fluency and higher level processing might affect L2 acquisition, especially fluency development.

The studies reviewed above showed that people's cognitive fluency for stimuli in a given domain can impact on how they make judgments about the stimuli they encounter. One can speculate that perhaps people's L2 cognitive fluency could contribute—in subtle ways that escape awareness—to how they evaluate and perceive their L2 contact environments. This could have important consequences for fluency development viewed through the lens of the dynamic framework described in Chapter 1 (Figure 1.3). Outside the classroom, L2 users often have to choose which L2 contact situations to enter into and to decide on just how involved they will become in those situations. For example, in a bilingual city such as Barcelona or Montreal, L2 users often have to decide which language to use when initiating conversations with strangers. They sometimes have to choose whether or not to use the L2 on the telephone, where the quality of acoustic transmission may be disadvantageous if their L2 cognitive processing fluency is already low. Some people may tend to avoid using the L2 in socially delicate situations, such as breaking bad news or discussing intimate topics, situations where a strong command of the language would be useful. By making such choices, L2 users might end up creating particular L2-usage niches for themselves (e.g., using the language only in face-to-face encounters with their neighborhood shop clerk). Restricting the use of the L2 to such niches could lead to processing fluency gains, but only for the limited set of expressions encountered in those niches. This processing fluency might—operating as a fluency heuristic—result in preferences for those particular aspects of the language and communication (e.g., people judging that it is more pleasant, and hence possibly more motivating, to use the L2 in context X than in context Y), resulting in further promoting fluency relevant for that niche. This situation resembles the Matthew Effect phenomenon discussed by Stanovich (1980) in relation to L1 reading fluency development. Readers can enter into an upward or downward spiral of fluency development, depending on whether their current level of reading fluency encourages or discourages increasing their volume of exposure to reading material; the same situation can obtain for language learners with respect to L2 fluency development.

In sum, the research reviewed here on general processing fluency, contributes the following to L2 fluency:

• Learning conditions can result in the acquisition of different levels of perceptual processing fluency, selectively for different stimuli.
• People have subjective experiences of the fluency of their own perceptual processing.
• People's subjective experience of their general processing fluency shapes decision-making about the stimuli they encounter, especially when required to make familiarity-based memory and/or evaluative judgments.

The studies reviewed above make clear that processing fluency is an issue of concern to cognitive psychologists generally, not just those interested in language. Those studies focused on aspects of *conceptual* and *perceptual* processing fluency; now we turn to *memory retrieval* processing fluency, another aspect of cognitive processing fluency that would be expected to have implications for L2 performance.

Transfer Appropriate Processing (TAP)

A basic issue concerning the retrieval of information from episodic memory—memory for past experienced events—is how the *relationship* between mental processes active at the time of encoding and at the moment of retrieval affects the ease or fluency of recollection. This issue has practical importance for skilled performance in virtually all domains, whether it be music, sport, medical diagnosis, chess, or L2 use. After all, when performing "on the fly," one wants fast and smooth retrieval of the information needed for the actions to be carried out. The goals of this section are to examine a key concept underlying encoding-retrieval relationships—the idea of *transfer appropriate processing* (TAP)—and to discuss how TAP might apply to questions about L2 fluency.

The nature of encoding-retrieval relationships has been the subject of research in psychology for decades (for reviews of TAP, see Roediger, Gallo, & Geraci, 2002; Roediger & Guynn, 1996; see Nairne, 2002, for some qualifications) but it has only been relatively recently discussed in a systematic way in the L2 literature (see Lightbown, 2007). A starting point for this discussion is the principle of "encoding specificity" in episodic memory (see Tulving & Thomson, 1973; Tulving, 1983), which holds that new information encountered at the time of learning is encoded in a context-sensitive manner, that is, specific to the conditions under which the information was encountered. By context is meant the set of cognitive and perceptual activities a person has engaged in during the time of learning. This means that encoding will be specific to the set of conditions prevailing at the time of intake. The principle of TAP holds that "memories are represented in terms of the cognitive operations engaged by an event as it is initially processed, and that successful memory retrieval occurs when those earlier operations are recapitulated" (Rugg, Johnson, Park, & Uncapher, 2008, p. 340). Important early demonstrations of this principle are to be found in studies by Kolers (1973, 1979) and Morris, Bransford, and Franks (1977). Kolers for example, manipulated cognitive operations at the time of encoding by asking participants to read stimuli written in geometrically transformed text (see Figure 3.2 for examples) and then to perform various reading and memory tasks with them.

Kolers (1979) reported a study in which he asked people to read aloud as quickly as possible a large number of 15- to 25-word sentences that appeared either in normal or inverted typographic orientation (N or I in Figure 3.2). Of these, the vast majority appeared in inverted form. Within the full set, one subset consisted of sentences appearing twice, the first time in normal orientation and the second time in inverted orientation.

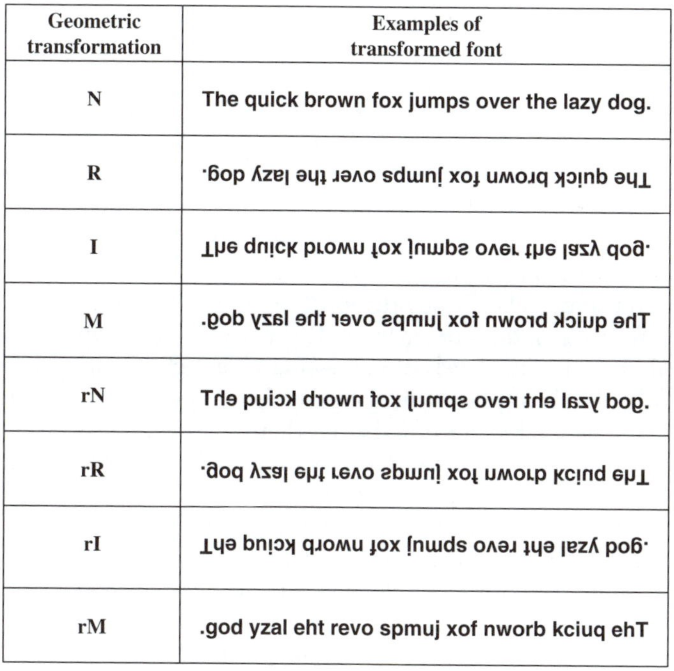

Geometric transformation	Examples of transformed font
N	The quick brown fox jumps over the lazy dog.
R	The quick brown fox jumps over the lazy dog.
I	The quick brown fox jumps over the lazy dog.
M	The quick brown fox jumps over the lazy dog.
rN	The quick brown fox jumps over the lazy dog.
rR	The quick brown fox jumps over the lazy dog.
rI	The quick brown fox jumps over the lazy dog.
rM	The quick brown fox jumps over the lazy dog.

Figure 3.2 Examples illustrating the types of font transformation used by Kolers (adapted with permission from Kolers, 1979, Figure 17.1, p. 365). N = Normal orientation; R = Reversed and then rotated to make the letters upside down; I = Inversion of each letter; M = Mirror image. Examples rN, rR, rI, and rM are the same as N, R, I, and M respectively, but with each individual letter reversed.

Another subset also consisted of sentences appearing twice, both times in inverted form. Thus, there were sentence pairs of an N-I type (first normal, then inverted) and other pairs of an I-I type (first inverted, then again inverted). The repeated versions of sentences reappeared at various lags after their first appearance. Of interest was the time taken to read the sentences aloud as a function of whether the typographical orientation remained the same or changed from the first to the second appearance. One outcome of the study was a facilitation effect for second readings of I-I sentences relative to first readings, as was expected, given that the second reading was of a sentence with the same words as the first. The most interesting finding, however, was that the second reading of I-I sentences (reading a sentence in inverted orthography that had been presented exactly the same way before) was even faster than the second reading of N-I sentences (reading a sentence in inverted orthography that had been seen before, but in normal orthography). This was noteworthy because one would not expect font orientation to have been particularly remembered when the sentence was read for the first time. Nevertheless, the transfer benefit from reading a normal version of the sentence was not as great as the benefit of reading an inverted version of the sentence, when the second reading was also an inverted version. Kolers' findings support the conclusion that participants encoded the cognitive/perceptual procedures by which they read the sentences, not just the meaning of the stimulus, and the match or mismatch of procedures impacted on the fluency of reading the second presentation of the sentence.

Another milestone in the TAP literature was the Morris et al. (1977) recognition study. Their study demonstrated that TAP had more explanatory power than did the then widely accepted account of memory retrieval known as the levels of processing approach (Craik & Lockhart, 1972). The levels approach held that deeper processing at the time of learning rendered recollection better than shallower processing (e.g., words processed at a semantic level would be better remembered than words processed at an orthographic or phonetic level). Morris et al. asked participants in an acquisition phase of their study to make either a semantic or phonetic judgment about sentences and words they heard. On a semantic trial, for example, participants heard a sentence with the word *blank* inserted in it, followed by a target word to be judged as to whether it fit semantically in the place of *blank* (e.g., *The BLANK had a silver engine … TRAIN*). On a phonetic trial they heard a sentence asking for a rhyming judgment (e.g., *Does BLANK rhyme with legal? … EAGLE*). For both types of trials they responded by answering *Yes* or *No*. Following this, half the participants were given a recognition test with instructions favoring recollection based on meaning (they were given the actual target words as heard during acquisition) and the other half were tested with instructions based on phonetics (they were given words not heard before that rhymed with the target words heard earlier). The results were that participants tested with rhyme recognition instructions showed better learning of Rhyme-*Yes* targets than of Semantic-*Yes* targets and the reverse for participants tested with the meaning-based instructions. These results raised troubling questions about the levels of processing approach to memory. Thus, Morris et al. showed that it is the match between learning and test—the encoding-retrieval overlap—that is crucial for successful memory (see also Blaxton, 1989).

More recently, Rugg et al. (2008) proposed a framework for understanding transfer-appropriate processing in terms of cortical reinstatement in the brain. Their framework is testable using functional magnetic resonance imaging (fMRI) techniques and they reviewed data from studies using such techniques to support the proposal. They pointed out, for example, that, according to TAP, encoding recruits cognitive-perceptual operations specifically needed by the task at hand, and is not handled by some kind of "dedicated encoding circuit" (p. 344). To support this conclusion, they reviewed several studies using fMRI.

Otten and Rugg (2001) asked people to perform a living/non-living judgment task on visually presented nouns or to judge whether a noun had an even or odd number of syllables. Different regions of the brain were activated by these different tasks. The living/non-living task activated primarily the medial and left inferior frontal cortex, whereas the syllable task activated primarily posterior cortical regions. Items that were subsequently recognized successfully were those associated with greater elicited activity at study time and items that were not successfully recognized were those associated with less elicited activity at study time. This outcome indicated that recognition did indeed depend on the nature of activation at the time of study. Moreover, the areas that were activated at the time of recognition overlapped with the areas that had been activated at the time of study, when the stimuli were being judged in the living/non-living and syllable tasks. Finally, Rugg et al. suggested that "retrieval cues need only elicit a fraction of [the] original activity in order to trigger the reinstatement of the entire pattern" (p. 341). Overall, their analyses add promising and complementary neuroimaging-based data to the behavioral data supporting a transfer appropriate perspective on memory retrieval.

In sum, the TAP perspective on memory retrieval provides an important message for understanding fluency in skilled performance. The TAP perspective holds that the ease of retrieval (and hence the fluency of action dependent on that retrieval) will depend in large measure on the degree to which brain region activation patterns at the time of retrieval overlap the patterns that were active at the time of study. This has implications for how skills, including L2 speech, should be acquired in order to optimize fluency (Gatbonton & Segalowitz, 2005; Lightbown, 2007; Segalowitz & Lightbown, 1999; Trofimovich & Gatbonton, 2006). These learning issues are addressed in Chapter 7. The basic idea, however, can be summarized as follows. L2 communication in the real world places various cognitive and perceptual processing demands on the L2 user. Fluent retrieval of earlier learned L2 knowledge and skills will depend in a significant way on the extent to which the cognitive and perceptual processes elicited at the time of communication match those that had been previously elicited at the time of learning. Of course, learning demands in the classroom do often differ markedly from communicative demands in the real world. Lightbown (2007) points out "that TAP helps to explain why learners are not always able to mobilize the knowledge they have acquired in certain situations when they face new ones" (p. 43) and she goes on to suggest that for this reason it may be important to diversify "the number of settings and processing types in which learners encounter the material they need to learn" (p. 43). In other words, the principles of TAP are relevant both for the acquisition of L2 fluency (and L2 knowledge) for use outside the classroom as well as for promoting learning inside the classroom.

The following general points can now be made about memory retrieval and fluency:

- One can speak about the fluency of memory retrieval in terms of its speed and ease of execution.
- According to the TAP principle, the fluency (and accuracy) of memory retrieval depends to a significant extent on the similarity between the mental processes currently active at the time of retrieval and those that were previously active at the time of study. This means that fluency-promoting learning conditions for L2 users should elicit cognitive and perceptual processing activities that are appropriate for transfer to the situations that will be encountered later when what has been learned is to be retrieved.

The last point raises a key follow-up question: *Which of the many processes active at the time of study will be the ones needing reinstatement at the time of retrieval?* This can be thought of, in part, as a question about the flexibility of processing—the ability to transfer skills to performance conditions that differ from those encountered during training, without significant loss in the quality of performance (see, e.g., MacKay, 1982). We turn now to this topic.

Processing Flexibility

Fluent performance of a skill does *not* imply rigid, mechanical execution of the skill. Rather, it is assumed that a fluent performer is also expert in adapting to changing circumstances in addition to being able to perform relatively quickly without loss of stability and accuracy. This issue of flexibility and its place in expertise and fluency is important in the skill literature (see Feltovich, Spiro, & Coulson, 1997, for discussion of competing views on this topic). In particular, two concepts related to flexibility arise from the general skill/expertise literature, each having implications for L2 fluency and its acquisition. These are *closed versus open environments* and *affordances*.

Closed versus Open Skills

In the literature on skilled movements (sport, dance, etc.), an important distinction is made between so-called "closed skills" and "open skills" (Allard & Starkes, 1991; Elliott & Lyons, 1998; Poulton, 1957; R.A. Schmidt & Lee, 2005). Closed skills are those taking place in environments that are relatively stable and where the goal of performance is to recreate as accurately as possible a physical or cognitive act that meets a particular standard or ideal form (Allard & Starkes, 1991, p. 127). Examples include motor movement activities such as weightlifting, diving, gymnastics, and cognitive activities such as mental arithmetic. In contrast, open skills take place in environments that are relatively unpredictable and where the goal of performance is to bring about some effect upon the environment (place the puck in the hockey net by overcoming the opponents' defensive moves; capture the opponent's king in chess), none of which involve repeating a particular motor movement or mental calculation according to some predefined standard. Of course, many skills involve aspects of both closed and open environments, so it is incorrect to think of all skilled activities as falling neatly into one or the other category. Nevertheless, the distinction is useful because it focuses attention on the different ways in which processes underlying performance must be recruited in order to execute skills fluently.

Some skills take place in predominantly open environments, such as competitive team sports where the goal is to produce some impact on the environment (score a goal) and the environment itself is continually changing as players and significant objects (e.g., the ball) move around in relatively unpredictable ways. To be successful, performers must adopt a stance with respect to the environment, treating it as essentially open or closed. Individuals can differ in the stance they take, especially in the case of L2 performance (Segalowitz, 1997). For example, L2 learners have the option of approaching the environment as essentially *closed*, requiring an emphasis on accuracy and precision, and involving a great deal of self-focus. In the extreme, it might be more accurate to talk about such L2 learners as *reciting* L2 utterances, rather than speaking spontaneously when using the language. It may be, for example, that certain types of classroom instruction encourage this way of relating to the language environment. In contrast, L2 learners can also view the environment as essentially open, requiring a focus on what communicative and social goals are to be accomplished with other speakers. Here the aim would be to fulfill communicative intentions and achieve goals that are not focused primarily on linguistic precision. In this case it might be more accurate to talk about L2 users *navigating* their communicative environment, and using the language as a tool for doing so. The closed and open skill stances will necessarily place different processing demands on the L2 user.

Research on motor skill learning has compared the learning of closed versus open skills, with some results relevant for L2 fluency issues. Elliott, Lyons, and Dyson (1997) investigated the acquisition of skilled target-aiming movements. In their study participants used a computer mouse to move a cursor on a computer screen from a home base to a target location as quickly and accurately as possible. Different groups of participants had different mouse-to-cursor speed ratios during the training phase (a "fast" cursor where a small mouse movement translated into a large cursor displacement [.5-to-1 mouse-cursor gain]; a "slow" cursor where the reverse occurred [2-to-1 gain]; a control condition where the ratio was 1-to-1, that is, 1 cm displacement of the mouse resulted in 1 cm displacement of the cursor). Performance during training was compared with performance in a transfer condition involving the intermediate mouse-to-cursor gain ratio (1-to-1 for everyone) and reduced visual information. Training involved closed skill performance, because all elements of the situation were predictable. Transfer involved learning to cope with unpredictability due to the new mouse speed and reduced visual information.

Three outcomes are of interest here. First, on transfer trials, where the mouse was calibrated as 1-to-1 for all participants, the control group which had already been trained with a 1-to-1 gain ratio outperformed the other two groups. This result supports the principle of specificity of learning (Proteau, 1992). In fact, the slow-cursor group actually performed significantly worse (more slowly) on these transfer trials compared to how they performed by the end of 100 training trials. Their performance indicated that, whatever it was they had learned during training, it did not transfer to the new 1-to-1 condition. Second, the data did not support an account of learning as progression from closed-loop control (performance dependent on sensory feedback) to open-loop control (performance dependent on higher level instructions for control and not on sensory feedback) (see Elliott & Lyons, 1998, for reviews of other studies with similar outcomes). This conclusion was based on the fact that the groups did not uniformly show gains on transfer trials. Uniform gains would be expected if a higher order motor program to control performance had emerged from the training phase. Finally, the authors concluded that performance on transfer trials was best when training provided an opportunity to acquire appropriate processing skills for the transfer situation, consistent with the principle of TAP discussed earlier. This conclusion was supported by the data from the slow cursor group who had very great difficulties on transfer trials, reaching the target far more slowly than on even the earliest practice trials. The authors concluded that these participants must have developed processing skills that were inappropriate for the transfer condition, in contrast to the other groups.

Elliot and Lyons (1998) discussed a study of motor learning that, unlike the aiming study just discussed, took place in an open environment. The task was ball catching, in which the ball had a slightly different trajectory on each of 200 trials. Participants wore liquid crystal goggles that could be programmed to occlude vision in various ways and thus limit their ability to gather the visual feedback information needed to improve their catching ability. The goggles could be programmed for alternating sequences of 20 ms ON followed by 80 ms OFF (predictable access to visual feedback), or 20 ms ON followed by 50, 80, or 110 ms OFF (randomly selected) (unpredictable access to visual information). For a given participant, training occurred under either predictable or unpredictable visual conditions. The next day, participants first received a new series of trials with the same type of visual access they had during training, followed by a transfer series with the visual access type (predictable, unpredictable) not experienced during training. Results were that participants trained with predictable access to visual information transferred better to the unpredictable visual access than vice versa. Elliott and Lyons concluded that in an open skill situation—where performance conditions are variable—learners benefit from predictable access to feedback that enhances the development of information-processing skills for dealing with the openness of the environment. In the ball-catching experiment, the participants had to adapt to the variable trajectory of the ball from trial to trial; having visual information available to them on a predictable basis—even with heavy visual occlusion—enabled them to develop the cognitive-perceptual control procedures needed to carry out the motor task of catching the ball skillfully. Participants who were not given that predictability of visual information were less able to perform the ball-catching skill on transfer trials.

It is interesting to consider what implications these motor skill learning studies might have for L2 fluency. One seems to be that the closed/open skill distinction is important to keep in mind because the nature of learning can vary as a function of this distinction, and that learning in a closed environment might not lead to the development of higher level general control mechanisms even as expertise develops. Another implication seems to be that, when learning takes place in an open environment (that is, where there is variability in performance conditions), it needs to allow the learner to acquire the complex information processing procedures required to perform well in an open environment transfer situation. This acquisition of complex information procedures is enhanced when there is the opportunity to receive reliable feedback during learning.

The distinction between closed and open skills originated in the literature on motor movement, not language. For this reason, the precise nature of what constitutes an open and closed environment in L2 fluency acquisition needs to be studied in its own right. Although this has yet to be done, it is possible at this point to identify some of the implications of the open/closed distinction for L2 fluency, especially when considered in conjunction with TAP. For most speakers, L2 use in the real world corresponds more to performing an open skill than a closed skill. Most utterances are made for communicative purposes and are thus embedded in a context of cognitive/perceptual processing for assessing the intentions of the interlocutor, for coping with variable and unpredictable turns of events, etc. Moreover, because the speaker is actively trying to bring about some change in the environment (e.g., to persuade, console, inform, etc.), these cognitive and perceptual processes do not simply occur alongside but otherwise independently of the linguistic processing required to produce the utterances. Rather, these cognitive and perceptual processes are part and parcel of utterance production itself. This is because the utterances are used as tools to bring about changes in the environment. To be successful in using these tools, speakers have to be perceptually attuned to much more than the basic sensory and motor aspects of speech (the phonetic and articulatory features required for accurate production). They have to be attuned to the ways the language permits them—or affords them the possibility—to accomplish their communicative goals. In other words, to communicate efficiently, speakers must be able to perceive and make use of the *affordances* of the language needed to achieve their communicative intentions. This brings us to the second concept underlying flexibility.

Affordances

The concept of affordances was introduced into the psychological literature by J.J. Gibson (see e.g., 1977). The general idea behind this concept is that an organism perceives more than the sensory array available to it from the environment; the organism perceives the possibilities and limitations the environment provides the organism with in respect to its goals. These perceived sets of possibilities and limitations constitute the affordances of the environment. (For background on affordances, see Greeno, 1994, and Jones, 2003; for discussion of issues with reference to non-linguistic examples see Chemero, 2003; E.J. Gibson & Pick, 2000; Heft, 2003; Michaels, 2003; Stoffregen, 2003; Turvey, 1992; and references contained therein.) Stoffregen points out that most theorists agree that a systems approach to behavior is implied by the theory of affordances (2003, p. 117). According to this systems view, affordances are considered to be a property of the organism-environment considered jointly as a system, where the property reflects opportunities for action.

An interesting non-language study of the perception of affordances is Warren's (1984) investigation into how people evaluate the climbability of a staircase from visual inspection. He asked people to judge a series of pictures of staircases varying in riser height as to whether they were climbable or unclimbable. Warren also measured optimal energy expenditure (oxygen consumption) during climbing as a function of riser height and climber leg length. The results indicated that across all participants, short and tall, the boundary between climbable and unclimbable stairways was defined at a riser height that was a specific constant proportion of leg length. Moreover, this relationship was independently predictable from the calculation of the requirement for minimum energy expenditure during climbing. Warren suggested that the findings provided "evidence that functional perceptual categories and preferences correspond to critical and optimal points in an animal-environment system" (p. 699). In other words, affordances reflect the functional relationships that obtain between an organism and its environment, considered as an organism-environment system, and animals and people perceive affordances in terms of these functional relationships.

Warren also pointed out that "an affordance may be selectively attended to" (p. 684), depending on the perceiver's needs at a given moment. Thus, stairs are available for climbing but they do not necessarily elicit climbing in the absence of an intention to use them for that purpose. The environment, then, can be seen as possessing a large number of affordances that permit—and limit—various kinds of action an organism may wish to engage in (and the same object will have different affordances for different types of organisms). Generally, when theorists discuss affordances and how organisms perceive and use them, they assume that the organism is actually capable of fluent action (e.g., Warren's adult participants were all experienced, "fluent" stair climbers). Once an action has been decided upon, it is assumed that the organism will know how to exploit the affordances with a minimum expenditure of energy to accomplish the goal in mind. The larger idea behind the theory of affordances is that this is how organisms, including humans, normally deal with their environment in a skillful way. If this is so, then these ideas may have interesting implications for how we might think about L2 fluency.

Using the term "affordance" in the context of L2 performance is somewhat unusual. As used in this book, the expression *linguistic affordances* will refer to *the resources within a language that provide the possibilities and set limitations for speakers wanting to use the language to fulfill specific communicative goals*. This is similar to the sense that J.J. Gibson had in mind when speaking about the affordances in the physical environment for an animal: "The affordances of the environment are what it offers animals, what it provides or furnishes" (1977, p. 68). Moreover, Gibson hypothesized "that the affordances may be more easily perceived by an animal than the properties in isolation, for the invariant combination of properties is 'meaningful' whereas any single property is not" (1977, pp. 67–68). Moreover, in Gibson's view, and as supported by Warren's research reported above, the affordances are not properties of either the object in the environment or of the organism but of the relationship between them. The affordances are a property of an organism-object system, where the organism has actions it wishes to carry out and the objects are potential resources for carrying out the intended action. Organisms (and people) appear to deal with the world this way—they perceive properties of the environment in terms of how those properties afford them possibilities of pursuing certain goals, as resources for possible action.

With respect to language, Van Lier (2000) puts it this way: "An affordance is a particular property of the environment that is relevant—for good or for ill—to an active, perceiving organism in that environment … If the language learner is active and engaged, she will perceive linguistic affordances and use them for linguistic action" (p. 252). Further on, Van Lier writes: "language learning is not a process of representing linguistic objects in the brain on the basis of input received. ... we do not 'have' or 'possess' language, but we learn to use it and to 'live in it'" (p. 253).

With respect to L2 fluency, an affordances approach would suggest that speech utterances and their features—their organization into words, sentences, their prosodic features, speech register properties, etc.—should not be viewed simply as arrays of sounds or articulatory gestures, but as vehicles for carrying out speech acts (Halliday, 1973) such as informing, requesting, commanding, apologizing, persuading, etc. These are speech acts for conveying information about the speaker's perspective on—or construal of—the situation being talked about. The language—its vocabulary, its fixed expressions, syntactic devices, prosody, sociolinguistic features, etc.—provides the vehicles for accomplishing these speech acts, that is, if the speaker knows how to exploit them appropriately. For example, an L2 user may wish to convey negative information in a tactful way. To do this successfully, he or she may want to use a particular syntactic construction (say, an impersonal construction to allow some emotional distancing from the negative content of the message). This construction would be an affordance of the language that a skillful L2 speaker could exploit to achieve a particular goal.

More generally the affordances of language have to do with providing speakers with means to manipulate the attention of interlocutors. As Tomasello (1999) put it, "linguistic reference is a *social* act in which one person attempts to get another person to focus her attention on something in the world" (p. 97). In Chapter 4 this idea is discussed further by including the focusing of attention in order to build construals of the world. An L2 speaker needs to be able to perceive and exploit the affordances of the language to make such attention focusing possible. If speakers are unable to retrieve a needed construction swiftly and without hesitation, they will deliver the message with reduced fluency. To be able to exploit these L2 affordances effectively, speakers require cognitive fluency in perceiving and handling the affordances.

Tomasello, agreeing with Langacker (1987), expressed the view "that language is a form of cognition; it is cognition packaged for purposes of interpersonal communication" (Tomasello, 1999, p. 150), and is not something separate from cognition that affects or is affected by or interacts with cognition. The goal of this chapter has been to consider some of the implications this perspective might have for thinking about L2 fluency. The chapter has reviewed research that touched on certain aspects of general cognitive functioning that was not specifically connected to L2 functioning per se. No claim is made here that all L2 fluency-relevant aspects of cognition have been taken into account. Rather, the idea was to identify a few aspects of general cognitive fluency that could also be relevant to L2 fluency, so that a more general approach to L2 fluency could be built from there. The present review proposed that the following ideas about general cognitive processing are relevant to L2 fluency:

- One can meaningfully talk about the fluency of general cognitive processing.
- Fluency heuristics associated with general cognitive fluency can shape judgments and preferences, with potential consequences for motivational aspects of fluency development.
- The fluency of memory retrieval depends on the extent to which at the time of study transfer appropriate processing was involved in the establishment of study-retrieval links.
- Skill development, including fluency development, can take place in either closed or open environments (or mixtures of the two), each having its own consequences for processing flexibility and transfer of learning to other contexts.
- Skilled performance involves being able to perceive and handle the affordances of the medium within which the skill is being performed.

Together, these generalizations provide a larger context in which the topic of L2 fluency may be situated. The chapters that follow explore these ideas further with direct reference to L2 fluency. The next chapter, in particular, examines the nature of *L2 cognitive fluency*, focusing on automaticity and attention.

Chapter Summary

This chapter examined several issues concerning general cognitive processing as they appear in the cognitive and skill learning literature unrelated to L2 functioning. These issues are, however, relevant to the development of L2 cognitive fluency. The following three points are ideas that will be brought forward to Chapter 7:

- *Fluency heuristics may affect how people assess their L2 experiences, with consequences for L2 cognitive fluency development, and for motivation to communicate in the L2.*
- *Transfer appropriate processing is a key aspect of memory retrieval fluency, and it may play an important role in the development of L2 cognitive fluency.*
- *Skill acquisition involves developing abilities to perceive and exploit the affordances of the skill medium. Open and closed skill acquisition environments shape this development differently, affecting the flexibility of processing. These considerations have consequences for L2 fluency development.*

4   Second Language Cognitive Fluency

> Expressions do not mean; they are prompts for us to construct meanings by working with processes we already know. In no sense is the meaning of [an] ... utterance "right there in the words."
>
> (Turner, 1991, p. 206)

The previous chapter examined cognitive fluency research by looking at performance in areas outside the field of L2 learning. This chapter shifts the focus back to L2 fluency by addressing the third anchor question, *Are there elements of cognitive fluency (cognitive fluidity) specific to L2 performance that underlie L2 utterance fluency?* In particular, this chapter looks at studies addressing the roles of what are commonly referred to as automatic and attention-based processing and how these may be considered components of cognitive fluency. It also examines the relationship between this cognitive fluency and L2 utterance fluency. The focus here is the cognitive-perceptual processing systems component (the "blueprint" component) of the dynamical systems framework shown in Figure 1.3 in Chapter 1. The goal is to identify elements of cognitive processing that would be expected to underlie utterance fluency and to explore how these elements can be operationalized so that their relation to utterance fluency can be studied directly.

This chapter first examines some general issues regarding the nature of L2 cognitive fluency. Then, it discusses automaticity and various ways it can be operationalized for empirical study. In particular, two views of automaticity are addressed—automaticity as ballistic processing and automaticity as processing stability. The next major section examines attention-based aspects of L2 cognitive fluency, with subsections on some cognitive linguistic considerations and ways of operationalizing this element of cognitive fluency. The final main section considers the link between cognitive fluency as discussed in this chapter and utterance fluency. The chapter ends with a summary and the identification of concluding points to bring forward to the final chapter. We begin with L2 cognitive fluency.

L2 Cognitive Fluency

As pointed out in N. Segalowitz and Hulstijn (2005), a central theme in virtually all discussions about L2 acquisition is that frequent exposure to elements in the target language (input repetition) and massive production practice (output repetition) are critical for attaining proficiency and fluency. Input and output repetition are believed to benefit language development by helping critical cognitive processing skills become automatic. N. Ellis (2002; N. Ellis & Ferreira, 2009), for example, emphasizes the crucial role that input frequency—the repeated encounters with target elements—plays in L2 acquisition. Bybee (2008) describes how frequent repetition can result in making grammar processes automatic, referring in fact to grammar as "automatized behavior" (p. 220). She even points out how frequent but incorrect repetition of certain language sequences can have a downside by leading to fossilization—that is, the acquisition of stable, permanent, but incorrect speech patterns that are very difficult to modify because they have become automatic (also, see Long, 2003). It is thus generally accepted that L2 mastery and high levels of utterance fluency require automatization, and a major route to automaticity is repetition. This automaticity enhances the fluidity and efficiency of underlying cognitive processing—that is, it enhances cognitive fluency.

Automaticity has been studied extensively, both in relation to general skill acquisition and L2 acquisition. (For general reviews on automaticity in L1 and other areas of skill acquisition, see Ackerman, 1988, 1989; Anderson, 1983; Anderson & Lebiere, 1998; LaBerge & Samuels, 1974; Levelt, 1989, 1999; Logan, 1988; Moors & De Houwer, 2006; Proctor & Dutta, 1995; Sanders, 1998; Schneider & Chein, 2003. See Pashler, 1998, Chapter 8, for an important review that is critical of the concept of automaticity. For reviews within the L2 acquisition literature, see DeKeyser, 2001; N. Ellis, 2002; Hulstijn, 2001; Johnson, 1996; McLaughlin & Heredia, 1996; McLaughlin, Rossman, & McLeod, 1983; N. Segalowitz, 1997, 2003; N. Segalowitz & Hulstijn, 2005.) Until recently, most studies of automaticity in L2 processing have focused on lexical access—that is, how people link L2 words to their meanings (e.g., accessing the mental lexicon component in Figure 1.2, Chapter 1). This is not surprising. The ability to link up words with meanings is fundamental to linguistic communication; without this ability, language simply cannot be used. Moreover, because word-meaning links are so central to using a language, overall L2 performance—including fluency—is likely to be compromised if the ability to make word-meaning links is itself inefficient. This is true whether the inefficiency is in productive speech encoding (corresponding to fluency vulnerability point $\{f_3\}$ in Figure 1.2, Chapter 1) or in receptive decoding of heard or read language (see, e.g., Cutler & Clifton, 1999; and Perfetti, 1999). Inefficient linking of words to meanings is likely to slow down processing overall, create overload problems (information "traffic jams") in short-term memory, require the speaker to reduce speech rate, and thus potentially be responsible for some speech hesitations and pausing. Generally, of course, L1 cognitive fluency is superior to L2 cognitive fluency. Therefore, by studying L1-L2 cognitive fluency differences regarding word-meaning links it might be possible to find useful clues about the organization of the two languages, and about the way the dominance of one language over the other may change as fluency develops. Specific examples of how one can study cognitive fluency related to lexical access are presented in this chapter.

Of course, L2 users need cognitive fluency for more than just making word-meaning links. Cognitive fluency is also needed for the more complex aspects of message formulation and comprehension, such as handling phrase and sentence constructions (corresponding to fluency vulnerability points $\{f_2\}$ and $\{f_4\}$ in Figure 1.2, Chapter 1). As will be explained later, this may involve attention-based mechanisms in a special way.

Thus, in broad terms, this chapter identifies two aspects of cognitive fluency—one related to the efficiency of making word-meaning links and the other related to the functioning of attention-based mechanisms involved in more complex language processing. Of course, there may be other important elements of L2 cognitive processing to study, but the two singled out here are the aspects of L2 cognitive processing that researchers have dealt with most to date.

It is worth considering why research on L2 cognitive fluency can be valuable, beyond contributing to an understanding of utterance fluency. One reason is that indices of cognitive fluency can serve as proxy measures for other aspects of L2 proficiency and language experience. Normally, lengthy testing is required to obtain measures of a person's general L2 proficiency, and of the length and intensity of that person's L2 experience. However, tests of processing *efficiency* in linking words to meanings—an aspect of cognitive fluency—can possibly serve as a stand-in measure of general proficiency and L2 experience. This is because the linking of words to meanings can only become very efficient if the L2 user has actually had a lot of exposure to and experience using the language in real communicative situations. Highly robust, efficient cognitive processing does not normally develop from formal instruction alone or from language study that excludes intensive social communication. This is because formal instruction and study rarely provide the massive and consistent training believed necessary to promote automaticity (Schneider & Chein, 2003) and thereby enhance the efficiency of mental processing (cognitive fluency). In contrast, formal instruction and study can lead to high levels of lexical *knowledge* and grammatical *accuracy*. For example, an English speaker can be explicitly taught that the rule for gender agreement in possessive pronouns (*his, her*, etc.) works differently in French versus English. One can acquire this knowledge with relatively little actual experience in real communicative settings, but cognitive fluency in processing this knowledge cannot be acquired without extensive experience in using it. Thus, evidence of strong L2 cognitive fluency can be taken as an indicator that the L2 user must have had a certain level of background experience, and it is in that sense that cognitive fluency measures might serve as a proxy measure for that experience.

Another reason for focusing on L2 cognitive fluency is that indices of efficient cognitive processing might serve as benchmarks for L2 development. Consider, for example, the Council of Europe's (2001) Common European Framework (CEF). The CEF provides illustrative descriptors of six different levels of L2 attainment within various qualitatively defined categories of speaking ability, one of which is fluency (Council of Europe, 2001, Table 3, pp. 28–29). These descriptors refer not only to the flow of speech but they also allude to underlying cognitive processes whose inefficient execution can disrupt that flow. Here are the descriptors, with the cognitive processing elements italicized for emphasis:

(A1) (lowest level): "Can manage very short ... utterances, with much pausing *to search* for expressions, to articulate less familiar words, and *to repair* communication."

(A2): "Can make him/herself understood in very short utterances, even though pauses, false starts and *reformulation* are very evident."

(B1): "Can keep going comprehensibly, even though pausing for *grammatical and lexical planning and repair* is very evident."

(B2): "Can produce stretches of language with fairly even tempo, although he/she can be hesitant as he/she *searches for* patterns and expressions ..."

(C1): "Can express him/herself fluently and *spontaneously, almost effortlessly*. Only a *conceptually difficult subject* can hinder a natural, smooth flow of language."

(C2) (highest level): "Can express him/herself *spontaneously* ... with a natural colloquial flow, *avoiding or backtracking around any difficulty* so smoothly that the interlocutor is hardly aware of it."

It is clear from these descriptors that beyond vocabulary and syntax knowledge there lies the issue of how smoothly the L2 user can execute that knowledge. Furthermore, the CEF descriptors indicate that how smoothly that knowledge is executed is itself a reflection of underlying cognitive skills such as searching, planning, etc. One can ask, then, if there are measures of L2 cognitive fluency that might serve as markers for these different levels of communicative fluency. Presumably, as the L2 user moves qualitatively from one skill level of communicative fluency to another, there is an associated parallel development in an underlying L2 cognitive fluency. What is needed are operational definitions of cognitive fluency to make it possible to investigate whether such cognitive fluency does indeed play a role in the level of utterance fluency attained.

Finally, with indices of L2 cognitive fluency in hand, it might become possible to assess the impact of specific teaching approaches and learning experiences (e.g., study-abroad programs) on the development of the cognitive skills needed for L2 utterance fluency. Such indices may lead to the emergence of new and useful evaluation criteria for assessing aspects of L2 training by allowing one to ask whether one learning experience enhances L2 cognitive efficiency more than does some other learning experience.

To fully realize the applied benefits of research on L2 cognitive fluency, there has to be consensus about what such terms as *automaticity* and *cognitive efficiency* should mean and how to define them operationally. Unfortunately, the field has not yet achieved that consensus. The next section takes up this issue.

Automaticity, Processing Efficiency, and L2 Cognitive Fluency

As mentioned earlier, a major theme in the fluency literature has been that L2 fluency develops because the supporting cognitive processes become increasingly automatic. But what is automatic processing exactly? Schneider, Dumais, and Shiffrin (1984) defined an automatic process as "a fast, parallel, fairly effortless process that is not limited by short-term memory (STM) capacity, is not under direct subject control, and is responsible for the performance of well-developed skill behaviors" (p. 1). Clearly, this definition presents multiple criteria for automaticity. The authors suggest that a cognitive process is automatic if it possesses a bundle of features referring to its speed (fast), its relationship to other ongoing cognitive activities (parallel; independent of external control), the resources it consumes (load independent; few attention resources required, hence low effort), and its association (possibly causal) with more macro-defined skilled behaviors (more global skill development).

This bundle has a certain intuitive appeal; it agrees with most people's personal experience in carrying out well-developed skills, such as speaking their L1 fluently, driving a car in a smooth, coordinated (fluent) way, playing a musical instrument well, and so on. People carry out such activities largely without thinking very much about what they are doing, without exerting very much effort, and they are usually able to carry on other normal activities at the same time. Over the years, researchers have tried to operationalize each of the features in the bundle separately. When features have been experimentally isolated in this way, the research has often revealed that the original picture of automatic processing needed major revision (e.g., see Pashler, 1998). The main difficulty facing a theory of automaticity is that the features in the "automaticity bundle" do not always co-occur as they should according to the original conceptions of automaticity. This leaves open the question of which one(s) should be retained as essential for automaticity.

Despite the now longstanding lack of consensus about what *automatic processing* should mean, the expression continues to be used widely by theorists and researchers, especially in the L2 acquisition literature. Often some behavior is labeled automatic without an operational definition of what that is supposed to mean, for example, ballistic processing or load independent processing. Instead, *automaticity* and related expressions are used generically, as in the following (to cite just one example): "it is very difficult to change the internal structure of this [fossilized] chunk once it has become automatized" (Bybee, 2008, p. 221). When used this way, the author usually means that the process under consideration (e.g., making word-meaning links) has changed in some non-trivial way by virtue of having become "automatic." The exact nature of the change, however, is not specified. The change can be considered non-trivial because, implicit in the claim about automaticity, the process has become more stable, more resistant to interference, and/or more independent, etc., compared to some reference point. All of these features usually also entail that the processing will be fast, but speed of operation of the process cannot be the sole justification for calling it automatic. This is because it is always possible to imagine two behaviors that differ in speed of operation even though neither is automatic in some deeper sense. Claiming some process has become automatic implies claiming that it has acquired properties beyond simply becoming faster.

This way of looking at automaticity leads to the possibility of operationally defining the term *automatic* without making precise claims about the exact nature of the automaticity. All of the more precise, operational definitions of automaticity (automaticity as ballistic processing, as load independent processing, etc.) imply greater processing *efficiency*. As well, evidence that the processing underlying one behavior is more efficient (not just faster) than that underlying another behavior implies that there must be some important difference in the way the two behaviors are organized. It seems reasonable enough, therefore, to say that a process is automatic, even if one cannot specify the exact nature of that automaticity, as long as one can say that the process is functioning more efficiently in some meaningful way compared to how it would have functioned if it were non-automatic. This is how the term *automatic* and related expressions will be used here—as a shorthand expression to mean that the process under consideration is functioning at some high level of efficiency that can be distinguished from some corresponding "non-automatic" reference point.

Several studies have shed light on the relationship between L2 fluency and automatic processing. Some authors have operationally defined automatic processing quite specifically as ballistic processing, whereas others have operationally defined automatic processing more generally as a gain in processing efficiency, leaving the specific nature of that efficiency unspecified for the moment. Examples of these studies are discussed now.

Automaticity Defined as Ballistic (Unstoppable) Processing

An early study of whether L2 fluency is supported by some form of automatic processing is Favreau and Segalowitz (1983). This study is interesting for two reasons. First, it appears to be the first ever to examine automaticity differences in L2 users differing in fluency by using a clear, operational definition of automatic processing, namely, automaticity as ballistic processing. Second, the study revealed that this form of automaticity differentiated more fluent from less fluent L2 users, whereas simple speed of processing of single word targets did not. This finding—that speed was less important than automatic processing—has implications for understanding L2 cognitive fluency (see below).

Favreau and Segalowitz (1983) operationally defined automatic processing as ballistic or unstoppable processing, in a manner proposed by Neely (1977), using a primed lexical decision task. They compared two groups of English/French bilinguals, both quite proficient in the sense that they could read screening texts in the L2 to the same level of comprehension as in the L1. However, one group—the less fluent group—read the L2 texts significantly more slowly than the L1 texts to achieve the same level of comprehension. In contrast, the other group—the more fluent group—read the L2 and L1 texts equally fast to achieve the same level of comprehension.

The participants performed a lexical decision task in which they judged whether a target stimulus shown in uppercase letters (e.g., "APPLE"; "OPPLE") was a real word in the language. The target stimulus was always preceded by a prime stimulus in lowercase letters designed to influence reaction time (RT) in some way. The prime stimulus could be the name of the category from which the target came (e.g., "fruit"), the name of a different category (e.g., "animal"), or a control prime with no semantic content (always "ooooo"). Participants were tested in separate language blocks (English, French). Normally in such experiments, when a prime is semantically related to the target, there is a facilitation effect in which RTs to judge the target are faster compared to the control condition (no prime, or a meaningless prime). In contrast, when the target is unrelated to the prime, there is an interference effect in which RTs are slower.

Favreau and Segalowitz (1983) also varied the interval between the onset of the prime and the onset of the target—the stimulus onset asynchrony (SOA)—across blocks of different SOA-condition combinations, the SOA being either short (200 ms) or long (1,150 ms) (prime duration was always 150 ms).

There were two conditions crossed with the above manipulations, delivered in separate blocks. One was the Expect-Related condition in which the participants were pre-trained to expect a category name (e.g., weapon) to be followed by the name of an exemplar from that category (e.g, GUN). In the Expect-Unrelated condition participants were pre-trained to expect a category name (e.g., fruit) to be followed by the name of an exemplar from a different specific category (e.g., CHAIR). Each subject participated in each expectancy condition. (To minimize confusion, for each participant the category names used in one condition were not used in another, nor were category exemplars used in more than one condition. Category and exemplar names were rotated across conditions and participants.)

This design yielded eight different testing blocks reflecting the different condition combinations: Language (L1, L2) by SOA (long, short) by Expectancy (related, unrelated) conditions. Within each condition block there were trials where the prime was a word naming the appropriate category (according to the expectancy condition) or was the meaningless control "ooooo." On half the trials the target was a real word and on half it was not. In each block, however, there were a small minority of surprise trials, where the word prime and the word target violated the expectancy rule for that condition. For example, the subject may have been trained to expect the name of a piece of furniture after the prime "fruit," but saw instead the surprise target "APPLE."

Of the many trial types involved in this study, the most relevant to the present discussion are the surprise trials in the Expect-Unrelated condition. Figure 4.1 shows the important results. As can be seen in the top panel of the figure, in the L1 condition in the long SOA condition (white bars), both fluency groups yielded interference effects, indicating that participants were slower when the surprise target violated expectations. In contrast, in the short SOA condition (black bars), there were facilitation effects, indicating that the SOA time interval was too short for expectations based on a recently learned rule (e.g., that the prime "fruit" would be followed by a target naming a piece of furniture) to overrule life-long experiences (e.g., associating "fruit" with the name of a piece of fruit). A short-SOA facilitation effect for a related but unexpected surprise target was interpreted as evidence of ballistic processing because it revealed that participants could not stop processing the usual meaning of the prime.

In the L2 condition, shown in the lower panel, the results were quite different in one important respect. The more fluent participants again showed a strong and significant facilitation effect for surprise targets in the short SOA condition, paralleling the result in the L1. In contrast, the less fluent participants showed no facilitation effect on the short SOA trials, indicating that there was no ballistic, automatic priming of potential targets semantically related to the prime. Favreau and Segalowitz (1983)

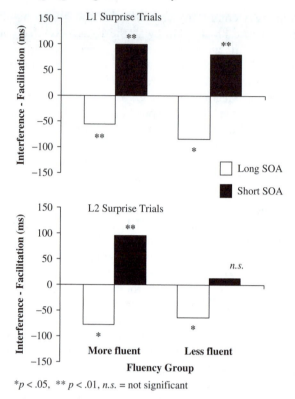

Figure 4.1 Results from Favreau and Segalowitz (1983) showing primed lexical decision facilitation and interference effects, relative to a control condition, on surprise trials in the Expect-Unrelated condition for more and less fluent groups of bilinguals, in the L1 and L2 and as a function of prime-target stimulus onset asynchrony. Asterisks indicate effects significantly different from zero.

concluded from this that the less fluent L2 users did not have, in the L2, the capacity to ballistically (automatically) link words and meanings the way they did in the L1.

A third result of interest with respect to fluency, mentioned in Favreau and Segalowitz (1983) but not highlighted, concerns the baseline conditions in the L2, where the semantically empty control prime ("ooooo") could exert no semantic effect on the processing of the target. As can be seen in Figure 4.2, there were *no* significant RT differences between the more fluent and the less fluent groups. This was true whether one looks at the data collapsed over all the L2 sub-conditions, over the long SOA conditions only, over the expect-unrelated conditions only, etc. This result indicates that, when semantic priming was not involved, there were no differences between these two groups in the speed of processing a single word target in this task situation.

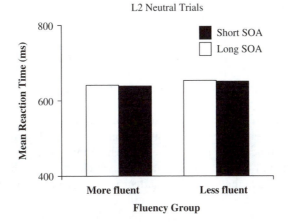

Figure 4.2 Results from Favreau and Segalowitz (1983) showing mean lexical decision reaction times in the L2 on neutral (control) trials in the Expect-Unrelated condition for the two fluency groups as a function of prime-target stimulus onset asynchrony (SOA) (there are no significant differences between the four means).

Taken together, the findings are interesting for the following reason. They indicate that, whereas ballistic processing was diagnostic of fluency differences, speed of processing was not. Of course, in many situations, one would normally expect different fluency groups to differ also on speed of processing. But the fact that this did not happen here suggests that speed of processing is not the critical element. These findings are fully consistent with the idea that high level fluency entails some reorganization of processes into a more efficient system, and not just the speeding up of all the individual components of processing. This idea is developed further below.

Another study, by Tzelgov, Henik, Sneg, and Baruch (1996), also investigated ballistic processing in fluent L1 versus less fluent L2 speakers. The focus of Tzelgov et al. was the nature of lexical access, but the results can also be interpreted as shedding light on fluency. In their study, the participants were Hebrew-English bilinguals dominant in Hebrew, their L1, and less fluent in English, their L2. The task was a version of the Stroop paradigm (Stroop, 1935) that is often used to study automatic and ballistic processing. In the version Tzelgov et al. used, they asked participants to name the font color of words shown on the screen. The words were themselves color names, written in the other language script. For example, the Hebrew word for red would be written using Latin letters (*adom*), and English color names would be written in Hebrew letters that sounded like English words when pronounced. Sometimes the meaning of the word corresponded to the font color (*adom* written in a red font; correct response = "red") and sometimes it conflicted with the font color (*adom* written in a green font; correct response = "green").

Tzelgov et al. (1996) reported several experiments, the goal of which was to find out if people access meaning via the phonological code of the word or link the visual code directly to the meaning. They found that there was a strong cross-script Stroop interference effect, for example, when the participant should report "green" for the stimulus *adom* (which means "red") written in a green font. In this example, the Hebrew word was written in a relatively unfamiliar form—in Latin letters—and so the interference must have come from the phonological representation that was elicited by the sound of /adom/, which triggered the concept of red. Interestingly, they found the effect to be asymmetrical in terms of language. The Stroop interference effect was always found when the phonological value of the stimulus was a color name in Hebrew, the L1, and the effect was either weaker or absent when the phonological value of the stimulus was a color name in English (written in Hebrew letters), the less fluent L2. The findings were interpreted as support for Kroll's asymmetric model of bilingual memory (Kroll & Stewart, 1994). In terms of fluency issues, the immediate interest here, the results demonstrated that in the more fluent L1, but not in the less fluent L2, there was *ballistic* processing of the phonological representation linking a stimulus to a particular meaning, even when the stimulus was written in an inappropriate script.

The Favreau and Segalowitz (1983) and Tzelgov et al. (1996) studies revealed that, in bilinguals for whom the L1 was dominant and more fluent, the processing of L1 words was ballistic (unstoppable), whereas the processing of words in the less fluent L2 was not. In addition, the Favreau and Segalowitz study also showed that, in highly proficient bilinguals who were as fluent or nearly as fluent in the L2 as the L1, processing was also ballistic in the L2. Thus, ballistic processing appears to be closely associated with fluency. The Favreau and Segalowitz study also indicated that, although the two groups differed in L2 fluency, they did not differ significantly in their speed of single L2 word processing in the neutral prime control condition. Hence, automaticity, operationally defined as ballistic processing, was diagnostic of fluency differences, whereas speed of processing was not.

A potential shortcoming of the Favreau and Segalowitz (1983) study and similar approaches to investigating automaticity and fluency is the complex research design used. This, together with the lack of consensus over which operational definition best captures what *automaticity* means, has made the study of automatic processing in L2 skill acquisition problematic.

In light of these concerns, N. Segalowitz and Segalowitz (1993) advocated a different strategy for investigating automaticity in relation to L2 skill. All approaches to skill learning appear to acknowledge that the responses of expert performers, in addition to being more accurate, generally differ from those of novice performers in being both faster and more stable. Put another way, the underlying system for producing responses during high-level performance operates more efficiently. Segalowitz and Segalowitz proposed looking at this processing efficiency by considering both speed (RT) and intraindividual variability of RTs at the same time. This idea has been independently advocated in other areas of human performance. For example, some researchers have studied cognitive decline—loss of efficient processing over and above cognitive slowing—as a function of age and neurocognitive compromise such as mild dementia (Christensen, Dear, Anstey, Parslow, Sachdev, & Jorm, 2005; Hultsch, MacDonald, & Dixon, 2002; Hultsch, MacDonald, Hunter, Levy-Bencheton, & Strauss, 2000). These studies are based on the premise that "intraindividual variability is a potentially useful indicator of cognitive functioning" (Hultsch et al., 2000, p. 597). In these studies, the researchers focused on *increased* intraindividual variability as a sign of cognitive decline. In contrast, N. Segalowitz and Segalowitz focused on *decreased* intraindividual variability as sign of gain in cognitive efficiency, the kind of gain expected under any theory of automaticity. Their approach, the first to use intraindividual variability in connection with L2 fluency, is taken up next. (For more on intraindividual variability, see Hultsch & MacDonald, 2004, and Slifkin & Newell, 1998.)

Automaticity as Processing Stability

N. Segalowitz and Segalowitz (1993) reasoned that one can study automaticity by distinguishing processing speed from processing stability (see Wingfield, Goodglass, & Lindfield, 1997, for a different strategy for dissociating speed from automaticity):

> One way in which practice may benefit performance is through a general *facilitory effect*. This effect involves change that is essentially quantitative, corresponding to an across-the-board acceleration or speed-up (Anderson's [1982] "strengthening"; see also MacKay, 1982) of the processes involved in executing a given task ...
>
> Practice can also lead to performance gains through qualitative changes in the functioning of the underlying processes through a *restructuring effect* [italics added]. Thus instead of simply speeding up the operation of the component processes, practice may set conditions for them to be organized differently; for selected, inefficient processes to drop out; for new, more efficient processes to replace older, less efficient ones; or for some mixture of all these possibilities to occur (e.g., Crossman, 1959).
>
> (N. Segalowitz and Segalowitz, 1993, pp. 371, 373–374)

In other words, one set of RTs might be faster than another for either of two reasons. The first is that there is a general across-the-board speedup of the underlying mechanisms responsible for the faster set (including the possibility of "speeded-up controlled performance"; Paradis, 2009, p. 6). The second is that there is restructuring or greater organizational efficiency in the way the action is carried out (see also Cheng, 1985), resulting in faster RTs. N. Segalowitz and Segalowitz argued that greater organizational efficiency would be marked not only by faster performance but also by greater processing *stability*. Processing stability could be operationalized in terms of RT variability—the intraindividual standard deviation (SD) corrected for mean RT—and that this measure could be used to determine if one set of RTs reflects greater processing stability than another.

The rationale behind this measure of processing stability is the following. Normally, there is a linear relationship between mean RTs and the SD associated with each mean RT (Wagenmakers & Brown, 2007, and Wagenmakers, Grasman, & Molenaar, 2005, provide both empirical and theoretical support for this). If the system underlying response execution speeds up without a change in the mixture or organization of the underlying contributory mechanisms, then RT variability will change linearly with RT. In other words, the SD changes proportionally to changes in the RT if the only thing that happens is that everything is executed faster. This means that the ratio of SD to RT (SD/RT) remains constant. This ratio is known as the coefficient of variation (CV) and it is this measure that N. Segalowitz and Segalowitz (1993) proposed might yield useful information.

They proposed recasting the question about the presence of automaticity indirectly, as a question about the viability of a *non-automatic* processing explanation as follows: *Given evidence of fast response times, do the data support rejection of simple, across-the-board speedup of underlying mechanisms as explanation of the faster RTs?* The speedup explanation for faster RTs is that all the processes underlying the production of those faster RTs are operating faster, more or less proportionally by the same amount, without any structural reorganization (and therefore without automatization). A speedup explanation, by itself, would be trivial and somewhat circular because it would amount to the claim that the faster RTs result from the underlying mechanisms operating faster. In recasting the question as an indirect one, Segalowitz and Segalowitz treat the speedup hypothesis as a null hypothesis to be rejected, leaving the alternative idea—that more than generalized speedup is at play—as a viable explanation for the data. Statistically significant changes or differences in the CV allow one to reject the speedup hypothesis.

Before proceeding further to look at how this was done, it is important to mention some constraints to keep in mind when interpreting the CV measure in this way. Suppose in a given case the CV measure fails to lead to rejection of the speedup null hypothesis. This outcome does *not*, by itself, support a positive claim in favor of across-the-board speedup (and against automaticity). The outcome only allows one to say there is no evidence to reject the simplest explanation for the data at hand, which is across-the-board speedup. Conceivably, a more sensitive test might have led to rejection of the speedup null hypothesis. On the other hand, if the CV measure does lead to rejection of the speedup null hypothesis, it would support a claim that some alternative explanation to simple across-the-board speedup is warranted, but it does not reveal what that explanation is. For example, it does not point specifically to ballistic processing or parallel processing or load independence as the operative factor. These are limitations on using the CV measure to reject the speedup null hypothesis, but they are not necessarily bothersome limitations. Often, one only wants to know whether the data are consistent with a non-trivial explanation for faster RTs, that is, the data are consistent with a claim of greater processing efficiency beyond simple, generalized speedup. In this case, the CV can be useful as a measure of processing stability.

For N. Segalowitz and Segalowitz (1993), when the CV permits a rejection of the speedup null hypothesis, the results can be interpreted as evidence for significant (and meaningful) processing stability. Another way to think about it is that there is always some level of noise or instability associated with how fast neural mechanisms operate (Faisal, Selen, & Wolpert, 2008; Slifkin & Newell, 1998). This instability will be reflected in behavioral variability in some way, such as in RTs, although the connection may be far from exact. The CV provides a useful index of this variability, insofar as it is a measure of the amount of variability there is per unit of response time. In this respect, the CV can be thought of as the SD per msec. of RT. The CV allows one to speak about response time stability after correcting for the absolute level of RT. Thus, if some training or practice experience significantly reduces the CV and the RT at the same time, then one can say that not only did performance become faster, but also that there was a net reduction in variability in the system. There was a gain in processing stability over and above the change expected by virtue of the linear connection between RT and its SD. Of course, as mentioned earlier, such an outcome does not point to the reason for the gain in processing stability. Segalowitz and Segalowitz argue, nevertheless, that regardless of the explanation (e.g., ballistic processing, parallel processing, increase in load independence, freedom from interference) the gain in processing stability "must have been brought about by the elimination of some of the processes whose variability-to-latency ratio is relatively high" (1993, p. 374). This means there has been a shift away from reliance on components of processing that are relatively slow and unstable (variable) toward greater involvement of the relatively faster and relatively more stable components of the underlying mechanisms.

In contrast, if the CV remains the same while RT becomes faster, this would indicate that, despite the faster responding, one cannot claim a gain in processing stability. The CV of reaction time thus potentially opens a window onto a very subtle aspect of a person's processing capability—the *processing stability* of the user's neurocognitive processing system in the L2.

N. Segalowitz and Segalowitz (1993) tested a basic hypothesis regarding the CV measure as an index of individual differences in processing efficiency. Participants were university students who were L2 users of English attending an English language program. They each performed two tasks. One involved a speeded reaction time task to detect the onset of a nonlinguistic visual stimulus. The authors hypothesized that there would be individual differences in RT, but not in the CV. This is because the detection task imposed such low level processing demands that individual differences in performance would only reflect differences in speed of simple underlying perceptual and cognitive processes, not in how efficiently they were organized. This result was obtained; the correlation between participants' CV and RT was not significantly different from zero, indicating no difference in CV as a function of RT (see Chocholle, 1940, for a similar result). The second task involved speeded lexical decision in English, the participants' L2. Here it was hypothesized that CV would vary as a function of individual differences in RT, because differences in L2 fluency would reflect differences in how efficiently underlying processes were organized (i.e., some L2 users being more automatic than others in word recognition). This is what they found. The correlation between participants' CV and RT was significantly different from zero ($r = .72$), indicating that faster responders exhibited greater processing stability overall. Similar results have been reported in other studies with L2 learners performing lexical decision tasks by Akamatsu (2008), N. Segalowitz, Watson, and Segalowitz (1995), and S. Segalowitz, Segalowitz, and Wood (1998).

Phillips, Segalowitz, O'Brien, and Yamasaki (2004), N. Segalowitz and de Almeida (2002), N. Segalowitz and Frenkiel-Fishman (2005), and N. Segalowitz, Trofimovich, Gatbonton, and Sokolovskaya (2008) also reported studies using the CV measure of cognitive fluency. These studies included two important changes in the procedures and method of analysis compared to N. Segalowitz and Segalowitz (1993). First, instead of a lexical decision task, where subjects have the somewhat unnatural task of distinguishing real words from non-words, these studies used an animacy judgment task where bilingual participants with varying levels of L2 proficiency had to focus on word meanings by judging whether nouns named living (e.g., *boy*) or non-living (e.g., *book*) referents.

Second, participants performed the animacy judgment tasks, once in the L1 and once in the L2, in separate blocks. This enabled the researchers to partial out performance in the L1 from performance in the L2, making it possible to remove sources of variance in the data due to individual differences in responding to task demands related to attention, motor control, general intelligence, general linguistic functioning, etc., not specifically related to L2 processing in the animacy judgment task. The residualized L2 RTs that remained after partialing represent the speed of response in the L2 after controlling for speed of response in the L1. The mean of these residuals taken across the sample of participants, of course, is zero. However, individuals with negative residuals can be regarded as those whose performance in the L2 was faster than would have been predicted on the basis of their L1 performance alone, and individuals with positive residuals were those whose performance in the L2 was slower than would have been predicted on the basis of their L1 performance alone. In this sense, those with negative residuals can be considered to be functioning at a cognitively superior level in the L2 than those with positive residuals, even though all may be performing in an absolute sense more slowly in the L2 than in the L1.

In the studies cited above, not only were L2 RTs residualized against L1. In a similar manner, L2 CVs were residualized to control for response stability in the L1. Participants' residualized RT and CV scores were used as their RT and CV data, instead of the original RT and CV scores. The residualized RT and CV data were then submitted to correlational analyses. In all of them, significant correlations were found between the *residualized* L2 CVs and RTs, paralleling the results reported earlier using just L2 measures alone (N. Segalowitz & Segalowitz, 1993; S. Segalowitz et al., 1998). The importance of these more recent results is that they underscore the L2-specific nature of the CV and RT measures, given that the measures of L1 performance had been statistically partialed out. These residualized measures served as measures of L2-*specific* cognitive fluency, and the correlations between residualized CVs and RTs indicated that, across the sample of bilinguals tested, individual differences in L2-specific speed of responding in a semantic judgment task was associated with individual differences in L2-specific processing stability.

It is interesting to compare these results with those of neuroimaging studies that look at the recruitment of processing areas in the brain as a function of expertise and of task complexity. The premise in those studies is that the less difficult the task—whether due to the inherent nature of the task itself or to the relative gain in expertise on the part of the subject—the smaller will be the neural regions recruited for performance (Haier et al., 1988, 1992). For example, Haier et al. (1992) trained participants on the computer game Tetris daily over a period of four to eight weeks. They found that improved performance was associated with glucose metabolic decreases. They concluded that the learning resulted in "decreased use of extraneous or inefficient brain areas" (p. 134). This finding is consistent with the assumption underlying the L2 behavioral studies, namely that processing stability reflects the underlying neurocognitive efficiency, lending support to the idea that measures of intraindividual processing stability speak to the issue of cognitive fluency.

In the literature, discussion of automaticity as fast, stable processing has not been restricted to lexical performance. Many have commented on the role automatic processing plays in grammatical performance. As mentioned earlier, Bybee (2008) referred to grammar as automatized behavior and commented on the implications this may have for L2 learners. Several researchers have investigated the role of automaticity in the learning of new grammatical rules by L2 learners or in the learning of artificial grammar-like rules (e.g., Bourne, Healy, Parker, & Rickard, 1999; Bybee, 2008; DeKeyser, 1997; N. Ellis & Schmidt, 1997; Healy, Barshi, Crutcher, et al., 1998; P. Robinson, 1997; P. Robinson & Ha, 1993). However, none of these studies has looked directly at whether automatic processing in grammar is associated with L2 proficiency as such; rather, these studies have focused on whether grammatical processing has become automatized during learning. Generally, the authors of these studies operationalized automaticity in terms of RT patterns following the power law of practice (Logan, 1992; Newell & Rosenbloom, 1981) (where response times follow a negative exponential as a function of the number of trials, gradually tapering off at some asymptotic value). The results of these studies of grammatical skill learning have been mixed (see N. Segalowitz & Hulstijn, 2005, for discussion), and at this time one cannot say definitively that these studies have implicated automaticity in grammatical learning.

Despite the inconclusiveness of the studies just referred to, there are strong reasons to suspect that, as speakers become more fluent in the L2, the cognitive mechanisms underlying the processing of grammatical relations become more efficient in some important sense, as was the case with lexical access. The next section examines the case of grammatical processing by taking an approach to the cognitive fluency assumed to underlie it that differs from many of the studies on this topic. The approach explored here, in the next section, links the processing of grammatical relations to *attention*-based mechanisms.

Attention-Based Aspects of L2 Cognitive Fluency and Grammatical Processing

As discussed earlier in Chapter 3, skilled performers often have to cope with the challenges of *open* environments—situations where information critical to successful performance changes in unpredictable ways, moment by moment. In order to meet such challenges a person must be able to focus and refocus attention on the fly in order to keep up with changing circumstances. In many non-linguistic areas of complex performance, it is easy to recognize that such abilities can be crucial to success.

For example, skilled driving, hockey playing, and chess playing are all examples where the goal is to bring about a change in an environment that is itself in a dynamic state (e.g., getting a car safely through a busy intersection, placing a puck in a well-defended goal, or overcoming a chess opponent's strategic defense moves).

A similar case can be made for L2 communication. Fluent speakers must be able to package information into appropriate language as thoughts come to mind, and they must do so in a relatively smooth manner or risk losing the floor. Moreover, in packaging thoughts into language, speakers often have to take into account feedback from the interlocutor about whether the message is being properly understood. This requires the ability to flexibly redirect the focus of attention in order to recruit the appropriate linguistic resources for formulating the message. In this sense, attention-based processing is a complementary aspect of the L2 cognitive fluency discussed earlier, complementary to the automatic aspects of processing. As will be explained shortly, L2 cognitive fluency needs to include both efficient processing (fast and stable) and flexibility of attention control.

As with automaticity, there are many different ways of thinking about attention and how it might play a role in L2 fluency. There is no universally accepted definition of attention (see Pashler, 1998, pp. 1–32). Nevertheless, there are common themes found throughout the literature that will serve the present discussion well. Cohen, Aston-Jones, and Gilzenrat (2004), for example, provide a useful global summary of what attention is, describing it as "the emergent property of the cognitive system that allows it to successfully process some sources of information to the exclusion of others, in the service of achieving some goals to the exclusion of others" (p. 71). Appropriate topics for attention research usually include the study of mechanisms involved in allocating cognitive resources to sustain processing on a particular target (staying on task), in focusing and concentrating processing on a particular target in the face of potential distractions (selective attention), in overseeing the sharing of resources in situations where more than one task is being performed (task sharing), in switching focus from one task to another (task switching), in preparing for an upcoming task, and other forms of cognitive control. Stuss, Shallice, Alexander, and Picton (1995) and Fischler (1998) discuss these and other functions of attention, and the possible neurocognitive mechanisms subserving them. Fan, McCandliss, Sommer, Raz, and Posner (2002) also discuss attention in terms of its alerting (noticing), orienting (shifting attention toward), and executive (controlling, decision-making) functions and the underlying neurocognitive mechanisms.

Tomlin and Villa (1994) provide a useful overview discussion about the treatment of attention in cognitive science and its relevance to L2 issues. They pointed out that L2 researchers interested in attention have tended to focus on questions about its role in learning and instruction, whereas researchers in mainstream cognitive science have focused more on the basic mechanisms underlying attention-based processes (see also R. Schmidt, 2001). It would appear that the situation they described in 1994 is still true nearly twenty years later. Tomlin and Villa review key issues in cognitive science approaches to attention and show their relevance to L2 acquisition. They point out that L2 researchers have four main conceptions of attention: as a limited-capacity system (i.e., a processing system that can handle only a small part of the information impacting on the individual), as a process of selecting critical information for further processing (selective attention), as a processing system that involves effort as opposed to less effortful automatic processing, and finally as a system involved in the control of information and action (p. 187). Their main point is that all of these aspects of attention are related to one another and can be understood in terms of an integrated attention system. Table 4.1 provides a list of some of the main functions of attention addressed in the L2 research literature. The functions listed are relevant to fluency insofar as disruption of these functions due to a lack of expertise in managing attention resources during L2 processing would be expected to result in reduced utterance fluency.

Applied linguists have recognized the functions of these attention skills for successful L2 acquisition and performance (see sources in Table 4.1). Leow (2007), for example, provides a thorough discussion and review of research on attention and awareness in L2 acquisition in general and in the context of receptive practice in particular.

These attention functions address real-time demands typically faced by L2 users in the real world, in instructional settings, and in test-taking/ evaluation contexts. If an L2 user is not able to meet these demands to some satisfactory level, it is reasonable to suppose that utterance fluency can become compromised. To meet the processing demands successfully, the L2 user needs both the processing stability described in the previous section, in order to escape certain pressures on cognitive resources, plus strong attention control and flexibility in order to be able to focus and refocus processing resources in a dynamically changing situation. This raises an interesting challenge for L2 researchers: How can attention be operationally defined so that one can study its relationship to L2 fluency? One way to answer this question is described below, but for the logic of that answer to be clear, it will be useful to first look at another functional distinction that can be made about attention, one that emerges from certain developments in the cognitive linguistic literature.

Broadly speaking, two categories of attention can be identified here. The first is *attention-to-language*. This category refers to situations where language is the object of attention, analogous to other perceptual situations where specific items in the environment become objects of attention. Non-language examples include trying to focus on one particular object

Table 4.1 Selected Examples of Attention-to-Language Involved in L2 Use and Learning

Examples of attention-to-language:	*Selected references*
Language selection (*choosing which language to use at given moment and maintaining focus on that language or switching as required*)	Green, 1998 Meuter, 2005
Noticing (*becoming aware of the structural regularities of a language, but not necessarily with metalinguistic knowledge*)	Leow, 2007 P. Robinson, 1995, 2003 Schmidt, 1995, 2001
Focus-on-form (*selective attention to details of linguistic form as opposed to semantics*)	Doughty, 2001 Doughty & Williams, 1998 N. Ellis, 2008 Long & Robinson, 1998 Ortega, 2007 Skehan & Foster, 2001
Planning (*preparation just prior to speaking*)	Ortega, 2005 Roberts & Kirsner, 2000 Skehan & Foster, 2005 Tavakoli & Skehan, 2005
Attention to instructional feedback (*e.g., teacher's recast*)	Ranta & Lyster, 2007 Trofimovich, Ammar, & Gatbonton, 2007
Attention and awareness during practice (*e.g., attending to feedback received during practice*)	Leow, 2007 Mackey, 2007a VanPatten, 2004
Selection during lexical access (*selecting appropriate words from among similar alternatives and selecting words in the appropriate language*)	Costa, 2005 De Bot, 1992 La Heij, 2005
Self-monitoring and self-repair (*checking and verifying one's own speech for errors in real time and making corrections as necessary*)	Kormos, 2000 Levelt, 1989, 1999 Postma, 2000 Skehan & Foster, 2005
Communicative strategies and problem-solving (*speakers' efforts to overcome difficulties encountered while speaking, such as dealing with word finding or grammatical complexity problems*)	Dörnyei & Scott, 1997 Kormos, 2006
Selective focusing on cues carrying sociolinguistic information (*attending to specific speech features that serve as social cues to emotion, politeness, register shifts, sarcasm, turn-taking, etc.*)	Levelt, 1989
Focusing on the speech stream as a channel of communication under noisy conditions (*selective attention to speech and ignoring irrelevant competing sounds – e.g., "cocktail party phenomenon," Cherry, 1953*)	Treisman, 1964

or spatial region to the exclusion of others, or to maintain focus on a target embedded within a noisy environment. The second category is *language-directed attention*. This category is qualitatively different from the first in certain respects. This category refers to situations where elements in the linguistic message itself modulate the processing of other elements within that very same message by directing attention in a selective manner in order to shape the construction of a mental representation of the meaning of the message (examples will be presented shortly). The distinction between these two ways of looking at attention and their relation to L2 fluency follows next, first by looking at attention-to-language and then to language-directed attention.

(Perhaps a third general category can also be identified—language-directed attention-to-the-world. This refers to how naming directs attention to the non-linguistic world. For example, upon hearing the utterance *Look at the ball!* a person will normally direct attention to that object. This aspect of attention has been exploited in interesting ways in eye tracking studies [e.g., Marian & Spivey, 2003], including studies of L2 comprehension, but it does not appear to be an aspect of L2-specific attention as such.)

Attention-to-Language

The attention skills listed in Table 4.1 refer to situations where general attention mechanisms common to all skill areas are invoked in L2 performance in order to use the language effectively. These are all cases of attention-to-language. For example, consider the situation where one has to monitor an incoming L2 speech signal for particular words or phonological elements that may have sociolinguistic significance. An example might be where it is important to know whether the speaker is using the familiar or formal form of "you" in French or Russian. This has parallels to monitoring the environment for non-speech targets, such as focusing on the sound of one particular instrument in a string quartet, or listening for some telltale sound of a car's motor indicating a badly needed tune-up. The word-monitoring example does, of course, have a linguistic aspect to it that the non-speech examples lack; the L2 user must be able to recognize the target element when it occurs. However, the attention mechanism for carrying out that monitoring could, in principle, be the same as that implicated in the non-speech examples. In this sense, attention-to-language can be thought of as a particular case of attention to the environment (here, the speech environment).

The story will be similar for the control of attention involved in language selection. L2 users need to control attention when deciding which particular language to use at a given moment and to keep using that language for the duration of the communication (Green, 1998). This example of selective attention also has parallels in non-speech domains.

For example, many computer users switch from one operating system to another, or from one word processing or statistical program to another, where task goals overlap greatly (e.g., save a file; move a paragraph; load data) but the action required differs slightly depending on the software being used. Musicians reading scores written in both treble and bass clef face a similar task demand; they see physically similar-looking dots on lines representing notes but have to assign to them systematically different interpretations depending on the clef sign that is operative. Again, vehicle drivers who frequently travel back and forth across the English Channel have to select a particular set of driving routines depending on whether the country goes by left- versus right-side driving rules.

All of the above examples require strong yet flexible control of the same basic attention functions in order to achieve a high level of performance. In language, a relatively poor ability to control these aspects of attention when using the L2 compared to the L1 will most likely result in reduced L2 utterance fluency. It is important, therefore, for L2 users to develop general attention-to-language skills, especially in attention-demanding contexts, if they are to use the L2 with high utterance fluency.

There is, however, another category of attention-based processing that is also relevant to L2 use. This one does not appear to fit directly into the categories of general attention such as those listed in Table 4.1. This category has been variously referred to as attentional competence in language (Talmy, 2008) and linguistic attention (Talmy, 2008; Taube-Schiff & Segalowitz, 2005a). Here it will be called *language-directed attention* in order to highlight what distinguishes it from attention-to-language. This category of attention skill, it has been claimed, is especially difficult to cultivate in the L2 (Talmy, 2008, p. 37). It will be argued here that it forms an essential component of L2 cognitive fluency.

Language-Directed Attention

In language-directed attention, the control of attention originates from within the linguistic message itself, and is directed back toward the mental representation that is associated with the meaning of the message. This contrasts with attention-to-language, described in the previous section, where control of attention originates from outside the message and is directed toward the surface level of the message. The distinction is illustrated in Figure 4.3.

Fauconnier (1994), Langacker (1987, 1991), and Talmy (2008), among others, write about attention in this language-directed attention sense, and they point out that every language is able to direct attention by modulating the saliency of the elements within the message. Talmy, for example, explains that the "attentional system in language includes a large number of basic factors, the 'building blocks' of the system, with over fifty identified to date. Each factor involves a particular linguistic mechanism that

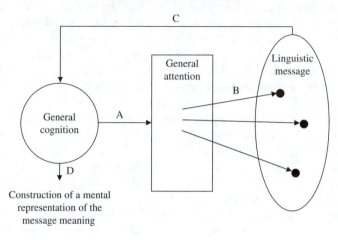

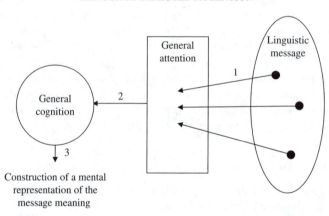

Figure 4.3 Schematic showing the difference between *attention-to-language* versus *language-directed attention*. In *attention-to-language* (top panel), the stimulus for attention originates in non-linguistic cognition which activates general attention (arrow A) to specific aspects of the linguistic message (arrow B), and the resulting information feeds back to general cognitive processes (arrow C), resulting in the construction of mental representation of meaning (arrow D). In *language-directed attention* (bottom panel), the stimulus for attention is contained in the linguistic message itself, which guides general attention (arrow 1) to guide general cognitive processes (arrow 2) in constructing a mental representation of meaning (arrow 3).

increases or decreases attention on a certain type of linguistic entity" (p. 27), and that the linguistic phenomena relevant to this discussion "pertain to the same single cognitive system of attention" (2008, p. 29). Talmy identifies several ways by which languages achieve their attention directing functions. These include the use of stress patterns and topicalizing by order of mention in an expression. He also discusses the different kinds of attention focusing that can be achieved by these mechanisms, such as foregrounding and backgrounding various types of information. Importantly, Talmy points out that different languages achieve these attention-directing goals in different ways (e.g., by word order in one language and word inflections in another) and this creates challenges for L2 users.

The cognitive linguist Gilles Fauconnier offers another useful perspective on attention and language. He writes:

> In order for thinking and communicating to take place, elaborate constructions must occur that draw on conceptual capacities, highly structured background and contextual knowledge, schema-induction, and mapping capabilities. Expressions of language do not in themselves represent or code such constructions ... Instead, languages are designed ... to prompt us into making the constructions appropriate for a given context.
>
> (Fauconnier, 1994, p. xviii)

In other words, linguistic expressions do not *contain* meanings; rather, they provoke and guide the construction of meaning (see Turner, 1991, cited by Fauconnier, 1994, and quoted at the top of this chapter). Fauconnier calls these constructions mental spaces. His idea is that communication involves setting up mental domains that are structured and connected: "The process is local: A multitude of such domains—mental spaces—are constructed for any stretch of thought, and language (grammar and lexicon) is a powerful means (but not the only one) of specifying or retrieving key aspects of this cognitive construction" (p. xxxvii).

Fauconnier's (1994, 1997) approach and similar ideas proposed by other cognitive linguists share the overarching idea that communicating is about using language to direct the attention of the listener/reader who is building a cognitive model of what the speaker/writer is thinking. An important aspect of this process is that communication is not just about naming particular objects, actions, and their attributes, or in stating propositions about them; rather, it is about conveying information about how the speaker wishes the recipient to construe the situation he or she is speaking about (Goldberg, 1995, 2006).

This is where grammar plays a central role as an attention-directing device. Grammatical forms serve as instructions to the recipient to foreground certain elements in the meaning representation that is being constructed; to background other elements; to specify spatial, temporal, identity, and other relationships between elements; to indicate the presence or absence of causal links between events, to convey information about the speaker's beliefs and attitudes about the veracity, probability, and plausibility of the events; and so on. By way of a simple illustration, contrast the following two sentences:

(a) John failed because he didn't study.
(b) John was failing despite supposedly having studied.

These sentences convey roughly the same basic information (both are about John, about his failure and about his studying). However, the speaker's construal about what is important is different in the two sentences. Sentence (a) specifies a causal connection between two events (*because*), whereas sentence (b) specifies a lack of causal connection (*despite*). In sentence (a) the failure is presented as a completed event (by the past tense *-ed*), whereas in sentence (b) it is presented as a process extended over time (by the past imperfect *was ... -ing*). Sentence (a) indicates nothing explicitly about the speaker's attitude regarding the situation, whereas sentence (b) indicates that the speaker has some doubts (*supposedly*) about claims regarding John's study habits. In these examples, the elements conveying the speaker's construal of the situation are morphemes that, to state it in a manner consistent with Fauconnier's approach, instruct the recipient how to construct a mental space for the meaning of the sentence.

In the past, the exact role of grammatical morphemes in language processing was seen as puzzling. William James observed (1890/1950): "We ought to say a feeling of *and*, a feeling of *if*, a feeling of *but*, and a feeling of *by*, quite as readily as we say a feeling of *blue* or a feeling of *cold*. Yet we do not: so inveterate has our habit become of recognizing the existence of the substantive parts alone, that language almost refuses to lend itself to any other use" (pp. 245–246). Here, James addresses the distinction between grammaticized words (*and, if, but, by*) and lexical elements (*blue, cold*). Talmy (2001, pp. 22–23) makes a similar distinction between elements such as noun, verb, and adjective roots that are open class items—members of a class that is large and to which it is relatively easy to add new members—and all other elements (generally grammatical) such as *and, if, but*, etc. that are closed class items—that is, members of a class that is relatively small and closed to the addition of new elements and that have a concept-structuring function. Slobin (1996) drew attention to this distinction by pointing out the special implications it has for L2 mastery. He argued that L2 lexical elements are inherently easier to master than L2 grammaticized elements. Lexical elements have a referential conceptual function, which is generally similar across languages (e.g., French *chien* and English *dog* by and large correspond to each other), whereas grammaticized elements have structural functions that typically do not correspond well across languages (e.g., prepositions in different languages typically have a weaker correspondence to one another compared to content words). This creates challenges for the L2 user.

To summarize so far, one can distinguish two fluency-relevant categories of attention—attention-to-language and language-directed attention. Attention-to-language appears to be not different, in principle, from general attention-to-the-world, other than the targets of attention-to-language are language and speech events. In contrast, language-directed attention involves elements within the linguistic message initiating and guiding the involvement of attention in the construction of mental representations of meaning. This form of attention is associated with the grammatical features of language. According to this view, grammatical devices direct the recipient's attention by modulating the focus and saliency of elements in the linguistic message and by directing the building of mental spaces or representations of the meaning of the message.

Incidentally, this account is not meant to imply that open class words—nouns, adjectives, verbs—do not also have important cognitive linguistic properties that may be implicated in attention direction and fluency. They certainly do have such properties and cross-linguistic differences may underlie some sources of utterance fluency. For example, *news* is a mass noun in English and takes a singular verb (*the good news is …*) but a count noun in French, and can take either singular or plural depending on whether one or more news items are being referred to (*nouvelle: La bonne nouvelle est …* "the piece of good news is …"; *les bonnes nouvelles sont …* "the items of good news are …"). By way of another example, verbs structure their sentences by governing the number and kinds of arguments they can take, and translation equivalents often differ in how they do this. For example, in English the verb *to comment on* always requires a prepositional phrase, not a direct object, as in *The President commented on the situation*, whereas the French verb *commenter* takes a direct object, as in *Le Président a commenté la situation*. Such cross-language differences can be challenging for L2 users and presumably could impact on utterance fluency. See Langacker (2008), Cadierno (2008), and Tyler (2008) for further examples and discussion on this topic.

As the brief review above has indicated, research work in this area by cognitive linguists (e.g., Fauconnier, Goldberg, Langacker, Talmy, among others) has concentrated primarily on identifying the kinds of attention-directing functions languages are capable of. Lists of such functions can be found in Croft and Cruse (2004, especially Chapter 3) and Evans and Green (2006, especially Chapter 15). Few researchers, however, have focused on L2 *fluency* from a language-directed attention point of view. Two such studies are reviewed now.

The first is a study by Taube-Schiff and Segalowitz (2005b). This study looked at flexibility in handling the attention-directing function of spatial prepositions (over and above primary knowledge of the meanings of the prepositions). The study found that flexibility of language-directed attention was weaker in the less fluent L2 compared to the more fluent L1. Participants in that study were English-French bilinguals, dominant in their L1 English, who use L2 French to varying degrees in daily life in Montreal. The task they had to perform was an attention-shift task modeled after the alternating runs design introduced by Rogers and Monsell (1995). The alternating runs design allows one to measure the processing burden of having to repeatedly shift attention focus from one task to a second task and back again compared with not making such shifts. This task provides a measure of a person's ability to focus and refocus attention, and this is relevant to the cognitive demands of processing language as messages unfold over time. As will be seen shortly, the experiment provided three important measures:

- measures of attention-shifting abilities with spatial prepositions (involving language-directed attention) in the L1 and L2
- measures of attention-shifting abilities with concrete nouns (not involving language-directed attention) in the L1 and L2
- measures of baseline performance in the L1 and L2 when attention-shifting demands were not involved.

The aim of the study was to see if there would be a dissociation between the L1 and L2 specifically in terms of the burden of managing shifts in language-directed attention.

The processing burden of attention control was assessed by means of a *shift cost* (the cost of having to shift attention focus compared to not having to do so). This shift cost allows one to look at the burden placed on the attention system after controlling for any processing burden arising from understanding the stimulus words in order to be able to do the task. This is an important point to keep in mind. The alternating runs design achieved this as follows. In a given condition, there were two tasks, A and B, each requiring a speeded response in making one of two choices (a speeded two-alternative forced-choice task). Participants received the trials in a predictable alternating sequence of tasks ... AABBAABB ... Of course, the actual stimuli used in the trials were not predictable, nor was the correct response predictable. Thus, on trial n the participant performed task A, then on trial n+1 she repeated task A, then on trial n+2 switched to task B, then repeated task B, then switched back to task A, etc. This created a sequence of trials following the pattern shift-repeat-shift-repeat, etc. There is now an extensive literature reporting that RTs on shift trials in this design are typically slower than RTs on repeat trials. The difference between the two—the shift cost—represents the burden on the individual of having to shift the focus of attention (for a brief review, see Pashler, Johnston, & Ruthruff, 2001). Using this design, Taube-Schiff and Segalowitz (2005b) assessed the burden of having to shift focus of attention within the more fluent L1 with shifting focus of attention within the less fluent L2, both when linguistic attention was involved and when it was not.

The specific conditions and tasks used were the following. One condition was a relational word condition involving relational stimuli—spatial location prepositional phrases that normally serve a language-directed attention function in the language. In the A task, the different phrases referred to vertical relationships (e.g., ... *was above the spot* ...). Participants had to judge on a given trial if that relationship was an example of verticality-up or verticality-down. In the B task, the phrases referred to proximity (e.g., ... *was near the* ...). Participants had to judge if that relationship was an example of proximity-close or proximity-distant. The other condition was a non-relational word condition involving non-relational stimuli—concrete nouns that named different means of conveyance. In the A task in this condition, participants had to judge whether a noun named a two-wheeled (e.g., *bicycle*) or a four-wheeled (e.g., *truck*) vehicle. In the B task, they had to judge whether the noun named a waterborne (e.g., *boat*) or an airborne (e.g., *airplane*) means of conveyance. The set of stimuli in each condition was relatively small— eight nouns, eight spatial preposition constructions—and so each participant viewed each item many times. In addition, the vocabulary used was very elementary and was well known to all participants in their L2.

The basic results are shown in Figure 4.4. The figure shows the shift cost, that is, the degree to which responses were slower on shift trials

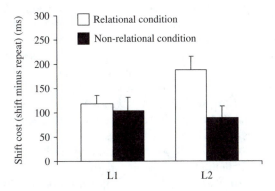

Figure 4.4 Results from Taube-Schiff and Segalowitz (2005b) showing mean attention shift costs (ms) in the relational word and non-relational word conditions in the more fluent (L1) and less fluent (L2) languages. All shift costs are statistically significantly different from zero and the L2 relational shift cost is significantly greater than the L2 non-relational shift cost.

than on repeat trials. The first important result is that in all conditions there was a significant shift cost, indicating that the experimental manipulation did indeed place a burden on the attention system. The second important result is that the shift cost in the *relational* condition in the L2 was greater than in the L1. This result is consistent with the expectation that engaging the language-directed attention system in an attention-shift task would place a special burden in the L2 relative to the L1. This result revealed that the flexibility of attention control with language-directed attention was weaker in the less fluent L2 than in the more fluent L1. Because shift costs represent performance on shift trials adjusted for performance on repeat trials, the shift cost does not reflect knowledge of the stimulus word meanings, but only the burden of having to shift attention between one category of stimuli and the other as required by the alternating tasks. The third important result was that the non-relational shift cost in the L2 was not significantly greater than in the L1; in fact, if anything, it was slightly smaller (but not statistically significant). This result indicates that the L1-L2 shift cost difference obtained in the relational condition was not due in some way to generalized reduced skills in lexical access in the L2; if that had been the case then there would have been a significant L1-L2 difference in the non-relational condition as well. Finally, there were no interaction effects between language and the stimulus sets used when the data from the repeat trials were analyzed alone (no attention shift involved); RTs were slower across the board in the L2 compared to the L1, but not more or less so for the concrete nouns than for the spatial prepositions. Overall, the results support the view that there is something special about the grammaticized elements of language and that, in particular, the ability to manage language-directed attention in the L2 is weaker than in the L1, and this difference is not related to general differences between the L1 and L2 in lexical access.

N. Segalowitz and Frenkiel-Fishman (2005) reported a similar attention shift study involving language-directed attention in the L2 and L1, again using the Rogers and Monsell (1995) alternating runs design with L2 users living in Montreal. In this case, Task A required a conjunction judgment and Task B a time adverbial judgment. In Task A, participants saw conjunctions such as *because* and *despite*, words that normally link clauses within a sentence by specifying something about the causal relationship between them. For example, in the sentence *John passed his exam because he studied all night*, the conjunction *because* indicates that the clauses are causally connected (the second clause should be construed as explaining the event in the first clause). In contrast, in the sentence *John passed his exam despite partying all night*, the conjunction *despite* indicates that the clauses are definitely not causally connected. There were four positive (e.g., *because*) and four negative (e.g., *despite*) conjunctions used. In Task B, participants saw time adverbials such as *now* and *later* that normally specify when the event named in the main clause takes place with respect to the present moment. Four relatively close-to-the-present moment (e.g., *now*) and four relatively far-from-present-moment (e.g., *later*) time adverbials were used. Participants were first instructed on how to classify all of these expressions. In addition to performing the attention-shifting task in English (L1) and in French (L2), participants performed the animacy (living–non-living) task described earlier in each language.

The authors partialed out L1 performance from L2 performance to obtain L2-specific measures of language-directed attention control, measures of lexical access speed (RT in the animacy task) and processing stability (CV in the animacy task). The most important result from this study is that the L2-specific measure of processing stability correlated significantly with the measure of L2-specific language-directed attention control (whereas the L2-specific speed of lexical access did not correlate significantly with attention control). The correlation indicated that there was 32 percent shared variance, after controlling for L1 performance. This suggests that cognitive fluency (processing stability) in terms of L2-specific lexical access was linearly associated with L2-specific attention control, although there remained a lot of unaccounted-for variance. This outcome suggests two points. First, language development experiences that result in high levels of processing stability in L2 lexical access will also result in high levels of skill in controlling language-directed attention related to the grammatical aspects of the L2. Second, L2 processing stability and L2 attentional control are nevertheless still relatively independent of each other (here, 68 percent of the variance was not shared). Future research needs to examine the relationship between these two aspects of L2 cognitive fluency using a wide variety of stimuli, and to investigate the impact of different L2 development experiences.

In sum, the studies reviewed above support the idea of an operationally definable, L2-specific, cognitive fluency that includes at least three components. These are:

- lexical access processing speed
- lexical access processing stability
- attention flexibility with the functions of language-directed attention linked to grammatical aspects of the L2.

There may, of course, be additional elements of cognitive fluency that should be considered, but these remain for future research to explore. This brings us back to the anchor question that is the focus of this chapter: *Are there elements of cognitive fluency specific to L2 performance that underlie L2 utterance fluency?* We now have identified three candidate elements of cognitive fluency, but what can we say about the relationship, if any, these elements have to L2 utterance fluency? This question is taken up in the next section.

Is There a Link between L2 Cognitive Fluency and L2 Utterance Fluency?

This chapter examined three ways of operationalizing elements of L2 cognitive fluency—in terms of the speed, processing stability, and attentional flexibility of the cognitive processes underlying L2 use—and it considered evidence of statistically significant relationships between these elements of cognitive fluency to overall L2 fluency and proficiency. However, no evidence has been presented yet of a direct association between measures of cognitive fluency and measures of utterance fluency such as those discussed in Chapter 2. The reason for this is that no one has conducted the necessary research. To my knowledge, only one published study has attempted this—N. Segalowitz and Freed (2004)— and it did find suggestive evidence in support of a link between cognitive fluency and specific measures of utterance fluency. Unfortunately, the study does not really meet certain crucial criteria that were discussed in Chapter 2 for such research. Specifically, there were no measures of L1 utterance fluency and so it was not possible to control for the contribution of individual differences in general speaking skills. Also, the speech samples were obtained using the Oral Proficiency Interview (Breiner-Sanders et al., 2000) and, as discussed in Chapter 2, this can be problematic because it results in a large amount of between-subject variability in the way the samples are obtained. Therefore, in the absence of relevant data at this time, it is appropriate to discuss what the relevant criteria and expectations might be for future studies attempting to relate L2 cognitive fluency to L2 utterance fluency.

In light of the discussions in Chapter 2 on the nature of L2 utterance fluency, and in this chapter on the nature of L2 cognitive fluency, we can identify the following four criteria as desirable guidelines for research on the links between the two.

- First, the operational definitions of cognitive fluency and utterance fluency should allow for measures to be taken in both the L1 and the L2. This will allow the L1 measures to be used as a baseline to control for individual differences in cognitive fluency and utterance fluency that are not specific to the L2. This is crucial if we wish to understand the fluency gaps spoken about in Chapter 1; namely, why the L2 seems to pose fluency challenges that the L1 does not.
- Second, it would be ideal to establish some generally agreed-upon measures for cognitive fluency and for utterance fluency. At the moment, it is not too much of an exaggeration to say that in many

studies variables are operationally defined somewhat idiosyncratically (e.g., silent pauses as periods of silence of 200 ms, 250 ms, 400 ms, 1 second). It is important for researchers to define variables in ways that make it easy to compare results across studies.

- Third, as was seen in Chapter 2, the kinds of utterance fluency features that a speech sample will exhibit can depend very much on the nature of the speaking task and the testing conditions. It is not likely that there is any one speaking task and set of conditions that alone could be *the* speech eliciting procedure. It is important, in fact, to recognize that under different conditions speakers will exhibit different amounts and kinds of utterance fluency. All of these need to be taken into account by any theory of how L2 cognitive fluency is linked to L2 utterance fluency.

- Finally, it is important to recognize that the link between L2 cognitive fluency and L2 utterance fluency will not be a rigidly tight one, for the reason that speakers are able to engage in various problem-solving strategies to compensate for what they perceive to be deficiencies in their own L2 utterance fluency. To the extent that L2 users can do this, they are able to mask the connections between basic aspects of L2 cognitive fluency (e.g., the speed, stability, and flexibility of processes related to lexical access and grammatical processing) and utterance fluency. For this reason, it is probably necessary to identify the situational limits that determine when such compensatory processing activities will and will not succeed. The compensatory strategies themselves should also be included among the elements of cognitive fluency that need to be considered just because they have an impact of utterance fluency too.

Hopefully, careful and systematic research along these lines will help identify which aspects of cognitive fluency are most germane to understanding utterance fluency, which elements of utterance fluency best reflect the operation of underlying cognitive processes, and how the link between the two manifests itself under different conditions.

Chapter Summary

This chapter discussed the cognitive fluency that is presumed to underlie L2 utterance fluency. Specifically, it looked at claims about automaticity and about the role of attention-based processing in L2 use. The main conclusions to emerge from this review for carrying forward to the final chapter are the following:

- *One can define, both theoretically and operationally, a form of L2-specific cognitive fluency (fast, efficient processing) that underlies fluency of L2 use. Three important distinguishable components* of cognitive fluency are L2-specific processing speed, processing stability, and processing flexibility.

- Processing speed is a necessary but not sufficient feature for defining cognitive fluency. Processing stability may be more important than processing speed as a feature of cognitive fluency. Flexibility of attention-based processing may be a more important feature of cognitive fluency than is processing speed, especially in grammatical processing.

5 Social, Attitudinal, and Motivational Factors Underlying Second Language Fluency

> A model of language must design it with a face toward communicative conduct and social life.
>
> (Hymes, 1972, p. 278)

So far, we have looked at fluency research from an applied linguistic perspective that focuses on the fluency characteristics of utterances (Chapter 2), on processing fluency in cognitive domains outside the L2 area (Chapter 3), and on L2 cognitive fluency understood in terms of processing efficiency specific to language (Chapter 4). However, as can be seen from the dynamical systems framework presented in Figure 1.3 in Chapter 1, there remains another important element underlying L2 fluency—a *social* component. This chapter examines some of the ways that social considerations might enter into the fluency picture by addressing the fourth anchor question posed at the beginning of this book; namely, *to what extent and in what way might social, motivational, and attitudinal factors serve as sources of influence on L2 fluency?* In examining whether and how social factors may be associated with fluency, this chapter breaks relatively new ground and is therefore necessarily somewhat speculative. In the past, few researchers have considered what links might exist between social and cognitive factors in L2 performance. In particular, there are few empirical studies of the social determinants of fluency although, as will be seen, it is widely assumed by researchers who take a socially oriented approach to language that the social aspects of communication actually do play a role in L2 fluency. The goal of this chapter, therefore, will be to explore why and how social factors may be expected to have an impact on the development of both L2 cognitive fluidity and L2 oral fluency and to propose a perspective that integrates these social considerations. This integrated perspective is summarized in a revision of the dynamical systems framework presented earlier in Figure 1.3. The chapter closes by identifying the main conclusions about the social dimension of fluency that will be carried forward to Chapter 7.

In brief, this chapter covers the following:

- The chapter opens by discussing *communicative competence*, a sociolinguistic perspective on language. This perspective challenges the view that a speaker's linguistic competence is primarily concerned with issues of grammaticality and how the underlying syntactic system shapes linguistic structure.
- Following on from the case made for the important place of socio-linguistic communicative competence in language acquisition, the chapter examines the role played by *formulaic sequences* or fixed expressions in shaping cognitive and utterance fluency. Formulaic sequences are inherently social in nature and they are not related to underlying knowledge of the structural properties of the language. The chapter focuses on the claim that the functions fulfilled by formulaic sequences serve to promote the speaker's communicative interests.
- Next, the chapter reports some empirical studies linking aspects of L2 proficiency and fluency to language identity issues. In particular, it is argued that *psycholinguistic factors* brought into play by the social environment will have an impact on the development of L2 cognitive fluency, and that this impact may be responsible for at least some of the association observed between social factors in L2 learning (e.g., sense of identity, motivation) and L2 fluency.
- Finally, building on the idea that speakers aim to promote the inter-ests of the self, including using language as an expression of identity, the chapter explores a recent proposal concerning the idea of an *L2 self*. This idea appears in the context of a motivational theory concerned with individual differences in willingness to learn and to use an L2. Although to date the theory of the L2 self has not focused directly on fluency issues as such, it will nevertheless be argued that the L2 self construct may provide a useful way for thinking about how social factors may impact on learners' acquisition and expression of fluency.

Communicative Competence and the Social Dimension of Communication

Nowadays, it is widely agreed that theories of language are incomplete without some recognition of the social dimension of communication. This was not always the case. In the 1960s and 1970s there was consid-erable debate between universal grammarians (Chomsky, 1965, 1975), whose theoretical approaches focused on the fluent, ideal speaker-hearer, and sociolinguists (Gumperz, 1972; Hymes, 1967, 1972; Labov, 1970), who were impressed with the number of socially shaped linguistic behav-iors that actually occurred in real communication. Sociolinguists pointed out that socially shaped linguistic behaviors often revealed language patterns that deviated from what is expected from the ideal speaker-hearer. Nowadays, a substantial part of the linguistics community, especially in applied linguistics, acknowledges the importance of the social dimension of communication for understanding language in general and for understanding L2 acquisition and performance in particular.

There are, of course, many ways to approach the social dimensions of communication that might be relevant to L2 fluency. The social psychology of bilingualism (Lambert, 1967) looks at the social influences impacting on L2 users' behavior and the social consequences that follow from their behavior. The sociology of language (e.g., Fishman, 1967) attempts to link the social factors that drive the use of two or more languages and the psychological processes that underlie a person's use of two or more languages. The sociocultural perspective (Lantolf & Thorne, 2006, 2007) applies Vygotsky's (1978) ideas about the social origins of mind to L2 learning. Discourse analysis examines the social nature of the flow of exchanges that take place in a conversation (e.g., Young & He, 1998). Pragmatics (House, 1996; Kasper & Rose, 1999) looks at the kinds of speech acts that people engage in. The ethnography of communication (Gumperz & Hymes, 1972) focuses on how speech communities develop and use group-specific speech codes. Finally, sociolinguistics is concerned with the role of social context in communication and, among other things, with phenomena of interlanguage variation, cross-cultural communication, conversational phenomena, and social identity (Young, 1999). All of these socially based approaches to language focus on the acquisition of L2 knowledge, but they seldom touch on L2 fluency as such. Nevertheless, there are, in particular, three social aspects of communication that turn out to be especially relevant to L2 fluency issues—*appropriateness*, *naturalness*, and *identity/self*. These are the focus of this chapter.

Appropriateness

Hymes (1967) made the case for a sociolinguistic approach to the study of language and in doing so he lamented the failure of the then current linguistic theories to recognize "the integrity of the message as an act" (p. 13). Hymes objected to the social decontextualizing of language that was so prevalent in much of linguistics and psycholinguistics. In his view, the goal of the scientific study of language should be to describe "the communicative competence that enables a member of the community to know when to speak and when to remain silent, which code to use, when, where and to whom, etc." (p. 13). In other words, communicative competence involves knowing how to speak in a socially appropriate way, and not just how to make grammatically correct sentences.

This idea has significant implications for fluency development. Because all speakers are part of some L1 speech community that has its own social norms of appropriateness, they will naturally expect to have to deal with similar norms in the L2 in some way. Many will, in fact, develop some ability to deal with such norms in the L2, but clearly many either will not or will do so to a limited extent only. To the extent that they do not, their speech might be marked by dysfluencies as they struggle—and often fail—to find the expressions appropriate for the moment. There are several kinds of social appropriateness that a communicatively competent person must be able to handle, whether in the L1 or L2. These include speaking with the appropriate level of politeness that takes into account the status of the hearer and the context in which the communication is taking place (e.g., using a formal versus casual speech register), and shifting from one register to another appropriately and at the right moment (e.g., switching to a casual code once some social rapport has been established with the hearer). Hymes (1967) summarized the components of this kind of communicative competence by means of the acronym *SPEAKING*, where the letters stand for the following eight categories of speech event components (pp. 20–25): Setting (or scene)—the time and place of the speech event; Participants—the interlocutors; Ends—goals, purposes, and outcomes; Art characteristics—message form and topic; Key—tone, manner, or spirit in which a speech act is carried out; Instrumentalities—medium of transmission and language or language variety used; Norms—norms of interaction and interpretation; and Genres—type of speech act. Hymes (1972) also stressed that the knowledge of how to speak appropriately is intimately bound up with the attitudes, values, and motivation the speaker has regarding the language and its uses. As he pointed out, this social dimension is not some sort of add-on that exists independently and in parallel with the grammatical and phonological dimensions of language. Rather, the "engagement of language in social life has a positive, productive aspect. There are rules of use without which the rules of grammar would be useless" (p. 278). For Hymes, acquiring the "competence of use" is as integral to language development as is acquiring competence for grammar. "Within the developmental matrix in which knowledge of the sentences of a language is acquired, children also acquire knowledge of a set of ways in which sentences are used. From a finite experience of speech acts and their interdependence with sociocultural features, they develop a general theory of [how to speak appropriately] in their community" (p. 279). This idea of sociolinguistic competence soon had an impact on the field of L2 acquisition in general. Canale and Swain (1980), for example, in a widely cited paper, explored the theoretical ramifications of such sociolinguistic competence for L2 learning, instruction, testing, and even the training of language teachers.

One can see, indirectly, some of the psychological implications of Hymes' idea for L2 fluency acquisition in the results of a study by Segalowitz (1976). That study began with the premise that L2 learners are often *not* socialized within the target language community but learn the L2 largely in the classroom and this only after having been first intensively immersed in communication patterns within their own L1 community. Consequently, such L2 learners often attain very low levels of sociolinguistic competence in the target language (Nadasdi, Mougeon, & Rehner, 2005). For example, many Canadian English speakers possess functionally adequate communicative skills in French but nevertheless experience difficulties in communicating with Canadian French speakers in terms of correctly using the formal and informal forms of the second person singular pronoun *you* (French *vous* and *tu*, respectively) or the first person plural pronoun *we* (where in French the impersonal third person singular *on* [= English *one*] tends to dominate over *nous* [*we*]). Unfortunately, there are very few empirical studies that have looked directly at the association between L2 sociolinguistic competence and aspects of L2 fluency. However, the study by Segalowitz illustrates one potentially indirect link between sociolinguistic competence and L2 fluency, a link that may have ramifications for fluency acquisition.

Segalowitz (1976) was interested in the consequences for L2 users of lacking skill with one of the most basic appropriateness rules of sociolinguistic competence—the ability to respond to an interlocutor's register shift from formal to casual speech. Often, such a shift signals friendliness, a reduction of social distance, and invites accommodation by the hearer, who normally would be expected to make a similar shift (Sachdev & Giles, 2004). The participants were English speakers in Montreal selected for having only moderate levels of skill in L2 French. The participants had functional communicative skills based on years of classroom learning but had relatively little experience by way of extended communication outside the classroom with native speakers of French, and hence little experience in modulating their L2 speech to meet the French-speaking community's sociolinguistic norms. In this study, the participants were required to interact twice with an unseen English-speaking interlocutor in another room linked by microphone, and then twice with an unseen French-speaking interlocutor. Unbeknownst to the participants, both "interlocutors" were actually prerecorded tape recordings of confederates made to sound like people in a live presentation. The English- and French-speaking "interlocutors" spoke on the first occasion using a formal speech register and on the second occasion they switched to a casual speech register.

The participants were divided into two groups—Listen-and-Speak, and Listen-Only. Participants in the Listen-and-Speak condition first heard the English-speaking interlocutor speak on "An Important Social Issue," after which the participant had to respond by doing the same thing in English. Next they rated the quality of the interaction and reported their impressions of various characteristics of the interlocutor. This whole procedure was repeated, again in English, with the same "interlocutor," except that this time the topic was "A Frightening Experience," for which the "interlocutor" shifted to a casual speech register, appropriate for recounting a personal experience of emotional significance. Finally, the entire procedure was repeated once more in French, the participants' L2, with the same topics and a similar shift in register. In the Listen-Only condition, a different group of participants went through the identical conditions but without having to speak at all.

The main results of interest concern the impact of the register shift on the participants' perceptions of the interlocutor and of the event. First, the participants revealed sensitivity to the register shifts insofar as that they gave different ratings before and after the shifts. Nevertheless, none of the participants reported being consciously aware of the register shift as such or of the purpose of the experiment. These findings in themselves are consistent with the idea that sociolinguistic factors operate in communication and can do so in the background without much awareness on the part of speakers. The main findings, however, were these. In the L1, both groups reported impressions that became more positive as the register shift went from formal to casual—that is, there were more positive perceptions of the interlocutor and more positive perceptions of the event as a whole. In the L2 this was also true, but for the Listen-Only participants. In contrast, for the Listen-and-Speak participants in the L2, the register shift had a *negative* impact. In the casual compared to the formal speech condition, the participants downgraded the perceived personal qualities of the French-speaking interlocutor, they reported that the communication was more difficult, and they reported believing themselves to have made a less favorable impression on the interlocutor.

The results of this study have ramifications for L2 fluency. They suggest that L2 speakers are sensitive to the sociolinguistic demand characteristics of the communicative situations. For example, at some level in the study just reported—possibly below awareness—participants were probably sensitive to the need to sound friendly, to use appropriate forms of respect and deference, to make appropriate register shifts, etc. This was expected because these are, after all, the normal demand characteristics of most communicative situations, whether in the L1 or the L2. However, in the present study the participants lacked the necessary sociolinguistic competence to fully meet these demand characteristics in the L2. This may have created a level of discomfort for the participants. As a result, they may have rationalized the discomfort to themselves by downgrading (in a sense, blaming) the interlocutor and by categorizing the encounter as relatively unpleasant. The L2 users may not have been aware of the reasons for feeling this way; nevertheless, this is what they may have experienced. Perhaps failure to be able to adequately meet the sociolinguistic demand characteristics of L2 communication affects many L2 users in this way. If so, then it is possible that such L2 users will be discouraged from participating in future L2 encounters. This could result in opportunities being missed for learning about and for practicing the use of sociolinguistically appropriate forms of speech in context, in addition to missing out on opportunities to learn and practice other aspects of the L2. All this could lead to lower levels of cognitive and oral fluency than otherwise could have been achieved. In this sense, lacking sociolinguistic competence can be seen to lead to a downward spiral in L2 fluency acquisition.

Clearly, there is an important opportunity here—as yet largely unrealized—for research on one of the ways the social dimension of communication interacts with fluency issues. It seems likely that there is a mutually supportive process involved here, where a certain threshold level of general cognitive and oral fluency is required before an L2 user will be able to attend to the sociolinguistic dimension of speaking and to learn from social encounters. Once achieved, however, this in turn opens up new possibilities for future and possibly even richer environments leading to even greater levels of fluency development. Wong Fillmore (1979) reported an example illustrating such a self-reinforcing learning cycle. She described the case of 5-year-old Nora, an Hispanic American in kindergarten learning English from a native English-speaking classmate. Nora was observed over a three-month period during which she made tremendous progress in English compared to four other learners, also being observed. Wong Fillmore noted in particular the cognitive and social strategies that Nora had adopted. Among these were the use of formulaic sequences in order to establish strong positive communicative bonds with her English-speaking friend, and this ensured that the friend became an important source of linguistic input. Nora's case illustrates how learning benefits from the positive feedback loop that can be established through mastery of the sociolinguistic dimension of communication (see also the discussion in Wray, 2002, pp. 159–161).

The sociolinguistic demand characteristics of L2 communication, however, represent only one aspect of the social factor referred to in the dynamical systems framework shown in Figure 3.1. Another important aspect is related to what gives speech the quality of nativelike *naturalness*, and it is to this topic we now turn.

Naturalness

Pawley and Syder (1983), in a seminal paper on nativelike naturalness in speech, wrote the following:

> fluent and idiomatic control of a language rests to a considerable extent on knowledge of a body of "sentence stems" which are "institutionalized" or "lexicalized". A lexicalized sentence stem is a unit of clause length or longer whose grammatical form and lexical

content is wholly or largely fixed; its fixed elements form a standard
label for a culturally recognized concept, a term in the language.
(1983, p. 191)

In other words, fluency depends on knowledge of *culturally* determined
fixed expressions. Such knowledge is not part of a person's competence
with the grammatical system underlying the language but is picked up
through social interaction with native speakers.

In focusing on this repertoire of fixed expressions, Pawley and Syder
identified two puzzles. The first is the puzzle of *nativelike selection.* Most
linguistic theories based on or derived from the generative grammar
approaches developed by Chomsky and others in the 1950s and 1960s
make the assumption that there is an infinitely large set of potential
sentences in a language and that a learner's task is to learn to distinguish
those that are structurally acceptable from those that are not. Thus, in
English, one would consider *I want to marry you* as grammatically
acceptable and *I marry-you want-to* to be grammatically not acceptable.
Theories of language based on the principles of generative grammar
explain how it is possible for people to use the finite means of language
(its finite vocabulary and grammatical devices) to create and comprehend an indefinitely large number of possible sentences in their language.
This, however, gives rise to an important puzzle. The puzzle is that,
despite the creative opportunities made possible by a generative grammar, most people do *not* make use of the vast potential for creating
sentences at their disposal. In fact, as Pawley and Syder pointed out, if
people did exploit this creative potential to the fullest extent possible,
"they would not be accepted as exhibiting nativelike control of the
language" (p. 193). Too large a variety of sentences would not sound
nativelike, despite the sentences all being grammatically acceptable.
Thus, to expand upon the previous marriage proposal example, the
expressions *My becoming your spouse is what I want* or *I want marriage
with you* would not be considered nativelike in English in most normal
contexts, despite being grammatically acceptable. Thus, nativelike selection of how to say something is not just a matter of correct application
of syntactic knowledge; it involves knowledge of social norms.

The second puzzle is that of *nativelike fluency.* Pawley and Syder
(1983) point out that it is a challenging task, even under the best of
circumstances, to keep speaking fluently for a short period of time, say,
even for 20 seconds or so. This is especially true for adult learners of an
L2. Part of the reason for this difficulty is that there are many processing
demands a speaker must attend to besides grammaticality. These include
making sure that what is said is coherent, is relevant to the topic under
discussion, is delivered with the right amount of precision or vagueness,
logic, humor, deference, etc. Native speakers are typically able to do all
this without compromising fluency; that is, without having to reduce

speech rate or make frequent pauses in the middle of clauses. They succeed because they have the facility of chaining together one clause at a time. Pawley and Syder consider this one-clause-at-a-time facility to be an "essential constituent of communicative competence" (p. 204). The puzzle, then, is how do language learners acquire this facility, given all the demands involved in producing continuous, coherent, and appropriate speech. Moreover, it turns out that in speech that is perceived as fluent by native speakers, there are many violations of the one-clause-at-a-time pattern; instead there are multiclause sequences that are also produced as fluent units. That is, the multiclause sequences are produced at a normal speech rate of around 200 ms per syllable and without internal pauses (see examples in Pawley & Syder, 1983, and in Goldman-Eisler, 1968). How do native speakers accomplish this and what are the implications for L2 speakers?

Pawley and Syder's (1983) solution to these two puzzles was to recognize that speakers possess knowledge that goes beyond what is specified in a grammar. This knowledge includes familiarity with habitually spoken, relatively fixed, or formulaic *sentence stems* and *phraseological units*. An example of a sentence stem would be "NP be-TENSE sorry to keep-TENSE you waiting" for sentences like "*I'm so sorry to keep you waiting*," "*John is sorry to have kept you waiting*," etc.). An example of a phraseological unit would be *It's raining cats and dogs* (see Pawley & Syder, 1983, and Wray, 2002, for more examples). Pawley and Syder argue that native speakers know perhaps hundreds of thousands of fixed and partially fixed expressions, many of them multiclausal, and that these "form the main building blocks of fluent connected speech" (p. 214). These expressions are not simply sequences that some speakers of the language will have memorized while others have not. Rather, these sequences have become lexicalized in the speech community's shared lexicon. They point out that

> What makes an expression a lexical item [as opposed to merely a memorized item], what makes it part of the speech community's common dictionary, is, firstly, that the meaning of the expression is not (totally) predictable from its form, secondly, that it behaves as a minimal unit for certain syntactic purposes, and third, that it is a *social institution*. This last characteristic is sometimes overlooked, but is basic to the distinction between lexicalized and non-lexicalized sequence.

> (1983, p. 209)

Thus, it is part of the English speaker's lexicon that one can say *I have a headache* whereas it is much less natural to say *I have an ache in my head*. In contrast, it is fairly unnatural to say *I have a thigh-ache* but natural to say *I have an ache in my thigh*. This kind of lexicalization of expressions contributes to fluency and nativelike naturalness of speech, and does so to a very major extent according to Pawley and Syder. The learning of such lexicalized expressions can only come about from social contact with the speech community, because one cannot distinguish natural-sounding from non-natural-sounding sequences from grammatical knowledge alone. Pawley and Syder thus argue that fixed or formulaic expressions are a central factor in speech fluency. This poses a challenge to L2 learners who lack the necessary breadth and intensity of socially driven communicative contact with speakers of the target language. The learners' failure to master critical formulaic expressions can compromise their ability to become fluent speakers. We turn now to a more detailed look at the possible significance of formulaic expressions for L2 fluency.

Formulaic and Fixed Sequences

The role and importance of formulaic and fixed sequences in speech fluency has been elaborated upon considerably since the appearance of Pawley and Syder's (1983) work. Alison Wray (2002, 2008), in two book-length treatments of formulaic language, expanded on the social nature of formulaic sequences. She argued that formulaic expressions serve three main functions—to reduce the speaker's processing effort, to mark discourse structure, and to enable the speaker to manipulate the interlocutor, including how that person perceives the speaker's identity. Wray (2002, Chapter 4, especially Table 1.4, p. 89) provides a detailed analysis of how formulaic sequences *serve as devices for manipulating the communicative situation*. This analysis led her to conclude that the three main functions of formulaic sequences can be summarized as fulfilling one overall priority—the speaker's promotion of the self.

Let's consider the three functions of formulaic sequences Wray has identified. First, there is the reduction in processing effort hypothesized to be associated with the use of formulaic sequences. Does this actually lead to measurable gains in processing? The volume edited by Schmitt (2004) reports several studies that have looked at such potential gains in cognitive efficiency. One study, by Underwood, Schmitt, and Galpin (2004), compared native and non-native speakers of English silently reading passages while eye movements were recorded. The study was able to compare the patterns of eye movements associated with sequences in the text that were formulaic with those that were not. The authors report that the native speakers, who were more familiar with formulaic sequences such as *by the skin of his teeth*, fixated less frequently and for a shorter duration on the terminal word of the sequence (here: *teeth*) relative to words in non-formulaic sequences, whereas the non-native speakers did not. This result suggests that there is indeed a measurable gain in processing efficiency in processing formulaic versus non-formulaic sequences.

Wray's second point concerns the marking of discourse. Formulaic expressions can be used to signal to the hearer the structure of the text that is about to be spoken (e.g., *There are three things*) onto which later spoken markers such as *first* and *second* can be mapped. Discourse markers also signal to the hearer when it is appropriate to jump in or to remain silent (e.g., *my point here is ___*). These devices help the speaker maintain control over the communication, and this too can aid fluency.

Finally, Wray's third point concerns the manipulation of the interlocutor. Wray argued that speakers use formulaic sequences to bring about changes in the environment through the use of commands, requests, bargains, politeness markers, and the like. They also try to establish their separate identity as a speaker to be paid attention to by the use of storytelling expressions (e.g., *once upon a time*), turn claimers (e.g., *Yes, but the thing is ...*) and holders (e.g., *The first thing you have to realize, of course, in addressing this issue is ...*), etc. They try to assert their group identity by using formulaic forms of address, hedges, quotations, and threats, among others, that are associated with their group. All these uses of formulaic utterances serve to promote the speaker's social and psychological interests (psychosocial goals). These interests include "being listened to and being taken seriously; having physical and emotional needs satisfactorily and promptly met; ... being perceived as important as an individual; being perceived as a full member of whichever groups are deemed desirable" (Wray, 2002, p. 96).

The *social* aspect of how formulaic sequences are learned and used is summed up in Wray's idea of speaker-hearer alignment (2002, pp. 99–100). This is the idea that interlocutors normally aim to maximize comprehension of each other's messages by reducing the processing load each person has to deal with when decoding the other person's message. To achieve this, speakers will use, whenever possible, fixed and partially fixed strings that the hearer is likely to be able to process as pre-assembled, lexicalized strings, in the hope that this will make the exchange of messages more efficient overall. The use of such strings reduces the processing load on the hearer (see Garrod & Pickering, 2007, on automaticity issues in L1 conversational interactive alignment). In addition, these strings can serve important functions that reduce processing loads even further, such as giving clues about the shape of the conversation (e.g., *I want to tell you a story*; *The first thing is that ...*) and signaling information about the speaker's identity as being a person from such and such a background (the speaker's generation, region of origin, first language, etc.). Information about the speaker's identity is important because it can indicate what kinds of lexicalized knowledge the speaker has access to, and this informs the interlocutor about what formulaic utterances would be appropriate to use with the speaker.

Interlocutors thus try to align themselves to each other by finding the appropriate types of devices needed to save each other processing costs in order to achieve efficient communication.

As Wray points out, it can be especially challenging for the L2 speaker to achieve such communicative efficiency (2002, p. 99). The L2 speaker may not have the appropriate repertoire of lexicalized formulaic sequences, and this can slow down the encoding of messages and place a heavy processing load on decoding what the interlocutor is saying. All this can compromise the L2 speaker's fluency in formulating appropriate responses. With respect to the fluency vulnerability points shown in Figure 1.2 in Chapter 1, this would correspond to $\{f_3\}$—accessing the mental lexicon. Such lexical access problems do not necessarily reflect the usual difficulties in L2 semantic retrieval that mental lexicon theorists normally discuss, such as accessing native language-target language translation equivalents; rather, they reflect difficulties in retrieving *socially appropriate* expressions for which the idea of translation equivalents is largely irrelevant.

The *social* dimension of speaker-hearer alignment lies in the following. Speaker and hearer negotiate with each other to determine what kinds of processing reduction devices they can use with each other. As explained by Wray,

> [A] non-native speaker who engages in prolonged genuine interaction with native speakers will be highly motivated to pick up the idiomatic turns of phrase of the host speech community. Using word strings which the native speaker, as hearer, can decode easily (because they are formulaic) will greatly enhance the success of the messages' interactional purpose, not least because, if the speaker has non-nativelike phonology, the hearer will need to engage in extra processing for the phonological decoding. In addition, though, the use of nativelike formulaic sequences will signal to native speakers that this non-native speaker is able to cope with their idiomatic output.
>
> (2002, p. 99)

This means that the process of acquiring a repertoire of formulaic sequences and of learning to use that repertoire to enhance fluency are intimately intertwined in the social exchanges that take place between interlocutors. This is why social factors play such an important role in the shaping of L2 fluency. Figure 5.1, taken from Wray (2000), summarizes the main elements in her model.

Wray (2002), in the quotation cited above, refers to the speaker's *motivation* to acquire a repertoire of formulaic utterances for fluency enhancing purposes and, as seen earlier, to promote personal interests in various ways. Perhaps this motivation involves more than just the energy

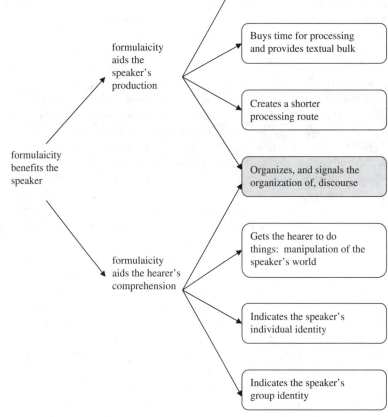

Figure 5.1 The functions of formulaic sequences in promoting the interests of the speaker's *Self*, as presented by Wray (2000, Figure 1, p. 478).

(effort) that moves the learner to focus on formulaic sequences. Instead, perhaps the motivation involves the way the L2 user more broadly orients him- or herself toward the target language and its community. If so, then the L2 learner's motivation might have deeper and longer-term consequences beyond simply affecting the likelihood of noticing and learning specific details about the language (about formulaic sequences, for example). There is one recently proposed theoretical approach to L2 learner motivation that might provide a fruitful way to think about these issues. This is Zoltán Dörnyei's (2005, 2009b) theory of the *Motivational L2 Self System*. We turn now to this socially grounded motivational perspective and the theoretical and empirical context in which it is located.

The Motivational L2 Self System

So far, we have seen that fluent communication requires knowledge and skills about appropriateness, naturalness, and the use of formulaic sequences, all of which can only be acquired through social interaction. These requirements represent linguistic demand characteristics that are inherent in all normal communication, and they can often pose significant challenges for L2 users, thereby compromising fluency. These demand characteristics concern the nature of the language to be used in communication. As such, they originate outside the L2 speaker. Put another way, they are part and parcel of what one has to do in order to communicate successfully, regardless of who is communicating.

Beyond these linguistic demand characteristics, however, there are other socially grounded factors that can affect fluency acquisition and its expression. These reflect something about the L2 speakers themselves as language users, as opposed to something about the language as such. In particular, these person-based considerations reflect L2 users' motivation to learn and to speak the language, motivations that are founded on socially constructed beliefs and attitudes about identity.

Over the years, researchers have reported associations between various aspects of L2 users' language performance—such as how they handle particular features of the target language or the amount and kind of language use they engage in—and their beliefs and attitudes about the language and the group speaking that language. (A cautionary note is in order here. Fluency, defined in terms of temporal and hesitation features of speech, has seldom been measured directly in the socially oriented studies cited in this section. Nevertheless, in light of the proficiency measures used in these studies, it is reasonable to speculate that fluency, as one aspect of proficiency, would also have varied as a function of the socially grounded beliefs these studies addressed.) For example, Taylor, Meynard, and Rhéault (1977) looked at the impact of perceived threat to ethnic identity on L2 learning outcomes. They studied native speakers of French from Quebec, Canada, where many believe that learning English poses a threat to the ethnic identity of French speakers. Participants filled out questionnaires regarding beliefs and attitudes toward English-speaking Canadians, about beliefs concerning threats to their ethnic identity, about motivation for learning an L2, and self-rating questionnaires concerning their abilities in English as an L2. The main result of interest here is that participants who felt that their cultural identity was under threat self-rated as less fluent in their L2 English.

Ellinger (2000) also reported evidence showing that ethnolinguistic identity was a significant predictor of L2 achievement in university students. By implication—because the achievement measures included teachers' evaluations and performance on reading comprehension, written expression, and cloze tasks—the results most likely also speak to fluency acquisition, although this was not specifically highlighted in the study. Ellinger conducted her study with Israeli Hebrew- and Russian-speaking students of English as an L2. Her results indicated that ethno-linguistic variables—including beliefs about the vitality of Hebrew and English, emotional distance from English speakers, and the strength of their own ethnolinguistic identities—were stronger predictors of L2 achievement than were more conventional motivational variables (e.g., interest in foreign languages, attitudes toward English, etc.).

Coupland, Bishop, Williams, Evans, and Garrett (2005) reported a study involving the learning of Welsh by high school students who varied in the degree to which they held feelings of ethnic affiliation and cultural engagement with the Welsh language and community. The researchers found that many of the social variables were significantly associated with self-reported competence in the Welsh language (and, by inference, with fluency). These and similar studies have demonstrated that learners' beliefs and attitudes about their personal social position in relation to the target language and its community can be associated with the level of language achievement attained.

In what may be the largest L2 study of its kind to date, involving some 13,000 participants, Dörnyei, Csizér, and Németh (2006) investigated Hungarian high school learners of different target L2s as a function of their attitudes towards these languages. The attitudes addressed by their questionnaires included, among others, integrativeness (the desire to become like the speakers of the target language), instrumentality (the desire to learn the language for pragmatic purposes), and other variables reflecting beliefs about and attitudes toward target language speakers and their community. Two outcome measures of interest here were the students' choice of language (e.g., English versus German) and the intended effort to learn it (e.g., the number of hours per week to be invested in it), reflecting the learner's motivation to learn the L2. By means of structure equation modeling, Dörnyei et al. found that integra-tiveness mediated the effects of all the other variables investigated and that the immediate antecedents of integrativeness were instrumentality and attitudes toward the target speakers' community. These results showed that social variables are not only involved in determining which language will be chosen to be learned, but—and this has implications for fluency development—beliefs and attitudes about the language, its speakers and their community were also associated with the amount of effort the learners reported intending to commit to learning. Clearly, this can have an impact on fluency development insofar as an effort to learn will affect the amount of exposure to the language a learner receives, which in turn will impact on fluency development. Additional support for this pattern of findings has been reported by Taguchi, Magid, and Papi (2009) in a study of Japanese, Chinese, and Farsi speakers learning English.

The results of other studies also suggest that the social role the L2 plays in a person's life may be strongly associated with learning outcomes and learning-related decisions. For example, Gatbonton and her colleagues have looked directly at the relation social identity might have with L2 attainment. In a recent article, they addressed the question of whether ethnolinguistic affiliation (the language community with which a person identifies) is associated with language learning motivation in such a way as to shape individual differences in L2 acquisition outcomes (Segalowitz, Gatbonton, & Trofimovich, 2009). That article reviewed several studies regarding the relationships between the strength and nature of beliefs about the target language and the target community, and it looked at detailed aspects of L2 attainment. The research also examined the possible role of psycholinguistic factors in mediating those relationships. The authors operationalized beliefs about the target language and its community with a questionnaire about L2 users' ethnic group affiliation (EGA) and their beliefs about the role language plays in EGA. In an earlier factor analytic study, Gatbonton and Trofimovich (2008) had found that four factors could be shown to underlie the feelings of EGA of the Canadian-based Quebec French participants in their study. For example, one of these factors was *Political EGA*, so called because it reflected support for a political program to achieve certain social and political goals of the ethnolinguistic group to which they claimed primary membership (e.g., beliefs regarding the enactment of laws to protect the French language in Quebec). These EGA measures served to quantify socially based beliefs and attitudes about their own L1 and the target L2 (here, French and English, respectively). The researchers also operationalized L2 attainment in a number of ways. One was in terms of the development of control over a particular sound in the target language—the voiced interdental fricative (voiced *th* sound in words like *other* and *there*)—which can serve as a marker of a speaker's ethnolinguistic identity (in Quebec, many L2 speakers frequently pronounce voiced *th* in a non-nativelike manner that is often perceived as pointing to *Québécois* French as being the L1).

Gatbonton (1978) and Trofimovich, Gatbonton, and Segalowitz (2007) had previously reported that the distribution of nativelike and non-nativelike pronunciations of voiced *th* in French Canadians' L2 English speech followed a particular pattern with respect to the phonetic environments in which the target sounds were embedded (e.g., word initial as in *there*; intervocalic as in *other*), in a manner predicted by a gradual diffusion framework for acquisition. This pattern reflected an implicational scale, in which nativelike pronunciations of voiced *th* appeared first in "easier" contexts and later in "harder" contexts, as opposed to simply appearing in speech in a random manner across all phonetic contexts equally. Trofimovich et al. (2007) discovered that the ordering of the contexts from "easy" to "hard" reflected two psycholinguistic factors: *frequency* of the context in the language (e.g., in English, voiced *th* occurs more frequently in word-initial contexts than in intervocalic contexts), and perceptual similarity/difference of the phonetic cluster (the target sound in its context) from phonetic elements it could potentially be confused with in the L1 (French) (e.g., the greater the difference, the easier the context; Flege, 1995). They also found that L2 speakers could be placed, in a statistically reliable way, on the implicational scale in a manner that reflected a stage of development in the mastery of voiced *th*. This made it possible to relate L2 speakers' level of development in using a specific phonetic target—one that has value as a cue to ethnolinguistic identity—to their EGA.

Gatbonton, Trofimovich, and Segalowitz (in press) reported that, across the sample of L2 users, speakers' Political EGA was significantly associated with where they were located in the implicational scale that reflected individual differences in control over the use of voiced *th*. Importantly, Segalowitz et al. (2009) reported that this association disappeared when the correlation between Political EGA and this measure of phonetic development was recomputed by first controlling for speakers' self-reported use of the L2 (as a percentage of time speaking throughout the day). This result indicated that L2 use appears to have mediated the relationship between the language-related political beliefs and phonetic control addressed in their study. Segalowitz et al. also reported that L2 use appeared to mediate the association between L2 speech rate and the belief that language is important in defining a person's identity. Of course, future research will need to address more directly the direction of causal links in these associations and it would be desirable to progress from measuring L2 use by self-report to more direct measures. Nevertheless, the findings are intriguing, and they invite further exploration of possible associations between social factors and L2 performance indicators, as well as investigation of whether and how L2 use might mediate such associations.

By way of an interim summary, we have seen that there are associations between various aspects of proficiency attainment—and by inference fluency attainment, although this needs to be explored more directly and in more detail—and socially grounded beliefs about language identity and beliefs about the relationship between one's own language community and that of the target community. Moreover, there was some suggestive evidence that the links between socially grounded beliefs and L2 performance are mediated, in part at least, by language use. It would be useful to put this picture of how social factors might impact on L2 performance into a larger theoretical framework of some kind. Such a framework might help shape the formulation of future research questions and might indicate how to work with the social dimensions of fluency in efforts to enhance fluency development. Dörnyei (2005, 2009b) recently presented one such framework—one that seems especially promising—and so it will be presented briefly here.

Dörnyei (2009b) is concerned with what drives a person to learn and use an L2 in the first place. He has proposed a theory of the *Motivational L2 Self System* to address this question. The theory draws on a number of recent advances in motivational psychology (from areas unrelated to L2 issues) and there is growing empirical support for his perspective (see Dörnyei 2005, 2009b for a fuller theoretical exposition, and papers in Dörnyei & Ushioda, 2009, for empirical support). Dörnyei's goal is to move thinking about motivation in L2 acquisition beyond simply ideas about incentives and needs that might drive a learner's behavior. Instead, Dörnyei sees motivational issues in L2 acquisition as being about the very fiber of a learner's being; that is, how learners see themselves—with respect to language—in relation to the world around them.

What, then, is it that motivates—energizes and guides—the L2 learner in deciding to learn the target language and to use that language to such an extent that there is an impact on fluency? In addressing this issue, Dörnyei has reconceptualized the previously dominant approach in the field—Gardner's (1985, 2001) motivational theory of the role played by integrative and instrumental goals in L2 learning. Dörnyei (2009b, especially pp. 23–25) argues that there is a need to move beyond integrative and instrumental goals. These goals refer, respectively, to the learner's desire to know the L2 in order to become like, and to be valued by, the members of the target linguistic community (an integrative goal), and to the desire to be able to use the language for practical purposes (an instrumental goal). Dörnyei suggests that these concepts largely no longer apply in a world in which boundaries between language groups have become extremely fluid and porous, where most societies have become multilingual, and where it is often difficult to define precisely which populations constitute the target language community. Indeed, on an individual level, as suggested by Gatbonton (2009, personal communication), such crossing of boundaries has served to foreground the problem of identity, making the link between language and identity all the more salient. Moreover, Dörnyei claims it is more appropriate to reformulate future-oriented *goals*, such as Gardner's integrative goal, as *future self-guides* that drive and direct behavior. The difference is that *goals* focus on end-states, and they can be rather abstract and hence not necessarily capable of providing strong motivational support. In contrast, *future self-guides* can focus on an individual's concrete, ongoing self-image as an L2 user. Moreover, because *future self-guides* do not depend in any way on whether an end-state has been achieved, they have the ability to exert a continuous impact on behavior.

Dörnyei's (2009b) theory of the *Motivational L2 Self System* starts with the idea, first elaborated in Markus and Nurius (1986), that people develop abilities to regulate their own behavior by setting goals and expectations. They had proposed the concept of *possible selves* as a mechanism by which people achieve this self-regulation. The basic idea is that people have images of themselves as they are and as how they could be, and such images motivate particular behaviors. Among the possible selves that people operate with are an *ideal* self—what it is they would like to become (e.g., rich, thin, successful); an *expected* self—what it is they are likely to become, a *feared* self—what it is they would like to avoid becoming (e.g., incompetent, lonely, alcoholic); and an *ought-to self*—an image of themselves they believe others have of them. Dörnyei singles out the *ought-to self* as being especially important because it reflects peer pressure stemming from the group(s) with which one identifies socially. Moreover, Dörnyei holds that these possible selves—and the *ought-to self*, in particular—are mentally represented in terms of imagery that is experienced as very real to the individual. This imagery, as Markus and Ruvolo put it (1989, p. 217; cited by Dörnyei, 2009b, p. 13), is "phenomenologically very close to the actual thoughts and feelings that individuals experience as they are in the process of motivated behaviour and instrumental action." The power of imagery to motivate performance enhancement and the regulation of behavior has been well documented in sports psychology (Gregg & Hall, 2006) where imagery techniques have been put to wide and effective use in the training of athletes. Dörnyei (2009b, pp. 16–17) specifically cites the significance and success of motivational imagery in sport as support for focusing on self-related imagery in L2 acquisition. He emphasizes that including such imagery in possible selves theory has opened up an innovative and promising conceptual breakthrough for a motivational theory of L2 learning. In particular, he writes, "Language learning is a sustained and often tedious process with lots of temporary ups and downs, and I felt that the secret of successful learners was their possession of a superordinate vision that kept them on track" (2009b, p. 25).

Dörnyei (2009b) further points out that the *ideal self* and the *ought-to self* function as future-guides in the individual's self-regulatory mechanisms for L2 use and acquisition. The *ideal self* provides a promotion focus related to goals to be achieved whereas the *ought-to self* provides a prevention focus related to avoiding negative outcomes. Sometimes the *ideal* and the *ought-to selves* are discrepant and, as suggested in *self-discrepancy theory* (Higgins, 1987, 1996), this discrepancy motivates people to act to bring the selves in line with each other. However, as Dörnyei points out, there exist situations in which the imagery associated with possible selves does not succeed in motivating behavior, contrary to the prediction of possible selves theory. Dörnyei identifies several conditions which, if not met, might lead to this happening. Among these, three seem especially relevant to fluency. These are *perceived plausibility*—the learner's need to believe that a particular possible self can indeed be achieved; *harmony between the ideal and ought-to selves*—the need for congruency between desired possible selves and social identities; and *accompanying procedural strategies*—the learner's need to have a path for achieving the hoped-for possible self.

To summarize, Dörnyei (2009b) posits an image-based, ongoing, L2 self that serves as a potentially powerful future-guide for self-regulation and for shaping L2-related behaviors. This L2 self comprises the following components. There is an *ideal L2 self*, which is the L2-specific aspect of a person's "ideal self." This self represents what people would like to become. There is an *ought-to L2 self*, which is the L2-specific aspect of the self that reflects what people believe others expect them to become and what outcomes they believe they are expected to avoid. This ought-to self is tied to the person's social identity; because the individual identifies with the social group that is the source of the expectations, he or she is strongly influenced by those expectations. Dörnyei sees these two components as operating in the context of *L2 Learning Experience*, "which concerns situated, 'executive' motives related to the immediate learning environment and experience" (2009b, p. 29). This means that the resolution of the discrepancy between the ideal self and the other selves must be viewed in light of the kinds of language interactions the learner has. Dörnyei's theory of the *Motivational L2 Self System* is a significant contribution to a cognitive science perspective on L2 fluency because it sets up the possibility for integrating the various social underpinnings of fluency that were discussed earlier—with each other and, as will be proposed next, with the non-social aspects of fluency too.

An Integrated Approach to the Social Dimension of Fluency

Four major points have been advanced in this chapter for including a social dimension among the determinants of fluency. The first is that a sociolinguistic competence underlies all L2 communication. This refers to a competence for knowing what is communicatively appropriate— knowing how the language is to be used for social purposes. L2 speakers who have not acquired an appropriate level of sociolinguistic competence will be left out of the social loop, so to speak, in their encounters with native speakers. This can result in dysfluencies as they search for sociolinguistically appropriate expressions, and it can affect the quality of their experience in communicating with others in the target language. This, ultimately, can affect the availability of opportunities to develop fluency.

The second point concerns control over the use of formulaic sequences or fixed utterances. The ability to correctly use formulaic sequences contributes to the nativelike naturalness of speech, and to modulating the message-processing load to make communication easier and more efficient. L2 speakers lacking appropriate control of formulaic sequences will not be able to enjoy the efficiency advantages that can accrue from using such sequences, and this can create processing burdens for them that might compromise fluency. Moreover, by not using formulaic sequences properly, the L2 speaker signals to the native speaker interlocutor that he or she has limited processing abilities, and this can result in the native speaker deciding to accommodate by simplifying his or her output, which again can deprive the L2 speaker of valuable opportunities to develop fluency.

The third point concerns the use of formulaic sequences to advance a personal social agenda, such as establishing their social position, and their individual and group identity vis-à-vis the interlocutor. This is a normal aspect of L1 communication and so it may be expected that L2 speakers will also experience the need to similarly advance a personal social agenda. However, to the extent that L2 speakers lack control over a wide range of formulaic sequences, they will miss out on sending and receiving of such messages, despite possessing a particular sense of self and having the wish to use the communication to advance the interests of that self. The result is that fluency of expression will suffer as L2 speakers attempt to compensate for the lack of skill in using formulaic sequences for social purposes, and L2 fluency acquisition will suffer as L2 speakers avoid encounters because of past failures to be able to use the language effectively to promote their interests.

The fourth point is one identified by the theory of the *Motivational L2 Self System*, based on recent developments in the social psychology of personality and motivation. This is the idea that L2 speakers have internalized images reflecting several possible selves as an L2 speaker, including an ideal self, an actual self, and an ought-to self. The theory assumes that these selves are linked with a sense of social identity—that is, as a member of some particular social group, including a community of speakers with a common language. One possible consequence of possessing a language-based social identity is to render the L2 speaker susceptible to various kinds of social pressures regarding how to behave with respect to the L2. According to the theory, these social pressures can impact on the L2 speaker's mental images of the self, including the L2-specific ideal-, actual-, and ought-to-selves. These images of self are highly imagistic and serve as future-guides that help to shape the L2 speaker's self-regulatory behavior with respect to the L2. This presumably would include the L2 speaker's behavior with respect to the sociolinguistic dimension of communication and the uses of formulaic sequences discussed earlier.

It is possible, of course, to think about these various sources of influence independently, as factors making separate contributions to the acquisition of fluency. In fact, this is how the literature currently tends to present the issues. However, given what is now known about the social influences on L2 performance, it is reasonable to speculate about how the various social factors described earlier may be viewed in an integrated way. Just such an integrated perspective is proposed here, and it is based on the following three main issues: L2 users have felt experiences related to their sense of self; languages possess affordances (resources) that make possible the promotion of the interests of the self; and fluency development requires exposure to psycholinguistically appropriate learning conditions.

> (1) *Sense of self—People invariably experience their exposure to and use of the L2 in terms that relate to a deeply felt, socially grounded, sense of self, and normally the goal of L2 communication (as it is for L1 communication) is to fulfill the needs of this self, in addition to any goals concerned with the direct exchange of cognitive information.*

This claim reflects the idea that L2 communication, as does L1 communication, is known to normally involve multiple levels simultaneously, including the sending and receiving of information about identity, social status, emotional states, etc., plus messages aimed at manipulating the social interaction in some way. All these socially grounded messages are part and parcel of the communication, in addition to the basic cognitive information that people usually think about as the principal content of the communication. As a result, communicating in the L2 is experienced in a wide-ranging and profoundly personal manner, most of which occurs below conscious awareness. This situation contrasts, for example, with the way most people experience exposure to and the use of other complex cognitive skills, such as when learning and performing mathematical, athletic, or artistic skills (although, perhaps for some very high level professionals, activities in these domains can also be felt as intensely personal). The nature of the sense of self that is mobilized by engaging in L2 communication has an impact on shaping the person's behavior in using the L2—in terms of the opportunities they seek for using the L2, their avoidance strategies, what they notice about the language when communicating, what they are able to learn from encounters, etc. It is important, therefore, from a research point of view, to understand the nature of the self that is implicated in L2 communication.

> (2) *Linguistic affordances—Languages afford their users particular ways for promoting the interests of the self, including a repertoire of fixed (formulaic) and partially fixed expressions, a range of alternate forms of phonetic and grammatical patterns that are associated with different speech registers, and socially conditioned rules for shifting from one speech pattern to another. L2 users need to master the use of these linguistic affordances in order to promote the interests of the self through the L2.*

This claim is based on the now well-established finding, as reviewed earlier, that languages possess a large and rich set of formulaic sequences that serve important communicative functions. In addition, language communities engage in speech accommodation, which involves the modulation of speech registers during the course of communication. An important goal of L2 research, therefore, should be to identify the specific details of formulaic sequences, speech registers, and speech accommodation as they relate to important communicative functions that L2 users must deal with at various stages along the path of L2 fluency acquisition.

> (3) *Appropriate learning conditions—Mastery of socially relevant linguistic affordances in the L2 requires exposure to the language under appropriate conditions that recruit psycholinguistically relevant cognitive and perceptual learning mechanisms.*

The conditions that promote language learning and fluency are, in large measure, fairly well known. These were reviewed earlier and they include high levels of repetition (frequency effects), exposure under conditions that promote transfer appropriate processing, conditions that make certain features of target language salient, etc. What is not well known— and therefore needs to be targeted by research—is what kinds of L2 use in natural social situations provide these conditions for successful learning.

These three points—the L2 user's sense of self, linguistic affordances, appropriate learning conditions—can be viewed as interconnected in terms of how they relate to fluency development (see Figure 5.2). As shown in the figure, the user's sense of self underlies how the person experiences and evaluates L2 encounters, determining the likelihood of future encounters and the nature of those encounters. Once in a situation, the language user has to take advantage of the appropriate affordances (or learn to do so) so that the interests and needs of the self may be properly served. However, fluency in the L2 will develop only to the extent that the user's motivation succeeds in bringing him or her into contact situations that are appropriate for learning to take place. If this learning includes mastery of linguistic affordances required to serve the needs of the self, then acquisition and fluency will continue to develop. If this learning fails to include such mastery, then language contact opportunities will decrease and acquisition and fluency will suffer correspondingly. In this way, the social, linguistic, and cognitive dimensions become intimately intertwined with respect to fluency development.

The relationships shown in Figure 5.2 go beyond those shown in Figure 1.3 (Chapter 1). For this reason, it is appropriate to update that figure somewhat so that it more fully reflects the operation of the social

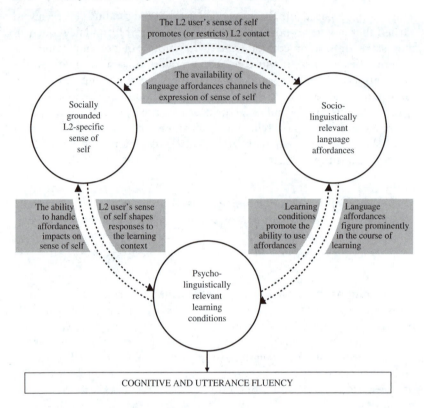

Figure 5.2 Interactive nature of the relationships between the L2 user's sense of
self, the target language's sociolinguistically relevant affordances and
the L2 contact environment's ability to promote learning and fluency.

factors described in this chapter. The updated version is presented below
in Figure 5.3.

Chapter Summary

This chapter looked at L2 fluency from a social perspective, including
contributions from sociolinguistics, from theories about the role of
formulaic language in L2 acquisition, and from a socially grounded
motivational theory of L2 acquisition and performance. The main
conclusions that emerged for carrying forward into the final chapter are
the following:

- *L2 users require fluency in terms of a sociolinguistic communicative
  competence to use the language appropriately.*
- *The L2 user's motivation to engage in L2 contact is founded on
  an L2-specific, socially based psychological sense of self, including
  sense of identity.*

Figure 5.3 Framework for thinking about the dynamic relationships among sources influencing L2 fluency (revised version of Figure 1.3).

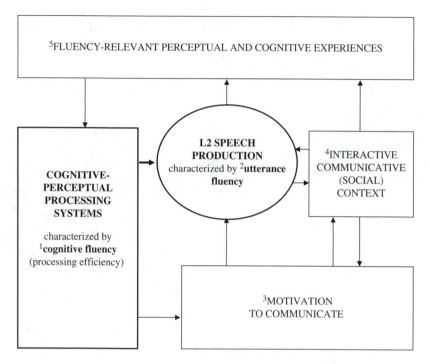

The act of producing *L2 speech* (central oval) is subject to at least four broadly defined influences that interact with one another, creating a system that is continuously changing and adapting over time, and that has the features of a dynamical system. L2 fluency is characterized by the relationship between cognitive and utterance fluency (the highlighted rectangle and oval). System components include: the *cognitive-perceptual systems* underlying speech production, *motivation to communicate*, the *interactive communicative* or *social context* created by the act of communicating, and the *perceptual and cognitive experiences* resulting from communicating and from the social context. These experiences affect utterance fluency by shaping cognitive fluency.

Notes
[1] Cognitive fluency features include processing speed, stability, and flexibility in the planning, assembly, and execution of utterances in terms of lexical access and the use of linguistic resources (linguistic affordances) to express construals, handle sociolinguistic functions, and pursue psychosocial goals.
[2] Utterance fluency features include speech rate, hesitation, and pausing phenomena, etc.
[3] Motivation includes willingness to communicate, beliefs about communication, language and identity, and the concept of the L2 self. Motivation influences speech production and the selection of social contexts in which to speak.
[4] The social context influences speech production by setting the cognitive task demands associated with communication and is the source for learning about linguistic affordances.
[5] Experiences include frequency of exposure, opportunities for repetition practice, etc.

- *The ability to use formulaic sequences or fixed expressions in a skilled manner to promote the interests of one's psychological sense of self is a fluency-relevant aspect of sociolinguistic communicative competence.*
- *The link between social aspects of one's psychological sense of self (e.g., one's sense of ethnic identity) and L2 performance is mediated by L2 use, presumably through the recruitment of cognitive and perceptual systems brought about by using the L2.*

6 Widening the Interdisciplinary Scope

Neuroscientific, Formal Modeling, and Philosophical Issues in Second Language Fluency

What people potentially are and what they in fact turn out to be are contingent, to an incalculable extent, on human intention, both individual and social, bounded only by available resources and the limits of ingenuity.

(Scheffler, 1985, p. 11)

So far, we have looked at basic studies attempting to measure L2 utterance fluency (Chapter 2), at how researchers have addressed fluency from a cognitive psychological and a general skills perspective (Chapters 3 and 4), and at research that takes into account the social dimensions of learning, identity, and motivation (Chapter 5). This chapter addresses the fifth anchor question—*What insights concerning L2 fluency can be gleaned from other branches of the cognitive sciences?*—by looking briefly at selected illustrative studies taken from three perspectives not yet represented. These are *neuroimaging studies* of fluency, *formal modeling* approaches to fluency, and *philosophical approaches* to expertise and fluency. These perspectives and the ones presented in earlier chapters should be considered as complementary; no one of them is the "correct" or the "most promising" way to address fluency issues. As will be discussed in the closing chapter, these approaches—because of the various ways they converge on fluency phenomena (Figure 1.3, Chapter 1)—together comprise a cognitive science approach to the study of fluency. It goes without saying that each of the three areas presented in this chapter has a much larger literature area behind it. The aim here is to briefly highlight the possibilities of convergence across three areas of thought where, at the moment, there is relatively little cross-communication.

Neuroimaging and Neurocognitive Studies of Fluency

The main limitation of fluency studies that focus just on oral behavior (see Chapter 2) is that it is hard to make inferences about the underlying brain processes and mechanisms. Fortunately, recent advances in non-invasive techniques for studying brain activity have made it possible to complement behavioral studies by investigating what happens in real time and space in the brain when a person uses the L2. There is a rapidly growing neuroimaging literature on bilingualism, and much of it has focused on trying to understand how multiple languages are represented in the brain and on the patterns of language loss in bilingual aphasia (for early work in the area, see Albert & Obler, 1978; Ojemann & Whitaker, 1978; Paradis, 1983; Zatorre, 1989; recent important sources include Abutalebi, 2008; Abutalebi, Cappa, & Perani, 2001, 2005; Abutalebi & Green, 2007, 2008; Costa & Santesteban, 2006; Green, 2001; Gullberg & Indefrey, 2006; Hull & Vaid, 2005; Paradis, 2004; and the references cited therein). The representation of multiple languages in the brain and the phenomena of bilingual aphasia are, of course, fundamental topics in L2 research, but they do not necessarily speak directly to questions about fluency. Nevertheless, brain-based studies can, in principle, offer insights into fluency not obtainable in any other way. For example, measures of event related potentials (ERP) and magneto-encephalography (MEG) allow one to measure neuroelectric and neuromagnetic responses, respectively, to stimuli that occur within hundredths of a second of stimulus presentation, and they do so in a way that is potentially free of many of the extraneous influences (sources of noise) that arise when a person has to speak or press a reaction time panel. Techniques such as functional magnetic resonance imaging (fMRI), positron emission tomography (PET), and to a lesser extent MEG, allow one to identify which regions of the brain are active during the performance of a task in a way that is not possible in studies relying solely on behavioral measures.

Moreover, sometimes it is even possible for imaging data to reveal distinctions about the underlying mental processes that are not at all evident in the behavioral data. For example, Bialystok et al. (2005) reported a study involving the Simon task (Simon, 1969) with bilinguals. The study used MEG to investigate which regions of the brain were implicated in the Simon task phenomenon and whether the activation patterns were the same in monolinguals and bilinguals. In the version of the Simon task Bialystok et al. used, participants saw red or green squares, and they had to press either the left or right reaction time panel to indicate which color they saw. The squares appeared on the left or right sides of the screen, sometimes congruent with the correct response (e.g., red square on the left side, congruent with pressing the left panel for "red") and sometimes incongruent (e.g., red square on the right side, incongruent with pressing the left panel for "red"). Typically in such a task, RTs on congruent trials are faster than on incongruent trials (see, e.g., Wascher, Schatz, Kuder, & Verleger, 2001). Subjects were either bilingual (Cantonese-English; French-English) or monolingual young adults, all bilinguals being "completely fluent in both languages"

(Bialystok et al., 2005, p. 42), having learned the L2 at a young age and using both languages daily. The finding of greatest interest here was that, although both bilinguals and monolinguals showed significant Simon effects (slower responding in the incongruent condition), the pattern of brain activation was systematically different in the two populations, something that could not be seen from an analysis of RTs alone. In the bilinguals, RTs correlated with activation over a larger set of regions (largely left hemisphere, superior and middle temporal, cingulate, and superior and inferior frontal regions), compared to the monolinguals (medial frontal regions). Bialystok et al. concluded that the regions implicated in the bilinguals' behavior reflected the areas that are normally engaged during the control of the two languages during language selection. Thus, their study showed that there exist individual differences in the way neural resources are recruited for performing a non-language task as a consequence of being a fluent bilingual, differences that the behavioral data were unable to reveal.

Generally speaking, in the bilingualism neuroimaging literature little distinction is made between *proficiency* and *fluency*, and so here the two terms will be used interchangeably. Of course, it should be remembered that the term *proficiency* normally includes reference to the *possession* of linguistic knowledge, which is distinct from the skill in being able to use that knowledge (fluency). The knowledge aspect of proficiency is usually reflected in performance accuracy; if the individual does not have the knowledge, then linguistic errors are made. Fluency, on the other hand, is usually reflected in performance delivery; the individual may have the knowledge to perform accurately, but not quickly or smoothly. Despite the strong reasons for distinguishing fluency from proficiency, using the terms interchangeably here is not altogether unreasonable. This is because, in brain-based studies of language, the focus of investigation is usually on individual differences in how efficiently people process information and which regions of the brain are recruited for that processing, not whether the individuals possess the knowledge in the first place. Experimental tasks typically do not tap into whether people are capable of understanding a particular word or a sentence, but rather what happens in the brain when people do indeed correctly process the target information and whether they exhibit fluency in doing so. In that sense, despite their often explicit focus on proficiency issues, the studies reviewed here qualify for our purposes as studies about fluency as well.

With these considerations in mind, this section will look at the following three main fluency-related issues:

- neural correlates of L2 fluency
- neural correlates of automaticity in L2 processing
- neural correlates of attention control in language selection.

Neural Correlates of L2 Fluency

Weber-Fox and Neville (2001) reported a study concerned with differences in brain functioning in more versus less fluent language users. The basic goal was to document neural correlates of processing English open and closed class words as a function of word class and of people's level of proficiency. Participants in the study were native English-speaking monolinguals and Chinese L2 speakers of English with different ages of acquisition for English ranging from the period 1–3 years of age to 15 years and older. Proficiency in English was assessed separately and found to correlate significantly with age of acquisition.

The linguistic stimuli were open class words with referential meaning (nouns, adjectives, verbs) and closed class words with structural/grammatical meaning (or relational meaning, as described earlier in Chapter 4: articles, determiners, prepositions, conjunctions). The words were presented in sentences, in the middle of a computer screen, one at a time every 700 ms. After the participants saw the final word of each sentence, they had to press a button to indicate whether, given that final word, the sentence made sense or not. Event related potential (ERP) recordings were taken while the participants read each sentence silently.

The results of most interest here concern how the ERPs to the open and closed class words (seen as the sentences were presented word by word) varied as a function of the participants' proficiency in English. Two sets of results can be highlighted here. First, it was found that, broadly speaking, the ERPs associated with open class (referential words) and closed class words (grammatical/relational words) differed from each other in the same way in both the bilingual and monolingual groups, and in the same manner as observed in previous research with monolinguals (Neville, Mills, & Lawson, 1992). In the time window from about 235 to 400 ms after the onset of the stimulus word, peak latency and amplitude of the ERP occurred significantly earlier for closed class words than for open class words. Also, the ERPs associated with closed class words were narrowly localized in recordings over anterior regions of the left hemisphere, whereas the ERPs associated with open class words were distributed over both hemispheres and were largest over posterior recording areas. These differences in patterns indicate that closed class and open class words recruit processing mechanisms that differ both temporally and spatially as reading unfolds in real time. The question of greatest interest here is whether these patterns differed in any interesting way as a function of English L2 proficiency. Such differences were indeed found for closed class words but, as we shall see, not for open class words.

In the case of the closed class words, the ERP of interest is the N280 (an ERP component with negativity peaking at about 280 ms after stimulus onset). In terms of spatial distribution (mostly at electrodes over left anterior hemisphere locations, as mentioned above) and peak amplitudes, Weber-Fox and Neville (2001) found that the N280 did not vary as a function of proficiency. Peak *latency*, however, did vary as a function of proficiency, indicating that longer latencies were associated with decreased proficiency. Also, for bilinguals who were immersed in English after the age of 7, the N280 latencies tended to be longer by more than 35 ms compared to the monolinguals. In other words, the processing of *grammatical/relational closed class words* was significantly slower for participants with weaker proficiency in English. In contrast, N350 effects (negativity peaking at around 350 ms), which is the ERP component of interest for open class words, did not show effects related to proficiency. In terms of spatial distribution (mostly posterior, bilateral), peak amplitudes and latencies, the N350 did not vary as a function of proficiency. Taken together, these results suggest that fluency is associated principally with the efficiency of processing grammatical/relational words (see also Weber-Fox, Davis, & Cuadrado, 2003), rather than the processing of the basic meaning of content words.

The results of Weber-Fox and Neville (2001) parallel those of the behavioral study by Taube-Schiff and Segalowitz (2005a) described earlier in Chapter 4. Recall that their study compared attention shift costs on trials where the target stimuli were relational words (closed class words: spatial prepositions expressing verticality versus proximity relationships) to shift costs on trials where the target stimuli were non-relational (open class words: names of two-/four-wheeled versus air/water vehicles). The processing demands were of a similar order of magnitude to those in Weber-Fox and Neville's study; namely, to understand short sentences (sentence fragments in Taube-Schiff & Segalowitz; short sentences in Weber-Fox & Neville). Taube-Schiff and Segalowitz found that in the L2, the less fluent language, shift costs on trials involving relational words were greater than in the L1, the more fluent language. Moreover, there were no L2-L1 (fluency) shift cost differences in the non-relational condition. Thus, both Weber-Fox and Neville (2001) and Taube-Schiff and Segalowitz (2005a) found that, in the L2, processing challenges are reflected in the domain of syntax or closed class words, and not in the processing of open class words. Although it is not clear how to map attention shift costs onto latencies of ERP peaks, the neuroimaging study results are nevertheless consistent with the conclusions presented in Chapter 4—namely, that one would expect to find processing to be challenged in the L2, especially in the domain of grammar compared to lexical semantics.

Finally, Weber-Fox and Neville (2001) also found differences related to proficiency when they looked at ERP patterns associated with the semantic violations produced by sentence-final words. In this case, subjects had to attempt to integrate the final word into the rest of the sentence, and of course they encountered difficulties when the word was inappropriate. It is well established that when a reader encounters an unexpected word—one that does not fit in a sentence—there is typically an N400 effect, an increased negativity at around 400 ms after onset of the eliciting word (Kutas & Dale, 1997). Weber-Fox and Neville observed that all the participants—monolinguals and bilinguals of various levels of proficiency—yielded significant N400 effects with sentences that contained a semantic violation in the final word, in comparison with control sentences where they did not. In the case of bilinguals, however, those who were immersed in L2 English at age 11 or later (i.e., whose L2 was weaker than their L1) had N400 peaks that occurred about 50 ms later than it did for monolingual participants. In other words, the weaker a bilingual's proficiency, the slower was the response to the semantic violation. This result, consistent with previous findings by Weber-Fox and Neville (1996), also suggests that the key neural manifestations of fluency are seen when processing requires integration or coordination of information, just as, for example, when processing grammatical/relational words or when integrating a target word into the meaning of a whole sentence, as opposed to simply performing a "look-up" of word meanings.

Patterns consistent with the above conclusions can be found as well in L2 imaging research using PET and fMRI techniques (for recent reviews, see Abutalebi, 2008, and Abutalebi et al., 2005). For example, Perani et al. (1996) tested adult native speakers of Italian with L2 proficiency in English that was weaker than in their L1. Their task involved comprehending stories in each language (on control trials they used Japanese, which none of the subjects knew). This task is more difficult than reading single words or isolated sentences because of the greater complexity of information integration required for story comprehension. When subjects listened to stories in the L1, similar activation patterns (compared against attentive rest) were found across all subjects, involving many areas, primarily in the left hemisphere (the angular gyrus—Brodmann Area [BA] 39; the superior and middle temporal gyri—BA 22 and 21; the inferior frontal gyrus—BA 45; the temporal pole—BA 38) and some in the right hemisphere (BA 21/22, BA 38, BA 31 and a focus in the right cerebellum) (p. 2441). When subjects listened to stories in the L2, activation was greatly reduced, involving significant activations in left and right BA 22 and 21, and minor bilateral activation of parahippocampal gyri (BA 36) that the authors attributed to increased involvement of memory structures (p. 2442). Thus, when bilinguals with non-nativelike L2 proficiency listened to stories—a task requiring the integration of complex information—activation was relatively restricted in the L2 condition compared to the L1 condition. It would appear that, when using the less fluent L2, the bilinguals were not able to recruit the necessary neural resources to handle complex information integration required by story listening.

In another study, Perani et al. (1998) tested high-proficient late-acquisition bilinguals (Italian speakers who acquired English after age 10 and used it daily in their work) and high-proficient early-acquisition bilinguals (Spanish-Catalan bilinguals who acquired the L2 before age 4 and who used both languages daily). The tasks involved story comprehension, similar to those used in Perani et al. (1996). They found that, across both groups, similar areas were activated by the L1 and the L2. Taken together, the two studies by Perani and her colleagues revealed that, when L2 fluency was low, the neural regions activated during comprehension of L2 stories were more restricted compared to those activated during comprehension of L1 stories, and that when L2 fluency was high, neural activation during L2 reading approached that of L1 reading. On the basis of these and similar results, Abutalebi et al. (2005) have suggested that it is fluency—not age of acquisition—that may be responsible for the different neural patterns of activation during complex processing in the L2. Abutalebi et al., for example, argue that when proficiency is very high "a common neural network is activated independent of age of acquisition" (p. 507). (It should be noted that sometimes failure to disentangle age of acquisition, years using the language, and age at time of testing, all of which can be highly correlated at times, can lead to incorrect conclusions about the relationship between age and fluency. See Stevens [2006] for discussion of this issue.)

Finally, Chee and his colleagues looked at how fluency is reflected in neural activation during the processing of single words. Chee, Hon, Lee, and Soon (2001) reported a study involving Mandarin-English bilinguals with varying proficiency levels in English. The experimental condition was a matching-to-sample task in which participants had to choose which of two words was closest in meaning to a sample word. Chee et al. recorded blood oxygen level dependent (BOLD) signal changes using fMRI as a function of task (L1, L2). They found an association between longer RTs, lower proficiency in the L2, and greater BOLD signal increases in the left prefrontal and parietal areas. They concluded that the greater neural recruitment reflected in the BOLD signal change indicated greater cognitive effort in the less fluent language in performing the semantic matching task (see also De Bleser et al., 2003). This result is consistent with other imaging studies that have shown greater neural recruitment for the execution of weakly automatized or less proficient skills (e.g., Raichle et al., 1994).

Overall, with respect to fluency, certain trends are beginning to emerge from the neuroimaging literature. When the task is in the L2 and requires the *integration* of information—as with closed class words (whose function it is to shape the integration of the content words in the phrases and sentences carrying them) and with sentences embedded in stories (requiring rich interconnections to be made across a text)—ERP latencies are faster and the regions activated are larger, reflecting better L2 fluency.

In tasks that are relatively simple—as with judgments about single word meaning—latencies are faster and the regions activated are smaller and more focused, reflecting more efficient and automatized processing. Moreover, as Paradis (2009) points out, different regions of the brain are implicated in automatic versus non-automatic processing (p. 19). Tasks involving single word processing are likely to require similar recruitment of declarative memory structures regardless of fluency level and therefore will yield small or no L1-L2 differences in the regions of the brain which become involved (see Paradis, 2004, for studies supporting this idea). In contrast, tasks involving more complex use of language are likely to require greater controlled processing in the L2 compared to greater automatic processing in the L1, resulting in differences in terms of brain activity involved.

Of course, there remain many unresolved issues. Alternative interpretations of some reports are possible, and some results are not fully consistent with other results, casting doubt on whether at this time we can pull *all* the findings together into one coherent account (see Paradis, 2009, for a comprehensive discussion of this situation). The "untidiness" of the field at this moment may in part be due to variation in the populations (e.g., early versus late acquirers; different levels of proficiency; and different ways of measuring proficiency), in the techniques used (ERPs and fMRI BOLD signals are far from being simple equivalents), stimuli used (single word versus sentence stimuli), and tasks used (ranging from simple to complex). One conclusion that may be drawn from the literature, however, is that, as bilinguals become more and more proficient in the L2, the neural processes recruited for performing semantic-based tasks in the L2 and L1 generally appear to become more similar to each other. A second conclusion is that challenges in grammatical processing appear to be especially important, and some have even suggested that, in the case of a late-learned L2, the neural recruitment for grammatical processing will never strongly resemble that of the L1.

Neural Correlates of Automaticity in L2 Processing

As already discussed, there are data suggesting that when processing is slow and inefficient—both hallmarks of poorly automatized processing—ERPs tend to have longer latencies and activation tends to involve larger regions. Nevertheless, as pointed out earlier in Chapter 4, simply demonstrating that some processing activity has occurred very rapidly is not sufficient evidence for concluding that it occurred automatically. Appeal must be made to some other characteristic beside speed in order to be certain that the processing mechanism is automatic in some meaningful sense. Almost no research to date has investigated the association between neural processes and automaticity, where automaticity has been defined more narrowly than just speed of processing. This is unfortunate, given the importance of automatic processing in skilled language performance (and in other domains as well).

A study by Golestani et al. (2006) used fMRI to investigate the neural correlates of syntactic processing in L1 and L2 of non-fluent French-English bilinguals. While in the scanner, participants viewed either three or five words in either the L1 or the L2. They were required either to silently read the words or to silently produce a simple grammatically correct sentence using the words. The researchers examined correlations between the strength of BOLD signal change and measures of language proficiency in the four conditions formed by crossing L1/L2 by read/sentence-generation task conditions. They found a number of interesting L1/L2 differences that speak to issues about differential recruitment of neural resources. Of most relevance to automaticity was the finding that the left putamen (basal ganglia) was activated only in the L1 sentence condition (after subtracting out the L1 word reading effect). They regarded this as due to the more automatic, procedural, rule-based nature of L1 grammatical processes, which others have suggested draw on subcortical structures for their execution (Ullman, 2001). In contrast, the L2—being less automatized—would not be expected to depend to the same extent on subcortical structures, the basal ganglia in particular. In this sense, the reliance on subcortical structures might be considered a neural correlate of the automaticity that underlies the more fluent L1. It would be most interesting to obtain independent behavioral measures of the automaticity of L2 processing in order to see if individual differences in automatic processing correlate with individual differences in dependence on subcortical structures. Such a study has not yet been carried out.

A study by Phillips et al. (2004, Experiment 2) investigated more directly whether intraindividual CV measures of processing efficiency (automaticity, as discussed earlier in Chapter 4) were associated with some property of the neural correlates of word processing. French-English bilinguals judged nouns as referring to living or non-living objects, where trials were organized so that half the target stimuli were preceded by a trial involving a high semantic associate and half by a low semantic associate. Interspersed among these stimuli were baseline filler words. Mean RT and the coefficient of variation of the RT were calculated for each participant in each language on baseline trials, on primed and on unprimed trials. These measures reflected the expected patterns and distinctions between high and low proficient bilinguals described in Segalowitz (2003) and in Chapter 4 (faster RTs, lower CVs, in more proficient bilinguals). Most importantly for the present discussion, however, was that the researchers also computed the CVs of N400 amplitudes separately for primed and unprimed trials (see Phillips et al., 2004, p. 255, for details of how this was done). They found that the pattern of N400 amplitude CVs for primed and unprimed L1 and L2 stimuli paralleled the pattern of results for priming effects across languages in the behavioral CV data (based on RTs). Based on this, they suggested that the N400 CV might "provide an important tool [for] ... future research on L2 skill acquisition" (p. 259). Overall, although efforts to find neural correlates of automaticity have only just begun (see also Kotz & Elston-Güttler, 2004), the results to date give some reason for cautious optimism.

Neural Correlates of Attention Control in Language Selection

This topic has received much consideration, both in the neurolinguistic and the cognitive behavioral literature. The question of how people keep their two (or more) languages separate and how they select which language to speak in at any given moment is a topic quite central to fluency. Clearly, if a person requires extra time and mental resources to stay on track in using one particular language and not another, this can compromise oral fluency.

A number of studies have shown that, in laboratory situations at least, when a bilingual is required to switch responses back and forth from one language to the other, there can be a longer latency to respond when switching back to the more fluent L1 (see Meuter, 2005, for a review). This somewhat counter-intuitive result was shown, for example, by Meuter and Allport (1999). In that study, bilingual participants had to name a digit shown on the screen, using the L1 or L2 as indicated by a color cue. On some trials, the current trial required the same language as had been required on the previous trial, while on other trials a language switch was required. Meuter and Allport found that latency to respond was longer when the current trial required an L1 response and the previous trial required an L2 response (i.e., an L2-L1 sequence) relative to the repeat sequence of L1-L1. This language shift cost was larger than the corresponding cost comparisons for L1-L2 relative to L2-L2 sequences. That is, there was an asymmetric shift cost whereby shifting to the L1 was more difficult than shifting to the L2. This result suggests that perhaps there is a strong inhibitory mechanism that springs into action to suppress an L1 response whenever an L2 response is required, and this inhibition does not lift immediately when the trial is over. If the subject has to now switch to the L1, it becomes necessary to overcome the strong inhibition and this incurs a delay in the response time. In contrast, when speaking in the L1, there is no need for such strong inhibition to suppress a potential L2 response, because that language is weaker and cannot compete strongly with the L1. Thus, if a switch to the L2 is required, there is no need to overcome residual inhibition from the previous trial.

It turns out, however, that the picture is far more complicated than it would seem to be at first glance. Costa and Santesteban (2004) reported a study with bilinguals highly proficient in their L1 and L2 and less proficient in an L3. They replicated the Meuter and Allport (1999) finding of an asymmetrical shift cost between a dominant L1 and a non-dominant L2. However, they did not find the asymmetrical shift cost between the more fluent L1 and less fluent L3. Also, Finkbeiner, Almeida, Janssen, and Caramazza (2006) reported a task in which bilinguals had to name numbers in the L1 or L2, cued by color, and to name interspersed pictures in the L1 only. The researchers found no shift cost for naming pictures in the L1 immediately following an L2 number-naming trial, relative to picture trials following an L1 number-naming trial. As Abutalebi and Green (2007) pointed out, however, that study confounded a language shift (L2 to L1) with a task shift (numbers to pictures) and this might have resulted in a different recruitment of neural processes. The complexity of the situation has been further underscored by recent neurolinguistic research in this area (see Green, 1998, for conceptual background and Abutalebi & Green, 2007, 2008, for important reviews of current research in this area). The interesting but complex picture that is emerging can only be partially summarized here. The situation can be summed up by reference to the following three key ideas coming out of imaging studies on bilingual language control:

(1) There is a basic left hemisphere system implicated in language selection control. According to Abutalebi and Green (2007), multiple levels of cognitive control underlie L2 speech production. They suggest that the anterior cingulate cortex is involved in monitoring conflict in general, including conflict that arises between languages and that has to be resolved through selection, including the detection of selection errors. Regions within the prefrontal cortex are implicated in that aspect of attention control involving response selection and inhibition. The inferior parietal lobe is involved in the contribution of working memory and the maintenance of representations required for carrying out the tasks. Finally, subcortical structures (basal ganglia) are involved in various aspects of language and lexical selection, especially where such activities take place in a more automatic and less controlled fashion. A summary of their model is presented in Figure 6.1 (based on Abutalebi & Green, 2007, Figure 1, p. 249).

(2) The system underlying the control of language selection is a dynamic one, changing in the way it functions as proficiency or fluency changes over time. As skill in the L2 becomes more automatized, there is a shift away from prefrontal activity to more subcortical activity. Abutalebi and Green (2007) made the point this way: "in order to interpret neuroimaging data correctly we need to take proficiency into account" (p. 252).

The third key idea follows directly from the second.

(3) Whereas questions about language representation and language control have typically been treated as separate, it may make more sense

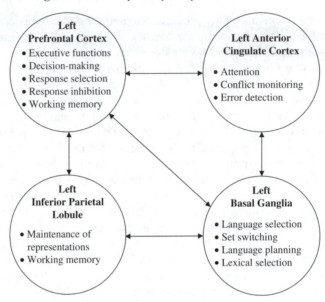

Figure 6.1 Schematic illustration of Abutalebi and Green's (2007, based on their Figure 1, p. 249) account of the multiple levels of cognitive control in bilingual language.

to consider these two questions as intimately interconnected. The representation question focuses more on "where" in the brain, and the control question focuses more on "how" in the brain. However, as just pointed out, in the early phases of (late) L2 acquisition, there is greater reliance on prefrontal mechanisms for representation and control, reflecting the initially low level of proficiency/fluency. As skill develops over time, the underlying processes become more automatized and shift to subcortical structures, more like those implicated in the L1. The result is a convergence whereby neural recruitment for L1 and L2 approach each other as L2 fluency approaches that of the L1. Interestingly, recent data has even challenged the critical period idea that the neural systems underlying L2 syntax in late learners necessarily remain distinct from those underlying L1 syntax. For example, Briellmann et al. (2004) report fMRI data showing that fluency, not age of acquisition, is more important in determining the spatial topography of language in multilinguals. This raises questions for interpreting the results of studies like that of Kim, Relkin, Lee, and Hirsch (1997), for example, where there is little information about subjects' fluency, leaving open the possibility of a confound between age of acquisition and fluency levels (see Abutalebi & Green, 2007, for a fuller discussion of these issues).

One possibly important aspect of the neural interactions not captured in Figure 6.1 is a time dimension that could reflect the dynamic interplay between the brain areas that are linked together. As Kutas, Federmeier, and Sereno (1999) put it, "In order to truly understand the processes underlying language, we need to know both *when* and where information becomes available in the brain, and our theories need to recognize the essential links between space *and time* for neural information processing" (p. 386; emphasis added). In recent years, some have proposed that rhythmic synchronization within neural networks is an essential element for the construction of various kinds of mental representations (e.g., Pulvermüller, Birbaumer, Lutzenberger, & Mohr, 1997; Tallon-Baudry & Bertrand, 1999), and this presumably would include the various objects of linguistic communication. If such coherence of neural activity across brain regions is an important aspect of brain functioning, one may speculate that it may also be important in the fluent operation of brain processes underlying L2 speech production.

Together, these key ideas provide two potential challenges to the fluency blueprint of the speaker represented in Figure 1.2 in Chapter 1. One challenge is whether to proceed with a functional blueprint at all, or whether to aim instead for a neural map. However, before we can even answer that question, there is another challenge to deal with. The neurolinguistic data can be read as calling into question an important assumption underlying most fluency research. This is the assumption that fluency is "just" a property of components of a structurally static network that underlies the system responsible for a bilingual's L2 performance. That is, the normal assumption is that the neurocognitive mechanisms underlying L2 performance involve particular neural structures and that each of these structures functions in a fluent manner to some particular degree. However, given Abutalebi and Green's (2007) caution to take fluency into account before interpreting neuroimaging data, perhaps there is a need to question the assumption about how fluency is reflected in a structurally static system and ask instead whether fluency is associated with some dynamic aspect of the organization of neurocognitive systems underlying L2 production and reception. Perhaps cognitive fluency is realized in the brain through improved *organizational* efficiency, not simply through faster or more stable processing of mechanisms without reorganization of the network. In light of the recent work reported earlier, perhaps it is appropriate to ask now whether the approach to fluency as shown in Figure 1.2, based on Levelt's (1999) "blueprint" of the speaker, needs to be revised.

The "blueprint" approach suggests—implicitly—that one should first identify the basic structures that underlie L2 performance and only after that has been worked out should one ask where there might be potential vulnerability points for fluency in those structures. This was the approach taken explicitly in constructing Figure 1.2 in Chapter 1. Now, however, perhaps one should ask whether variation in fluency reflects variation in the very structural details of the "blueprint," as opposed to the efficiency of operation of particular local elements viewed in isolation from the rest of the network. One might speculate that perhaps gains in fluency reflect changes in processing efficiency that result from some sort of reorganization of the system responsible for speech production, possibly involving recruitment of different brain regions and possibly also involving increased coherence patterns, as opposed to reflecting gains in processing efficiency that take place at very local levels. This idea would be consistent with Paradis' (2009) suggestion, for example, that automatization does not involve non-automatic controlled mechanisms becoming gradually more automatic but rather involves replacing non-automatic mechanisms with other mechanisms (i.e., restructuring) that meet the criteria for automaticity. This possibility is interesting because of the implication that fluency implicates structural and temporal reorganization of the brain. Future research needs to address this possibility and to explore just how fluency reflects the organizational efficiency of the brain subserving multiple languages.

Formal Modeling

For the past several decades an important research technique in the arsenal of cognitive scientists has been formal modeling of cognitive processes and computer simulation to test these models. Modeling and simulation have delivered many benefits, especially in the case of language studies. As many have noted, computer modeling of language processes provides an excellent way to put theoretical assumptions to rigorous test by forcing one to be very explicit; vagueness and ambiguity are not tolerated by the unforgiving computers through which the simulations are implemented. Another benefit of computer modeling is that sometimes it can provide an existence proof, namely, a demonstration that in principle some particular assumption works (or doesn't, as the case may be).

For example, consider a developmental pattern that involves what appears to be a qualitative improvement in performance followed by a plateau period where performance seems to remain stable, followed by more periods of improvement and plateaus. It is often assumed that such a developmental trajectory is evidence of development through stages, where consolidation of learning takes place during the plateau, resulting in the qualitative change that marks the onset of a new stage of development. This is how, for example, the development of children's performance on the Piagetian balance beam task has been understood and, conceivably, the idea of stages may apply to L2 development as well. Some formal modelers, however, have been able to simulate such development—with periods of improvement followed by plateaus—without appealing to underlying "stages" (McClelland, 1989; see Quinlan, van der Maas, Jansen, Booij, & Rendell, 2007, for recent discussion of this topic). McClelland offered his simulations to demonstrate that, in the case of the balance beam problem, in principle there can be incremental quantitative change that looks like—but is not—passage through qualitatively different stages. There is similar debate among psycholinguists about the acquisition of skill in using the English past tense, some arguing that development here involves a qualitative change (internalization of a past tense rule) and others that development involves only incremental changes in connections (no emergence of rules), as demonstrated by the behavior of simulation models (see McClelland & Patterson, 2002; Pinker & Ullman, 2002).

In the case of computer modeling of bilingualism phenomena, the greatest effort has gone into questions about how words in two languages might be acquired, stored, and accessed, and in debates concerning the utility of Universal Grammar approaches to second language acquisition. Most computational models used in simulations aim to reflect, in some theoretically satisfying way, the basic properties of real neural systems (see Broeder & Plunkett, 1994; Gasser, 1990), but models can nevertheless differ from one another in important ways. Thomas (2005) reviews the dominant models found in bilingualism research and the assumptions that underlie these models. These assumptions include whether the model posits separate, language-specific mechanisms for detecting whole words, or a single integrated language-neutral system of mechanisms for detecting the component features of words (e.g., phonemes, letters). As Thomas points out, and as will be pointed out again shortly, this has consequences; depending on one's assumptions, a model may or may not permit addressing particular questions.

All computational models involve a network of elements that are interconnected in ways that allow them to activate or inhibit each other with some particular level of strength or probability. However, models can be divided into two broad classes—*localist* and *distributed*—depending on how they conceive the networking of the constituent elements. Localist and distributed models differ from each other in fundamental ways. As a result, one may be better suited for addressing certain questions than the other, including bilingualism.

Localist models generally assume discrete layers of elements specialized for different types of information, such as basic orthographic features (straight lines, curved lines, etc.), orthographic symbols (letters, characters), words, etc. The elements in the model are connected to each other with various connection strengths, usually set initially by the researcher, and they do not change with experience. In effect, strict localist models provide a snapshot of the processing system at one moment in time and they do not address how the system changes with development. Distributed models, on the other hand, conceive of the objects under study (say, words or phrases) as represented in the activity of many elements distributed widely over the network. In a distributed network there is not, for example, one particular node that corresponds to a specific word in a given language. Moreover, the pattern of distributed activity changes over time as a function of experience (there is feedback about whether the output of the network is correct, given the input). In distributed models, connection strength between elements is usually set randomly initially and the system normally converges over time on a particular pattern of connection strengths as a function of experience.

Because localist models do not incorporate change, they tend not to be useful for addressing questions about development. On the other hand, because the layers of elements have clear meanings (there might be layers for letter features, word identity, etc.), it is generally easier to assign theoretical meaning to configurations within the network. Also, information moves through localist networks in ways that can be interpreted as modeling processing time. In contrast, distributed models change their configurations over time and so they are useful for addressing questions about development (say, word acquisition). On the other hand, they often posit "hidden" banks of units that form into processing units over time, units that mediate between input and output. The theoretical meaning of these hidden unit patterns of activation can, however, be difficult to interpret. Moreover, it is usually difficult to model response time in a meaningful way in distributed models.

Thomas (2005, p. 205) has identified eight general categories of questions about bilingualism that modeling theorists have attempted to address. These are:

- How many processing systems are there? Is there one for both languages, two separate ones, or partially overlapping systems?
- How are lexical items identified as belonging to a particular language?
- Does having two languages result in interference?
- How does the language "switch" operate and how does language dominance affect this?
- How is each language acquired and does this involve issues of critical periods and language transfer?
- How are patterns of dominance and differential proficiency maintained?
- Are there modality specific characteristics of bilingualism (e.g., does dominance of one language over another differ from one modality to another across various modalities—speaking, listening, reading, writing)?
- How are languages lost through brain damage (aphasia) or disuse (attrition) and how are they recovered?

The last three of these categories deal to some extent with fluency issues, insofar as they touch upon dominance and proficiency differences between languages.

No attempt will be made here to review in depth the major computational models that are currently found in the bilingualism literature; Thomas (2005) has done that in a chapter that provides a valuable source outlining the principal models, comparing their assumptions, achievements, and relative strengths and shortcomings (see also N. Ellis, 2003; MacWhinney 2008). Among the principal localist models that Thomas reviews are the Bilingual Interactive Activation (BIA) model (Dijkstra & Van Heuven, 1998), the Bilingual Model of Lexical Access (BIMOLA) (Léwy & Grosjean, 1997, cited in Thomas, 2005), and the Semantic, Orthographic, and Phonological Interactive Activation Model (SOPHIA) (Dijkstra & Van Heuven, 2002), based on an extension of the BIA (the BIA+) model. Among the principal distributed models are the Bilingual Single Network Model (BSNM) (Thomas, 1998, cited in Thomas, 2005), the Bilingual Simple Recurrent Network (BSRN) (French, 1998, cited in Thomas, 2005), and the Self-Organizing Model of Bilingual Processing (SOMBIP) (Li & Farkas, 2002; see also the DEVLEX model of Hernandez, Li, & MacWhinney, 2005). The overall picture is that these models are generally in a relatively early phase of development, and that no one localist or distributed model has to date emerged as clearly capable of addressing all bilingual processing phenomena successfully. Thomas also points out areas in which bilingual models could benefit from the considerable advances that have taken place in the development of monolingual models of language processing and development, such as incorporating the modeling of the automatization of naming that takes place with experience.

What about L2 fluency? By and large, except for attempts to model language dominance, computational models of bilingual processing have not focused on matters touching directly on fluency. In principle, localist models provide more possibilities than do distributed models for addressing timing issues implicated in fluency, but to date there are no computational models simulating oral fluency phenomena such as speech rate or pause and hesitation phenomena. Distributed models appear, in principle, to be better suited than localist models for modeling fluency development over time and how network organization might reflect fluency level (this may be important in light of the neuroimaging research pointing to a possible association between fluency and neural organization). Thomas (2005) further points out that to date models of bilingual comprehension have not dealt successfully with L2 development that takes place long after L1 acquisition has been completed (e.g., simulating adult learning of an L2). Generally speaking, computational models treat the L2 either as developing along with or as already existing alongside the L1, with L1 dominance accounted for by giving it more prominence (e.g., greater connection strengths; more practice cycles).

In addition to turning attention to fluency issues, a more general challenge for theorists working with computational models (in all areas of bilingualism) is to bring model building to a point where the models reveal *new* phenomena and yield testable predictions that have hitherto escaped the attention of theorists not using computational models. To date, the vast majority of modeling has been concerned with simulating existing empirical findings and testing the viability of various assumptions about L1-L2 relationships after the fact and—with one possible exception—none appear to have succeeded in identifying new phenomena to study. The possible exception is in the work by Paul Meara.

Meara (2004, 2006, 2007) has been working with a class of formal models—Random Autonomous Boolean Networks (Kauffman, 1993)—that differ in significant ways from the types of computational models just described. His models are meant to simulate the activity of a vocabulary network of interconnected words. Meara makes no claims about the models being psychologically or neurally realistic in some essential way, as do connectionist theorists about their models. On the contrary, Boolean networks are designed to be as simple as possible—some might even say simplistic (e.g., Laufer, 2005)—precisely in order to discover what interesting properties will emerge from networks with a minimum of built-in assumptions. In this sense, Meara's use of modeling reverses the strategy employed more generally in the field of L2 computational modeling. There, the goal has been to build into the localist or distributed models the machinery necessary to simulate some phenomenon of bilingual performance. In contrast, research with Boolean networks aims to see what properties very simple networks appear to have that might help us understand bilingualism phenomena.

Meara's Boolean networks function as follows. A network starts out with some number of nodes representing words (say, 2,500). In the simplest instantiation of the network, each word has a permanent input link from exactly two other words (and output links to a small number of words, which may or may not be the same as the input words). Each word is one of two types, reflecting the activation rule that governs it. One rule is that a word is activated only when both its input words are themselves currently active, corresponding to logical AND. Otherwise this word is deactivated. The other rule is that a word is activated when it receives a signal from either or both of its inputs, corresponding to logical OR. Initially, the network links are randomly determined, as are the designations of which words are to be AND or OR words. Also, initially half the words are randomly determined to be activated and half deactivated. The network is then put a through a series of cycles. On each cycle the activation state for each word in the next cycle is computed as a function of its AND/OR type and the current activation state of its two inputs; following this, all the changes are made and the next cycle begins. As the network goes through its cycles, one can keep track of how many words are active or inactive in each cycle, which items change and don't change, etc.

Meara has found that such networks can display interesting properties, some of which are directly relevant to fluency. For example, Meara (2004) found that with just two inputs per word, as described earlier, running the network through about 50 cycles results in a stable configuration—an attractor state—in which some words remain activated, others remain deactivated, and some cycle back and forth. This might seem surprising; intuitively, we might have expected an unstable outcome with words appearing to turn on and off randomly in successive cycles. Furthermore, Meara reports that, once a network has achieved an attractor state, it appears to remain rather resistant to change thereafter. For example, when a target word is deliberately deactivated, a network that has achieved an attractor state usually just reactivates that word on a subsequent cycle. Meara draws the following important conclusion from this: "lexical attrition is NOT a property of the individual words that make up a lexicon: rather, it is a property of the network of relationships between the words" (2004, p. 141). Thus, one result of Meara's simulation research is that vocabulary loss—and, by extension, some aspects of fluency—need to be viewed in terms of the *structures* that support words and the objects of fluency. Vocabulary loss should not be viewed just in terms of the words and objects themselves in isolation.

Meara (2004) was also able to model some aspects of vocabulary loss by introducing a very small change to the network. For example, on every fifth cycle, a randomly selected OR word was converted to an AND word. This made it just a bit more difficult for that word to achieve an activated state, because now both its inputs had to come from activated words instead of just one of the inputs. After the change was made on a given cycle, the network was allowed to run through five iterations to "absorb" the impact of the change before another attrition event (conversion of an OR word to an AND word) was imposed on it. The results were very interesting. Meara discussed 10 cases—10 simulation runs representing 10 virtual subjects—where this kind of vocabulary loss was imposed. The first result of note was that there were large individual differences in outcome across the 10 cases. Second, most of the cases showed stable and large activated vocabularies over many iterations, until suddenly there were precipitous drops in the number of activated words. Third, averaging the data across cases provided a completely misleading picture. Averaging the data suggested there was gradual attrition over time, when in fact, for nine out of the ten cases, there were dramatic losses over the span of a relatively few iterations. These simulation results allowed Meara to make the important observation that "vocabulary loss is always triggered by attrition events, but attrition events do not always trigger vocabulary loss" (2004, p. 145). Again, we have evidence of the importance of viewing vocabulary accessibility and fluency in *structural* terms, not simply in terms of items considered out of context. It would appear then that networks of this sort are vulnerable to small changes that can undermine fluency in dramatic ways.

Meara (2006) further investigated the emergent properties of these networks. In this literature review, he drew the important conclusion that it is by no means certain that simulating the building of vocabularies with small networks using just a few items will invariably scale up to large, bilingual systems. Meara (2006) explored how to give a network an L1, an L2, and even an L3, and how these different "languages" might be operationally defined within the network (he proposed rules of "entanglement" between languages).

Meara (2007) explored, via Boolean networks, how vocabularies might grow from initially very small networks. The work is clearly exploratory and preliminary, but already some interesting conclusions have emerged. For example, he reported that it is possible for a network to start out with items that are not linked to each other but rather form a base to which newly acquired items attach themselves. Apparently the size of this base affects the emerging structure of the network as a whole. Meara was able to show that, with appropriate, simple assumptions about how words link together and are activated, a *self-sustaining* set of activated units can emerge in a simple network. Echoing conclusions reported earlier, the self-sustaining nature of these elements appears to be a property of the network structure rather than of the elements themselves. In particular, his simulations indicate that this self-sustaining vocabulary grows when the links between elements are formed at a faster rate than the rate of acquisition of new elements (in his model, acquisition of new words and the formation of new links between words are independent events). As Meara points out, the link-making process (as distinct from encounters with new words) may be crucial in vocabulary development, with obvious implications for L2 vocabulary development.

It is interesting to speculate about the implications this may have for fluency. If indeed stable, self-sustaining sub-networks emerge under the right circumstances, it may be that their self-sustaining nature is akin to massive reactivations of the links on each cycle. A consequence of such repeated reactivations in a real neural system could be increased automaticity that would enhance fluency. One could further speculate about whether certain learning activities could promote the link-making that leads to the emergence of such self-sustaining sub-networks—"islands" of fluency, if you will—thereby boosting vocabulary acquisition. Such a process might even develop into a kind of feed-forward loop, where "fluent" regions of the network support new vocabulary acquisition, resulting in growth of those regions, leading to enhanced vocabulary growth, and so on. This speculation requires empirical data about real learners, of course, but the idea is quite consistent with the ideas discussed earlier concerning transfer of appropriate learning in Chapter 3, and with suggestions by Meara (1993), Mezynski (1983), Nation (1993),

Segalowitz and Gatbonton (1995), among others, about the importance of fluency of access for vocabulary growth. This idea will be taken up again in the final chapter, where pedagogical issues for promoting L2 fluency are discussed. What Meara's work with Boolean models adds to the discussion, is a much-needed tool for exploring how fluency might impact on vocabulary growth and how this impact might be an emergent feature of simple networks. A simulation tool, such as Boolean networks, allows one to explore of the boundary conditions for this phenomenon. The simulation tool also allows for discussion to move from relatively imprecise speculation to more rigorous tests where researchers have to carefully operationalize the variables involved.

In summary, the formal modeling of fluency has barely begun, although some examples can be found. Such modeling promises to provide ways of testing assumptions about the ways languages relate to each other and the impact this might have on fluency. As well, some of the more recent developments in modeling have begun to generate new hypotheses that one hopes will ultimately be explored further in behavioral studies with real language users. Perhaps the most interesting general conclusion to emerge from recent work is the idea that some fluency phenomena may reflect the structural aspects of the supporting networks more than they reflect the properties of individual words and phrases viewed in isolation. These developments make dynamical systems thinking all the more relevant to understanding fluency issues.

Philosophical Approaches

One of the pillars of cognitive science is philosophy of mind, a discipline that addresses fundamental questions about brain/mind/body relationships. These include questions about meaning and the nature of mental representation, about consciousness and subjective experience, about mental causation, and about the relation between language and thought, among others. Interestingly, while questions about language figure prominently on the agenda of philosophers of mind (Beakley & Ludlow, 1992; Chalmers, 2002; McLaughlin & Cohen, 2007), the topic of language *fluency* (or even of fluency-related issues) is hardly represented, if at all. This may reflect the preoccupation that philosophers of mind have with problems of knowledge as opposed to skilled performance (that is, issues concerned with putting knowledge into action in real time). Indeed, one does not normally think about fluency, let alone *L2* fluency, as a *philosophical* issue. However, as will be explained in this section, there are certain issues that some philosophers have addressed that, while perhaps not directly related to L2 fluency, may nevertheless have important implications for understanding it. For this reason, this section includes a brief look at some philosophical approaches that make a contribution to a cognitive science perspective on L2 fluency.

Although no philosopher (to my knowledge) has directly addressed L2 fluency, some philosophers of education have addressed the related problems of how to realize human potential and how to promote skill development. The notion of "fluency gap," discussed in Chapter 1, can be seen as a specific example of these problems. A "fluency gap" can be seen as a case of failure to realize human potential and to develop skill successfully. After all, one's fluency in the L1 can be taken as a reasonable indicator of the level one is potentially capable of reaching in language performance. The nearly universal observation that L2 fluency attainment falls short of L1 fluency may be taken as an example of failure to fulfill human potential, as a failure in a particular area of skill development. Why is there this fluency gap and why is it so widespread? Perhaps philosophical investigations into the nature of human potential can offer some insight into these questions.

Educational philosopher Israel Scheffler (1985) points out that philosophical interest in human potential has been around for a long time and that, as a notion, human potential is something nearly everyone has an opinion about. Ideas about human potential are wrapped up in beliefs about human nature—ideas that can have a direct link with one's value system when acting in the educational sphere. For example, many believe that it is part of human nature to either to have or to lack the potential to learn particular skills to a particular level (some have innate talent, some don't), including achieving a high degree of L2 fluency. According to this belief, only some people "have an ear" for languages. Given that a student is considered to have the requisite potential, it would be considered a good thing to invest resources in helping this student to realize that potential. By the same token, one should not waste resources by investing them where the potential is lacking. In this way, beliefs about human nature regarding potential can make an important difference; they can shape educational policy decisions and pedagogical practices. It is also possible that particular beliefs about the nature of human potential can affect research by shaping the choice and framing of the questions investigated. That is why philosophical issues matter here.

Scheffler (1985) suggests that historically there have been three myths about the nature of human potential that need to be disposed of if researchers and educators are to successfully help people attain high levels of performance. These myths apply to the problem of fluency development, just as they do to other areas of skill acquisition. These are the myths of fixed potentials, of harmonious potentials, and of uniformly valued potentials.

The idea of *fixed potentials* negates the possibility that a person's stock or repertoire of potentials can change over time, both quantitatively and qualitatively. This is a myth, according to Scheffler (1985). He argues that, just because one cannot find ways to realize a person's potential at this moment does not mean that the potential cannot be realized or even acquired at a later time. Rather than being fixed, potentials may vary over time.

This alternative means that, to enhance fulfillment, one would have to figure out what the appropriate training would be. For example, one would have to create suitable experiences to promote the right kinds of motivation to engage the learner in practice in a sustained way. Within this frame of reference, one would not simply dismiss the low performing student as simply lacking some essential quality (innate potential, talent) needed for learning. Moreover, the idea that potential can be variable rather than fixed leads to the idea that potentials are interlinked. That is, enhancing one potential today may create new potentials later. As Scheffler puts it, the "Realization [of potential], in short, is prospective and not merely retrospective" (1985, p. 12). In terms of helping learners overcome fluency gaps, this means acknowledging that people are never *inherently* incapable of achieving high levels of L2 fluency. One simply must find the right circumstances and conditions to promote learning, although this might require different approaches for different people. Scheffler's idea about the variability of potential is in fact fully consistent with the dynamical systems view represented in Figure 5.3 (Chapter 5).

The idea of *harmonious potentials* is that all of a student's potentials are realizable at the same time—that they are all harmoniously realizable. This too is a myth, according to Scheffler. A person may have many different potentials and, while these may be compatible with one another as potentials, their realizations might not be. This means, as he puts it, "[o]ne cannot literally be all that one can be" (1985, p. 15). Choices have to be made. One consequence of the belief in the myth of harmonious potentials is that it leads educators to shrink from distinguishing among a learner's many potentials and from making the necessary, but difficult, selection about which of a person's current potentials to enhance. The implications of this for addressing fluency gaps is that one needs a deep and detailed understanding of the complex underpinnings of fluency, so that learners' individual differences with respect to these underpinnings can be properly addressed.

Finally, there is the idea of *uniformly valued potentials*. This idea holds that all potentials are equally positive, that the educator need not take into account negative potentials. As Scheffler (1985) points out, however, "people are potentially insightful and intelligent, and potentially boorish and stupid. We need, in short, to take account not only of incompatible values but also of positive disvalues" (p. 15). Because there exist negative potentials alongside positive potentials, the educator must make careful choices when attempting to construct optimal learning conditions and experiences.

Scheffler contends that adherence to these three myths is not only mistaken but harmful, because they "offer untestable devices for projecting a limited and rigid view of human possibilities" (1985, p. 45). To replace them, he proposes a new conceptual framework for understanding human potential. We can also think about this framework as relevant for understanding and developing practices to promote successful (i.e., high level, fluent) L2 acquisition. Scheffler's framework contains a number of complexly interrelated concepts that need not be fully described here. The most pertinent ideas, however, are the following.

First, potential is not to be considered a metaphysical essence that is a fixed and an enduring feature of a person's makeup. This means that individual differences in fluency attainment do not reflect individual differences in people's fixed, intrinsic capacities to become skilled or fluent language users but rather in capacities that are variable and open to change over time. Second, Scheffler's approach is to think, instead, about "enhancing potential through negation of impediments: i.e., through *eliminating* them or, rather, through *circumventing* them" (1985, p. 75; his emphasis). Here, of course, is where research from each of the different domains of the cognitive sciences has a special role to play—identifying the sources of interference and impediments that must be avoided or overcome if skill acquisition is to be successful. Third, "the enhancement of potential is the empowering of learning" (p. 83). This means that the realization of potential to become highly skilled requires the learner/performer to become an agent of his or her own development. As Scheffler says, the enhancement of potential is not about development in general but about *self*-development. Each of these three ideas is, in principle, testable, and together they contribute to a special view of skill development—including fluency development.

There is a final observation from the philosophical literature on skilled activity that merits consideration. Michael Polanyi (1962; Polanyi & Prosch, 1975) has made interesting and important observations—applicable to L2 fluency—concerning the special kinds of knowledge and awareness people have when performing skilled acts of any kind. He gives the following example to illustrate what he means, best described in his own words:

> When we use a hammer to drive in a nail, we attend to both nail and hammer, *but in a different way.* We *watch* the effect of our strokes on the nail and try to wield the hammer so as to hit the nail most effectively. When we bring down the hammer we do not feel that its handle has struck our palm but that its head has struck the nail. Yet in a sense we are certainly alert to the feelings in our palm and the fingers that hold the hammer. They guide us in handling it effectively, and the degree of attention that we give to the nail is given to the same extent but in a different way to these feelings. The difference may be stated by saying that the latter are not, like the nail, objects of our attention, but instruments of it. They are not watched

in themselves; we watch something else while keeping intensely aware of them. I have a *subsidiary awareness* of the feeling in the palm of my hand which is merged into my *focal awareness* of my driving the nail.

(Polanyi, 1962, p.55)

Another example that Polanyi gives is that of the blind man using a cane as a probe to feel his way. For the expert user, the cane becomes an extension of his or her hand. In yet another example, Polanyi writes "[i]f a pianist shifts his attention from the piece he is playing [the object of focal awareness] to the observation of what he is doing with his fingers while playing it [the object of subsidiary awareness], he gets confused and may have to stop" (Polanyi, 1962, p. 56). Vernon Howard (2008) makes the same point by saying that "with practice we come to *inhabit* the tools ... of our trade ... Similarly for performing artists, they identify with their instruments—the piano, violin, or clarinet becomes, quite literally, the bodily extension of the performer's focal awareness, that *from* which he or she attends *to* the music itself" (p. 66). As Howard puts it, the performer *becomes* the instrument.

Perhaps there is sense in which using a language fluently parallels the skilled use of tools and musical instruments as described by Polanyi and Howard. When we use language fluently to convey a message or to probe another person's mind for information, we normally are not aware of the structure and texture of the language as such (its sounds, the articulatory routines invoked, the grammatical patterns, the effort involved in retrieving words and phrases, etc.). The language feels more like an extension of ourselves; it is as if we *inhabit* the language in the way that Howard suggested the virtuoso musician inhabits the piano or violin. Focal awareness is on the meanings being conveyed, whereas there is subsidiary awareness on the tool (the language) being used to convey those meanings. In contrast, when fluency is lacking, one might say that there is focal awareness of the language itself as a tool, and this interferes with using it skillfully. No doubt part of what distinguishes fluent from nonfluent use of language is the effortless, unconscious—i.e., automatic—character of the underlying fluent linguistic processing. But there may be more to it than just heightened mechanical automaticity of language processing. With fluent language there is a feeling of immediacy of the meanings, of direct contact with the mind of the interlocutor, that is muted or lacking with nonfluent language use (consider, for example, the reduced impact of highly emotive language when delivered or received in the L2, even when the words are fully understood, rapidly encoded, and otherwise fluently handled; Pavlenko, 2005; Segalowitz, Trofimovich, Gatbonton, & Sokolovskaya, 2008). Is this fluent-nonfluent difference fully accounted for by differences in automaticity or is there more to it than this, as might be suggested by this perspective on skills? To date, there has been no empirical research on this question.

In summary, to date there has been very little in the area of philosophy of mind or education within the cognitive sciences that has addressed problems of L2 fluency. What there is concerns the nature of human potential and skill development, but their implications for L2 fluency have hardly been dealt with. However, if this philosophical work were focused on L2 fluency, it would hold that failure to develop L2 fluency is not a reflection of a lack of intrinsic linguistic talent or potential to do so. Rather, this failure would reflect not having properly cultivated the various potentials for skill development that do exist in the individual and that could be acquired in time. The failure would also reflect not having addressed internal sources of interference blocking or undermining the development of fluency. This philosophical analysis of the nature of skills also suggests that expert performance involves a special relationship that forms between the performer, the target object of the performance and the medium (tool, instrument) through which that performance is carried out. This view may hold implications for an understanding of L2 fluency as a special case of expert performance.

Chapter Summary

This chapter covered perspectives on L2 fluency from three branches of the cognitive sciences not addressed in the previous chapters—neuro-imaging studies, formal modeling of fluency phenomena, and philo-sophical approaches. The main conclusions to emerge from the works reviewed for carrying forward to the final chapter are the following:

- *There exist neurolinguistic markers of L2 fluency difficulties for different aspects of fluency (e.g., word finding; syntactic integra-tion; sentence integration; larger-scale text integration; language selection). The spatial and temporal organization of neurological structures supporting L2 processing are intimately bound up with fluency. (This idea has implications for the provisional model of the L2 speaker presented in Chapter 1.)*
- *Whereas most computational modeling has not yet directly addressed L2 fluency issues, recent work with Boolean networks may have implications for understanding fluency. Very simple networks can have emergent properties contributing to network stability/ instability in ways relevant to fluency. The behavior of locally defined elements in networks—the availability/non-availability of words, phrases, grammatical constructions, etc.—may be more a function of network relationships than of the properties of indi-vidual network elements. Growth in a network may involve a special role for link-making between elements, over and above the direct acquisition of new elements.*

- *Philosophical approaches to human potential and skill acquisition—including L2 fluency acquisition—suggest that failure to develop performance expertise reflects failure to overcome internal sources of interference and to cultivate an individual's existing and future potential, and is not a deficit in some intrinsic ability to learn.*

7   Toward a Cognitive Science of Second Language Fluency

The most significant feature of a functional system is that, as a rule, it is based on a complex dynamic "constellation" of connections, situated at different levels of the nervous system, that, in the performance of the adaptive task, may be changed with the task itself remaining unchanged.

(Luria, 1980, p. 22)

[O]ne would expect that various social attitudes and motives are intimately involved in learning a foreign language. Furthermore, the whole process of becoming bilingual can be expected to involve major conflicts of values and allegiances, and bilinguals could make various types of adjustments to the bicultural demands made on them.

(Lambert, 1967, pp. 91–92)

The goal of this book is to develop a cognitive science perspective on L2 fluency. There are two reasons why this goal is worth pursuing. The first reason is that L2 fluency in the real world matters for all sorts of social, economic, and personal reasons. Although not all L2 speakers aspire to—or should aspire to—nativelike or near-nativelike levels of speaking ability, an L2 user's fluency level can have socioeconomic consequences. For this reason fluency development is not something peripheral to successful language development. The second reason is that if we want to understand and do something about increasing L2 fluency, then we need to shed piecemeal approaches to this issue, such as looking at fluency from one relatively narrow angle at a time. We should seek, instead, an overarching perspective capable of bringing to light crucial questions that otherwise might be missed. The ideal framework is one in which different disciplines are involved in a mutually supportive way, not just complementary and independent of each other. The cognitive science framework proposed in this volume is intended as a starting point for achieving this. This chapter will review the conclusions drawn from the studies examined earlier in an effort to weave them together into a comprehensive, cognitive-science-based account of L2 fluency.

It will also explore some of the implications of this account. However, before getting into the main substance of this chapter, a few words are necessary about why, in the much larger scheme of things, it is important to think seriously about L2 fluency.

The pace of population movement and the mixing of language groups over the last century have accelerated to levels never experienced before in human history. There are virtually no countries remaining that are truly monolingual or nearly so, and those regions of the planet where monolingualism is still prevalent appear to be diversifying linguistically. Moreover, by all evidence, the pace of language contact is only going to increase in the future. This means that knowing an L2 is no longer simply a luxury that one might just take up, say, to enjoy foreign travel. Rather, having skills in an L2 (or L3, L4, etc.) is becoming more and more an economic and social necessity—it is, as Bourdieu (1991) put it, a social capital (see also Pool, 1993, on economic and linguistic power).

Bourdieu (1991) has written at length about how language enters into human interaction in ways that go beyond the simple exchange of basic cognitive messages. He writes,

> Linguistic exchange—a relation of communication between a sender and a receiver, based on enciphering and deciphering, and therefore on the implementation of a code or a generative competence—is also an economic exchange which is established within a particular symbolic relation of power between a producer, endowed with a certain linguistic capital, and a consumer (or a market), and which is capable of procuring a certain material or symbolic profit. In other words, utterances are not only ... signs to be understood and deciphered; they are also *signs of wealth*, intended to be evaluated and appreciated, and *signs of authority*, intended to be believed and obeyed. Quite apart from the literary (and especially poetic) uses of language, it is rare in everyday life for language to function as a pure instrument of communication. The pursuit of maximum informative efficiency is only exceptionally the exclusive goal of linguistic production and the distinctly instrumental use of language which it implies generally clashes with the often unconscious pursuit of symbolic profit. For in addition to the information expressly declared, linguistic practice inevitably communicates information about the (differential) manner of communicating, i.e. about the *expressive style*, which, being perceived and appreciated with reference to the universe of theoretically or practically competing styles, takes on a social value and a symbolic efficacy.
>
> (Bourdieu, 1991, pp. 66–67)

Bourdieu is drawing attention here to the fact that knowing a language, and being able to use it appropriately (this includes speaking with an appropriate level of fluency) can open doors in life, whereas not having these language skills can effectively close doors. The fluency aspect of the "manner of communicating" that he referred to includes the *perceived fluency* discussed in Chapter 2. Listeners make inferences about speakers' cognitive fluency and possibly use this as the basis for inferences about their general intellectual abilities, their identity, their relationships to the community in which they live, etc. In this way language takes on a special social significance, one in which listeners interpret fluency as reflecting much more than the speaker's overall competence in using a language (even though some of these interpretations may be quite mistaken).

Recently, some economists have been developing the idea of language as a form of capital even further. Chiswick and Miller (2007) write that language skills meet the economic criteria for any resource to be considered a form of *human* capital because, as they point out, language skills are productive (i.e., they bring value to the person), they are acquired at a cost (i.e., there is an outlay in terms of time, effort, and often money), and they are embodied in the person (i.e., they qualify as *human* capital because they cannot be separated from the person the way land, equipment, or company shares can be) (2007, p. xx). Chiswick and Miller argue that "spoken language skill … is the most basic form of human capital" (p. 78) and they go on to document, with examples from around the world, how the ability or inability to use a language can have significant economic consequences for speakers.

Language issues are increasingly inserting themselves into many everyday walks of life, and particular types and levels of language fluency are now part of the skill sets of certain jobs. For example, communication between air traffic controllers and pilots often involves at least one person speaking in an L2. Here, lack of fluency—even in this highly circumscribed context—can have disastrous results (International Civil Aviation Organization [ICAO], 2004a, 2004b). In ICAO (2004b), for example, it was reported that there were 1,100 deaths in the period 1976–2000 from aviation mishaps involving language miscommunication, in addition to numerous other language-related mishaps reported annually. (For examples of research into L2 communication issues in this area, see Barshi & Healy, 1998, and Farris, Trofimovich, Segalowitz, & Gatbonton, 2008.) Or, to cite another example, in the health sector—because of growing linguistic diversity in the population—medical professionals and personnel increasingly have to deal with patients who speak other languages. As a result, they must either rely on translators or learn to speak the language of their patients in order to provide appropriate services (see, e.g., M. Robinson, 2002). Language issues arise in many other settings, too, including in the fields of business, education, law, government, and politics. Many countries and regions have recognized multiple official national languages and by law have to provide linguistically equitable services for more than one group within their borders. Because of all these profound social implications associated with linguistic diversity, it is important that issues of fluency be studied as broadly as possible.

The rest of this chapter is organized into three main sections. The first section, entitled *An Emerging Cognitive Science Perspective*, reviews the conclusions that were identified at the end of each of the previous chapters, stimulated by the anchor questions guiding the organization of this book. The aim of this review is to show how it is possible to articulate a comprehensive cognitive science perspective on fluency. Because this part of the discussion will need to refer to Figure 5.3 several times, for ease of reference that figure is reproduced here as Figure 7.1. The second section, *Some Implications for Instructed Learning*, briefly explores some of the practical implications for language pedagogy of the cognitive science approach espoused here. The final section, *Conclusions*, wraps up the presentation, and includes a brief statement about future directions.

An Emerging Cognitive Science Perspective

This section presents the view of L2 fluency that emerges from the conclusions provided at the end of the previous chapters. These conclusions are listed in Table 7.1, reordered and grouped in order to facilitate linking them with the summary in this section. The review below begins with a consideration of the general nature of L2 fluency that emerges from these conclusions.

A Cognitive Science Perspective on the Nature of L2 Fluency

What is L2 fluency in light of the cognitive science perspective advocated here? We can start by considering what observable characteristics of L2 speech might indicate something about a speaker's fluency. Chapter 2 explored ways of addressing these questions, and it yielded three main conclusions (see 1, 2, and 3 in Table 7.1). First, a distinction was made among possible referents for the word "fluency," two of which are immediately important (see Figure 2.1, Chapter 2). One of these two referents is speech *fluidity*—this is the *utterance fluency* of the output. This fluidity is a property of the actual speech and is reflected in its temporal characteristics (speech rate, patterns of hesitations, etc.). It is possible to measure these characteristics objectively in addition to relying on listeners' impressions about them. However, it is important, when studying the nature of the speech output, to take into account two other matters: the nature of the elicitation tasks used for gathering speech samples (e.g., describing pictures, retelling a story, reading a text, responding to an interview) and the task difficulty and processing load placed on the speaker (e.g., time available to plan what to say;

Figure 7.1 Framework for thinking about the dynamic relationships among sources influencing L2 fluency (same as Figure 5.3).

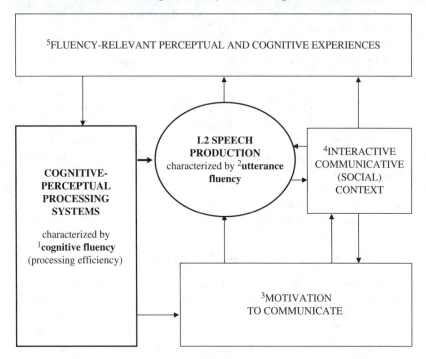

The act of producing L2 speech (central oval) is subject to at least four broadly defined influences that interact with one another, creating a system that is continuously changing and adapting over time, and that has the features of a dynamical system. L2 fluency is characterized by the relationship between cognitive and utterance fluency (the highlighted rectangle and oval). System components include: the cognitive-perceptual systems underlying speech production, motivation to communicate, the interactive communicative or social context created by the act of communicating, and the perceptual and cognitive experiences resulting from communicating and from the social context. These experiences affect utterance fluency by shaping cognitive fluency.

Notes

[1] Cognitive fluency features include processing speed, stability, and flexibility in the planning, assembly, and execution of utterances in terms of lexical access, and the use of linguistic resources (linguistic affordances) to express construals, handle sociolinguistic functions, and pursue psychosocial goals.

[2] Utterance fluency features include speech rate, hesitation, and pausing phenomena, etc.

[3] Motivation includes willingness to communicate, beliefs about communication, language and identity, and the concept of the L2 self. Motivation influences speech production and the selection of social contexts in which to speak.

[4] The social context influences speech production by setting the cognitive task demands associated with communication and is the source for learning about linguistic affordances.

[5] Experiences include frequency of exposure, opportunities for repetition practice, etc.

Table 7.1 The 15 Main Conclusions from the Previous Chapters. Reordered and Grouped into Four Categories to Reflect the Accompanying Discussion

ON THE NATURE OF L2 FLUENCY
A Cognitive Science Perspective

1. *The search for oral correlates of fluency needs to focus on features of L2 performance that are reliable indicators of how efficiently a speaker is able to mobilize and temporally integrate, in a nearly simultaneous way, the underlying processes of planning and assembling an utterance in order to perform a communicatively acceptable speech act.* (From Chapter 2)
2. *One needs to distinguish among (a) cognitive fluency—the efficiency of operation of the underlying processes responsible for the production of utterances; (b) utterance fluency—the features of utterances that reflect the speaker's cognitive fluency; and (c) perceived fluency—the inferences listeners make about speakers' cognitive fluency based on their perceptions of their utterance fluency.* (From Chapter 2)
3. *The study of the relation between cognitive and utterance fluency requires controlling for individual differences in processing that are not specific to the L2, and taking into account task-specific effects related to the speech elicitation methods used and to the testing conditions under which they are administered.* (From Chapter 2)
4. *One can define, both theoretically and operationally, a form of L2-specific cognitive fluency (fast, efficient processing) that underlies fluency of L2 use. Three important distinguishable components of cognitive fluency are L2-specific processing speed, processing stability, and processing flexibility.* (From Chapter 4)
5. *Processing speed is a necessary but not sufficient feature for defining cognitive fluency. Processing stability may be more important than processing speed as a feature of cognitive fluency. Flexibility of attention-based processing may be a more important feature of cognitive fluency than is processing speed, especially in grammatical processing.* (From Chapter 4)

CONTEXT
What are the Fluency-Relevant Situations in Which L2 Users Communicate?

6. *The L2 user's motivation to engage in L2 contact is founded on an L2-specific, socially based psychological sense of self, including sense of identity.* (From Chapter 5)
7. *Fluency heuristics may affect how people assess their L2 experiences, with consequences for L2 cognitive fluency development and for motivation to communicate in the L2.* (From Chapter 3)
8. *The link between social aspects of one's psychological sense of self (e.g., one's sense of ethnic identity) and L2 performance is mediated by L2 use, presumably through the recruitment of cognitive and perceptual systems brought about by using the L2.* (From Chapter 5)

CONTENT
What do L2 Speakers Communicate about in These Contexts?

9. *Skill acquisition involves developing abilities to perceive and exploit the affordances of the performance medium. Open and closed skill acquisition environments shape this development differently, affecting the flexibility of processing. These considerations have consequences for L2 fluency development.* (From Chapter 3)

Continued

Table 7.1 (Cont'd)

10. *L2 users require fluency in terms of a sociolinguistic communicative competence to use the language appropriately.* (From Chapter 5)
11. *The ability to use formulaic sequences or fixed expressions in a skilled manner to promote personal psychosocial interests (interests of the self) is a fluency-relevant aspect of sociolinguistic communicative competence.* (From Chapter 5)

PROCESS
What are the Processing Requirements, from a Cognitive Science Point of View, for Communication of this Content to be Fluent?

12. *Transfer appropriate processing is a key aspect of memory retrieval fluency, and it may play an important role in the development of L2 cognitive fluency.* (From Chapter 3)
13. *There exist neurolinguistic markers of L2 fluency difficulties for different aspects of fluency (e.g., word finding; syntactic integration; sentence integration; larger-scale text integration; language selection). The spatial and temporal organization of neurological structures supporting L2 processing are intimately bound up with fluency.* (From Chapter 6)
14. *Whereas most computational modeling has not yet directly addressed L2 fluency issues, recent work with Boolean networks may have implications for understanding fluency. Very simple networks can have emergent properties contributing to network stability/instability in ways relevant to fluency. The behavior of locally defined elements in networks—the availability/non-availability of words, phrases, grammatical constructions, etc.—may be more a function of network relationships than of the properties of individual network elements. Growth in a network may involve a special role for link making between elements, over and above the direct acquisition of new elements.* (From Chapter 6)
15. *Philosophical approaches to human potential and skill acquisition— including L2 fluency acquisition—suggest that failure to develop performance expertise reflects failure to overcome internal sources of interference and to cultivate an individual's existing and future potential, and is not a deficit in some intrinsic ability to learn.* (From Chapter 6)

---

complexity of the task). As pointed out in Chapter 2, researchers have begun to understand how these factors affect speech output, but a more systematic study of these effects will be crucial if we are to have a fuller understanding of L2 fluency. Skehan's (1998) advice on this still rings true, that "it is no longer feasible to use tests to sample performance to gain an indirect insight into the underlying competence and the structure of abilities ... [and that instead] ... it is important to have systematic ways of approaching performance itself, and how processing factors influence it" (p. 5).

The second referent for "fluency" is the *efficiency* with which the L2 user's underlying cognitive-perceptual system operates while planning, assembling, and executing L2 utterances. This was labeled the speaker's *cognitive fluency* in Chapter 2. This aspect of fluency characterizes the mechanisms responsible for producing the output and that helps give the output the features that it has (e.g., unstably executed cognitive processing might lead to speech hesitations). Cognitive fluency is thus a property of the individual's cognitive system, which is reflected in the temporal characteristics of the underlying processes. These properties of the underlying processes need to be measured separately from the temporal features of the speaker's speech output.

The key idea here is that, to understand L2 fluency overall, one should not simply provide a description of the output (e.g., that a given speech sample is slow, marked by hesitations, etc.), but go beyond and develop instead a theoretically grounded account linking output utterance fluency to the cognitive fluency of the mechanisms underlying utterance production. This idea is reflected in the framework depicted in Figure 7.1. The oval in the centre of the figure represents L2 speech output events. The utterance fluency of these output events can be characterized in terms of such features as speech rate, pausing, and hesitation phenomena, and so on. The list of potential features characterizing utterance fluency that could be studied is very long. However, not all of them may actually turn out to be relevant. For example, there is a lack of consensus in the literature about whether both filled pauses and silent pauses should be accorded equal importance as features in fluency descriptions of L2 utterances. To decide on which features are truly crucial for understanding L2 fluency, some decision rules are needed. Without such decision rules, there is the risk that studies of utterance fluency will proliferate for lack of a theoretical compass to guide the focus of research. Two decision rules (based on Conclusions 1, 2 and 3 in Table 7.1) are the following:

Decision rules:

(1) *Retain those measures of L2 utterance fluency (e.g., speech rate, hesitation rate) and of L2 cognitive fluency (e.g., processing speed, processing stability) that are L2 specific—that is, that take into account corresponding L1 baseline values.*

(2) *Retain those measures of L2-specific utterance fluency that are linked to L2-specific measures of cognitive fluency.*

The first rule might appear to be overly constraining. After all, it could be argued that if a person's L2 speech is marked by undue hesitations, that should be sign enough of dysfluency. However, if the person in question is equally hesitating when speaking in the L1, then the matter may not be an issue of L2 fluency at all, but a general problem of speaking. The same logic applies to cognitive fluency. This logic underscores the importance of obtaining L2-*specific* measures of utterance and cognitive fluency.

Another important reason for referencing L2 measures to L1 measures is that doing so will help address the question raised about fluency gaps in Chapter 1. The reader will recall that "fluency gap" refers to the widely acknowledged observation that people typically seem less able to achieve the same level of fluency in their L2 as in their L1 (the within-individual fluency gap) and that across people there are greater individual differences in fluency achievement in the L2 than in the L1 (the between-individual fluency gap). The study of L2 fluency is, to a large extent, about understanding the sources of these fluency gaps; if the gaps did not exist, there would be no need for special study of L2 fluency, because L2 fluency issues would reduce to language-general fluency issues. (Note that this is not to discount the potential importance of individual differences in basic cognitive processing resources, such as speed of processing and working memory capacity, in L2 proficiency attainment. P. Robinson [2002a], for example, proposes that there exist *aptitude complexes* for which there are individual differences that may underlie L2 proficiency attainment in instructed settings.)

Figure 7.1 can help point to the possible sources for these two fluency gaps. The *within-person fluency gap* might reflect the fact that the four components of the dynamical system identified in the figure (the cognitive-perceptual processing systems, the motivation to communicate, the social context, and the fluency-relevant cognitive and perceptual experiences) typically exert influence for more hours per day and in a richer manner (that is, with more input, more output, more feedback, etc.) in the L1 than in the L2. In fact, if one considers just the time-on-task estimates alone that some theorists have made regarding the acquisition of high level expertise, it is not difficult to understand why L2 fluency often lags behind L1 fluency. Ericsson, Krampe, and Tesch-Romer (1993), for example, have suggested that typically 10,000 hours of deliberate practice—that is, focused activity using the skill under conditions that challenge performance so that it improves—are needed to achieve high levels of expertise. Most children easily log in that many hours within three to five years in their L1, because most of the waking day is spent communicating or rehearsing their communication in that language. In contrast, most people, especially older children and adults, simply don't have that much time to devote to the L2. The *between-person fluency gap*—the relatively large individual differences in L2 fluency attainment (Segalowitz, 1997)—can be understood as reflecting differing amounts of time across individuals devoted to the L2, compared to the relatively similar amounts of time spent in the L1, time that approaches optimal levels. Of course, there may be many other reasons for the two fluency gaps, but as a first approximation the time-on-task explanation provides a plausible account.

The second decision rule above reflects how L2 fluency came to be described in the first anchor question (Chapter 2). This description was arrived at specifically for the purpose of developing an integrated, cognitive science approach to fluency. Under this approach, L2 fluency—as a general construct—is held to be a property of the system linking cognitive fluency and utterance fluency. Here the focus is on how the speaker's ability "to mobilize and temporally integrate, in a nearly simultaneous way, the underlying processes of planning and assembling an utterance" (the cognitive fluency) results in that utterance having the particular properties it does have (the utterance fluency). These components of the proposed cognitive science framework are shown as the heavily outlined rectangle and oval in Figure 7.1.

This second decision rule is central to the cognitive science perspective on L2 fluency; without such a rule it will not be possible to have a focused approach. Instead, there will be studies of fluency in cognition and—separately—studies of the fluidity of second language speech, with no close links drawn between them. This is not to say that measures of cognitive fluency cannot be useful on their own. As discussed in Chapter 4, L2-specific measures of cognitive fluency can sometimes be used as proxy measures for the extent and depth of a person's experience in using the L2. Also, as discussed in Chapter 3 under the heading of fluency heuristics, general processing fluency phenomena sometimes have interesting behavioral consequences. Nevertheless, in terms of a cognitive science approach to L2 *fluency*, the advantage in constraining the topic as suggested by this decision rule is that it motivates explanation in terms of how the processes underlying L2 speech output result in giving it the features that it has.

Chapter 2 also looked at specific aspects of utterance fluency that researchers have investigated. From the findings available to date, it is difficult to say which of the many potential temporal characteristics of L2 speech will ultimately turn out to be the most promising for fluency studies, especially for L2-specific measures of utterance fluency. At the moment, measures of speech rate based on (pruned) syllables per second and of the relative amount (e.g., percentage) of silent durations 200 ms or longer seemed to have worked well in several recent studies (Cucchiarini et al., 2000, 2002; De Jong et al., 2009; Derwing et al., 2004; Tavakoli & Skehan, 2005). However, no study has yet looked at fluency measures taking into account the provisions of the two decision rules described above at the same time. Clearly, a great deal more work needs to be done in this area. New computer-based techniques for automatically analyzing speech samples acoustically for various features, although still in their infancy, hold promise for examining this issue in greater detail.

Chapter 4 looked at specific aspects of cognitive fluency, the mechanisms responsible for producing the output (conclusions 4 and 5 on Table 7.1). It was proposed that processing speed, processing stability, and processing flexibility are good candidate elements of cognitive fluency and that these can be measured in a way that yields

L2-specific indices. It was further suggested that, although processing speed is not, by itself, diagnostic of fluency, processing stability combined with processing speed might be a good measure of cognitive fluency in lexical access, and processing flexibility might be a good measure of cognitive fluency in grammatical processing. Again, it must be pointed out that as yet no studies have investigated both cognitive and utterance fluency measures together, guided by the two decision rules described above. Clearly much more work needs to be done in this area too.

To sum up so far, we now have a definition of L2 fluency that recognizes the relationship between cognitive fluency and utterance fluency, we have two retention rules for deciding which operationalized measures of cognitive and utterance fluency to keep, and we have a (conceptual) dynamical systems framework (as shown in Figure 7.1) to guide thinking about L2 fluency from a cognitive science perspective. The next step is to develop an account of L2 fluency based on the remaining conclusions (6–15) shown in Table 7.1. As a way of organizing this information, we can group the conclusion points under three basic headings:

- Context: What are the fluency-relevant situations in which L2 users communicate?
- Content: What do L2 speakers communicate about in these contexts?
- Process: What are the processing requirements, from a cognitive science point of view, for communication of this content to be fluent?

Each of these will be considered briefly in turn, beginning with the context question.

Context

The contexts in which L2 speakers use the target language place specific communicative task demands on them. These task demands determine which cognitive resources they must recruit in order to speak fluently. Broadly speaking, there are two classes of L2 usage contexts—instructional settings and natural settings. Instructional settings frequently—but not necessarily always—differ from natural settings in terms of the task demands they place on speakers (an issue discussed later in this chapter). Natural settings will be the first focus here because these are the contexts in which people ultimately end up using the L2 (see the next major section for discussion of instructional settings).

People enter into L2 contact because they are motivated to do so in a variety of ways including, for example, wanting to obtain or convey specific information, desiring to interact with members of the target language social group, obtaining pleasure from using the language, etc. The framework shown in Figure 7.1 indicates this by showing that motivation influences the generation of speech output and also influences the selection of social context in which to use the L2. In all cases, the L2 speaker has to establish and maintain some kind of social relation with the interlocutor and this shapes, in part, the content of the communication.

Content

As discussed in Chapters 4 and 5 and in several of the conclusions shown in Table 7.1, there are at least four categories of information content that are fluency-relevant in L2 communication. These four are simultaneously present in virtually every natural L2 communicative event, and they include the following:

- conveying the basic cognitive message by referring to objects, events and their attributes
- communicating construals (perspectives on the situation being talked about)
- handling sociolinguistic functions (e.g., to maintain appropriate social relations with the interlocutor)
- promoting personal psychosocial interests (including maintaining one's status, and conveying information related to personal and group identity).

As a set, these four categories make clear that, while communication may involve the exchange of words intended to transmit basic cognitive information, it is normally about much more than that. Skilled L2 users have to be fluent not only in retrieving learned associations between names and their referents, but to be able to do so while, at the same time, conveying construal information, handling sociolinguistic functions, and promoting personal psychosocial interests. To accomplish this, the L2 user needs to draw on the resources provided by the language medium for dealing with these different aspects of message content and to use these resources fluently in the process of planning, assembling, and executing speech production. As indicated in the framework in Figure 7.1, the interactive social context is both the source of situational demands that shape communicative content and the source for learning about the resources (linguistic affordances) available for meeting these demands. This brings us to the next important question—the *processing* considerations for being fluent in handling these categories of content.

Process

What are the cognitive processing requirements for fluent delivery of the four categories of communicative content? As discussed in Chapters 3, 4, and 6 (Conclusions 4, 5, 12, 13, 14, and 15 in Table 7.1), the cognitive processing requirements for fluency include:

- high levels of efficiency in speed and stability of processing (related to "automaticity")
- high levels of efficiency in attentional control and flexibility (related to the role of attention in skilled performance)
- fluency-related changes in the functioning of the underlying neuro-linguistic system (e.g., neural reorganization as significant gains are made in processing fluency [cognitive fluency])
- efficient (or fluent) memory retrieval due to transfer appropriate processing (TAP).

In terms of the dynamical systems framework, these processing requirements address the cognitive fluency of the cognitive-perceptual processing systems component. There has been a lot of cognitive research conducted on the four aspects of processing efficiency and memory retrieval just listed above, but this research has focused primarily on those aspects of processing skill that are related to word selection, word retrieval, sentence comprehension, and the like—that is, processing that relates to the cognitive message contained in a stimulus. Unfortunately, there has been little parallel work concerning processing related to the handling of information related to cognitive linguistic issues (e.g., construals). Neither has there been much work on cognitive processing efficiency in handling sociolinguistic aspects of messages. However, the same considerations should be expected to apply to these aspects of communicative content as they do to the primary cognitive content of stimuli.

It can be seen from this brief review that a cognitive science perspective on L2 fluency can suggest possibilities not likely to come to mind when one adopts an isolated, single-discipline perspective on fluency. For example, sociolinguists have been in a better position to identify the ways languages afford possibilities for conveying social messages in parallel with cognitive messages, whereas cognitive psychologists have rarely taken this dimension of language into account when studying processing efficiency (and vice versa). Yet both groups of researchers hold important pieces of the fluency puzzle. One can imagine other combinations of disciplines giving rise to questions that would not otherwise be asked. For example, as discussed in Chapter 6, work in formal modeling of artificial vocabulary networks suggests that under some conditions stable, self-sustaining sub-networks can emerge, producing results similar to massive reactivations of network links. Such a phenom-enon may possibly increase efficiency within the network and enhance its processing fluency. Based on this, applied linguists might ask if there are elements of real languages that might make such self-sustaining sub-networks a possibility, for example, through fixed expressions and formulaic sequences that have become highly stable and efficiently processed.

The cognitive science perspective presented here is meant to serve as a framework for thinking about fluency, not as a full theory of L2 fluency. There are, consequently, many important topics that have been left out, but that will eventually have to be integrated into the framework, too. A few of these can be listed here; their ultimate relevance to L2 fluency is obvious, but treatment of these topics would require several more chapters at least. These topics include, among others, declarative versus procedural memory in learning (Paradis, 2009); implicit and explicit learning and knowledge (DeKeyser, 2003; N. Ellis, 1994; R. Ellis et al., 2009; Hulstijn, 2005; Paradis, 2009); mental representation within and across languages (Kroll & Tokowicz, 2005; Paradis, 2009); individual differences (Dörnyei, 2005, 2009a; Michael & Gollan, 2005; P. Robinson, 2002b; Segalowitz, 1997) and working memory (Michael & Gollan, 2005).

Before closing this chapter, it is appropriate to look at one more important topic: the implications a cognitive science framework might have for improving L2 fluency through teaching.

Some Implications for Instructed Learning

A practical question regarding the proposed cognitive science perspective on L2 fluency presented here is whether it has any implications for improving L2 fluency through instruction. A full treatment of this topic would require an examination of the long and rich history of L2 instruction, something that is beyond the scope of this book. However, some of the principles and conclusions presented so far are clearly relevant to instructional concerns and so this section will explore a few of these. Broadly speaking, a cognitive science perspective would hold that instruction succeeds in improving fluency when instruction enhances the cognitive fluency of the processes underlying L2 speech production. This is not an entirely new idea. Gatbonton and Segalowitz (1988, 2005) presented an earlier treatment of certain aspects of the ideas presented below where they discussed fluency development and automatization in the context of communicative approaches in language teaching (ACCESS—Automatization in Communicative Contexts of Essential Speech Segments). However, the cognitive psychological perspective on which that treatment was based can now be expanded. The goal here is to situate the issues within a much broader cognitive science perspective.

Three main ideas emerge from the cognitive science perspective regarding how L2 fluency can be promoted through instruction. The first idea concerns *transfer appropriate processing*. TAP, it will be recalled (Chapter 3), is the principle that transfer of learning to a new setting will be most effective if the kinds of mental processing required at the time of learning match those that will be elicited in the transfer context. To apply the TAP principle to L2 instructional settings requires first identifying what processing activities will be activated in the transfer setting (i.e., in natural communicative settings) and then considering how instruction can be designed to elicit these same processing activities during learning (see Lightbown, 2007, for discussion of TAP in relation to L2 instruction; see Trofimovich & Gatbonton, 2006, for discussion of TAP in pronunciation learning). The processing activities from natural settings that need to be identified will be those elicited by the kinds of content associated with communication in those settings, namely the four categories mentioned earlier. These categories include information that refers to the objects, events, and attributes being talked about; information regarding the speaker's construals or perspectives about the relationships between those things being talked about; information related to sociolinguistic functions; and information designed to promote the speaker's psychosocial goals. These categories of information are normally always part and parcel of communication in natural settings.

Although many language-teaching paradigms exist at the present moment (see Lightbown & Spada, 2006, for a useful review of the issues), the dominant approaches today are communicative language teaching (CLT) and task-based language teaching (TBLT), as they are sometimes known (Van den Branden, Bygate, & Norris, 2009). These approaches (there are many versions) focus on meaning, trying to recreate in the classroom the natural communicative conditions that may be expected to elicit genuine communication as it is thought to occur outside the classroom. CLT-based methods have enjoyed a great deal of success, but there remain important issues that researchers and theorists continue to address. For example, there are concerns about how teaching should target particular language structures (e.g., Pienemann, 1999; VanPatten, 2004), how practice activities might best be built into a CLT approach (e.g., DeKeyser, 2007a), how corrective feedback functions in a CLT setting (e.g., Mackey, 2007b), and where planning for speaking fits into language instruction (e.g., R. Ellis, 2005). Although the above and many other issues relevant to CLT have been the subject of attention in recent years, what has not been always explicit in discussions about CLT is the role of communication in L2 learning and, in particular, what exactly is learned when learners engage in communication. A cognitive science perspective can make a contribution to this issue by addressing the nature of the fluency-relevant mental processing that presumably takes place during communication and, therefore, can help decide what is learned that could be transferred to new settings. This perspective can also bring to light knowledge that may be useful for developing learning activities for the classroom.

Tomasello's (2003) usage-based approach to language acquisition provides a useful context for understanding the nature of mental processing implicated in communication. According to this approach, the learner and interlocutor engage in *joint attention*—that is, they intentionally monitor each other's attention and they both attend to the objects and events that are being talked about. They also engage in *intention reading*—that is, they try to understand the social intentions of the other person. Tomasello discusses joint attention and intention reading in the context of infant L1 acquisition; however, these concepts apply also to L2 communication. This engagement of joint attention and intention reading is what distinguishes the mental activity underlying the *genuine communication* found in natural settings from the mental activity underlying the activities often found in instructional settings. This is because, in natural settings, the L2 user engages in language contact in order to accomplish goals that are personally important and where success in reaching these goals requires precisely this involvement in joint attention and in intention reading. In contrast, in those particular instructional settings where communication is highly decontextualized (e.g., in role-playing activities involving speaking from fixed or memorized scripts), the speaker's actual involvement in joint attention and intention reading is not aligned with the teacher's intended goal of the communicative activity. This situation—involving fixed scripts—would be more akin to a closed than to an open skill environment, as discussed in Chapter 3. Here, the learner's goal is usually to satisfy the teacher that the material has been learned, or to avoid embarrassment in front of the class; the learner's goal will not be aligned with the assumed intentions of the various characters in the role play activity (see Gatbonton & Segalowitz, 2005, for more discussion about how classroom activities can succeed or fail to be genuinely communicative and what can be done to ensure genuine communication in the classroom).

In sum, natural settings involve the communication of the four types of content identified earlier. Communicating these four types of content requires speakers to engage in particular types of cognitive processing (i.e., joint attention and intention reading). According to the TAP principle, the likelihood of retrieving any learned L2 material at a later time increases when the cognitive processing demands experienced during learning match the demands that will be experienced later. This brings us to the second important idea regarding instruction from a cognitive science perspective on L2 fluency—what the to-be-learned material should be.

The second idea concerns learning to perceive and use *linguistic resources*. To successfully use the L2 in order to convey information related to construals, sociolinguistic functions, and personal psychosocial goals, it is not sufficient to just acquire a particular vocabulary and master syntax. As noted in Chapters 4 and 5, languages provide a wide range of opportunities for handling these communicative goals. These resources can draw on different aspects of the language, often going far beyond individual aspects of vocabulary and syntax. Moreover, different languages handle this in different ways. These resources were referred to as "linguistic affordances" in Chapter 3 because they make it possible (or limit possibilities) for speakers to fulfill various intentional, communicative goals. To put it another way, as discussed in Chapter 4, people have to package the thoughts they want to communicate in a way that meshes with the possibilities afforded by the language—they have to engage in "thinking for speaking," as Slobin (1996) put it. Language learners need to learn, therefore, how the target language requires them to think for speaking. For this, they have to be able to perceive and exploit the linguistic resources (affordances) available to them at the moment they are needed. What is important for learning, according to the cognitive science perspective, is that exposure to these resources should occur in a context where learners have to use them to fulfill genuinely communicative goals. This is necessary in order to optimize transfer of learning outside the instructional setting.

The third idea concerns *cognitive fluency*, that is, the highly efficient operation of the cognitive processing mechanisms underlying the planning, assembly, and execution of the target L2 utterance. The single elicitation of mental processing activities, however transfer appropriate, will not be sufficient to make them operate efficiently. As discussed in Chapter 4, there must be a significant amount of consistent repetition of these processes for them to gain significantly in speed and stability (i.e., become more "automatic"; Schneider & Chein, 2003). Thus, a cognitive science perspective would hold that learning activities in the classroom should not only recreate the mental processing involved in communication in the real world (TAP principle), but they should also provide learners with opportunities for systematic repetition in order to activate and reactivate the same set of cognitive processes. It is important to note that what must be repeated is the whole set of mental processes involved in the planning, assembling, and execution of the speech act, and this must occur within genuinely communicative contexts (otherwise, the nature of the underlying cognitive processing could change significantly). Gatbonton discusses how to design instructional tasks that are genuinely communicative and naturally repetitive at the same time (Gatbonton & Segalowitz, 1988, 2005). She argues that the learning activity must be *inherently repetitive* in the sense that repetition needs to become a means for the learner to attain the task goal (not repetition for its own sake but in order to accomplish the communicative goal). In this way, the learner remains involved in genuine communication while engaged in repetition. (For other discussions regarding the use of practice and repetition in language learning, see DeKeyser, 2007b, 2007c; Lightbown, 2007; Mackey, 2007a; Ortega, 2007; P. Robinson, 2001b; and Trofimovich & Gatbonton, 2006.)

In addition to promoting processing speed and stability, activities meeting the criteria outlined here, including inherent repetition, can be useful for promoting *processing flexibility*. This is because, in the process of pursuing genuine communication goals, learners' attention will inevitably shift from one aspect of cognitive processing to another as they choose which means to select and what to suppress. Because of the frequent shifting of attention due to the inherent repetition in the learning activity, learners can develop cognitive fluency in attention focusing as it applies to the planning, assembly, and execution of utterances—in ways that should transfer outside the instructional setting.

This cognitive science perspective on L2 fluency can also be related to instructional settings in at least two other ways. One has to do with motivation which, as can be seen in Figure 7.1, is a major component in the framework. It will be recalled from Chapter 5 that Dörnyei (2009b) has elaborated a theory about people's L2-specific sense of self—their sense of themselves as second language users. Figure 5.2 presented a schema of the interacting influences in which this L2-specific sense of self plays an important role in the acquisition process leading to fluency, and that this L2-specific sense of self can change (grow) as learning progresses. A possible implication for instruction is that this element of motivation might be explicitly harnessed within the design of fluency activities (it is not clear yet how this might be done; Dörnyei, 2009b, alluded to the imagery techniques elite athletes use to enhance performance—perhaps something similar could work in L2 fluency development). By augmenting this aspect of motivation, learners might become more attuned to learning about the linguistic resources of the target language, because by developing skill with these linguistic resources they will be better able to pursue communicative goals that are congruent with the goals of the L2-specific self.

The second point concerns an effect that was alluded to in Chapter 6. This is the idea that processing fluency can beget more processing fluency. Vocabulary researchers have discussed such effects in relation to the learning of new words through reading (Meara, 1993; Mezynski, 1983; Nation, 1993). They have suggested that new words in a text can be added easily to one's vocabulary if one already has fluent access to some threshold level (e.g., 90 percent) of the words in the text as a whole. Likewise, perhaps by achieving high levels of cognitive fluency through instruction, the neurocognitive network underlying the planning, assembly, and execution of L2 utterances can become more self-sustaining. Meara (2007) demonstrated the theoretical possibility of this with his simple vocabulary network models.

To conclude, we have seen that a cognitive science perspective on L2 fluency has yielded a number of ideas that might serve as criteria for instructional activities designed to promote fluency in instructional settings (see Table 7.2 for a summary). To the extent that the variables underlying these criteria can be operationalized and measured, it may be possible to test their usefulness.

Table 7.2 Summary of the Implications for Promoting L2 Fluency in Instructional Settings that Emerge from a Cognitive Science Perspective (See Text for Details)

Criteria for instructional Activities for Promoting L2 Fluency, Based on a Cognitive Science Perspective

- *The activity involves transfer appropriate processing.*
- *The activity is genuinely communicative, eliciting joint attention and intention reading with interlocutors.*
- *The activity promotes skill in perceiving and using linguistic resources that afford possibilities and limitations for pursuing communicative goals (linguistic affordances).*
- *The activity is inherently repetitive in order to promote cognitive fluency in the handling of linguistic resources (gains in processing speed, stability, and flexibility).*

Activities meeting the above criteria have the potential of creating the following benefits for fluency development:

- *The cognitive processing system may experience self-supporting gains in cognitive fluency, resulting in greater neurocognitive network stability and in self-sustaining activation, further enhancing cognitive fluency.*
- *Gains in cognitive fluency may enhance the learner's motivational (L2-specific self) system, thereby facilitating performance gains in the rest of the system.*

Conclusions

This chapter began with two quotations from nearly half a century ago: one from Luria, the neuroscientist and aphasiologist, and the other from Lambert, the social psychologist of bilingualism. In one sense the two quotations could not be more different—the former addressing functional systems in the brain, and the latter touching on social and cultural factors in second language learning. However, it should now be evident from the cognitive science perspective presented in this book that the two are fully compatible and complementary. Interestingly, by today's standards, neither statement would be considered particularly controversial, even though at the time they were written the statements were rightly viewed as insightful and thought provoking. Their value for us today is that, by thinking about how neurocognitive science and social science are indeed compatible and complementary, a way opens up for thinking about the problem of L2 fluency that is broader in scope and more integrated than have been most approaches on this subject.

The principal aim of this book has been to place thinking about L2 fluency within a multidisciplinary, cognitive science framework. Represented here are the social sciences (especially sociolinguistics and applied linguistics), the formal disciplines (linguistics, cognitive linguistics, formal modeling sciences), philosophy, and, of course, the behavioral and neurocognitive sciences. The approach does not privilege any one discipline over another, because they are in true complementary relationship. As pointed out earlier, certain interesting ideas about fluency would not have emerged without borrowing concepts across disciplinary boundaries. This is perhaps the major take-home message.

An important feature of the cognitive science perspective presented here is that what underlies L2 fluency is extremely complex. It involves a constellation of elements that are in dynamic interaction with each other. It is just not appropriate to apply linear thinking (X causes Y, end of story) to questions about fluency. The challenge of fluency is that it requires a dynamical systems way of thinking about it, with the recognition that changes in the system reflect continual system-wide adaptations. This does not mean, however, that predictions cannot be made and that falsification of hypotheses is not possible. What I have tried to show is that there are identifiable elements in this system—captured by constructs such as *cognitive fluency, utterance fluency, linguistic affordances, processing efficiency, L2-self,* etc.—that can indeed be given operational definitions. In principle—and in some cases, already in fact—these constructs and their interactions can be studied. What I have also tried to show, despite the daunting complexity of the situation—some might be tempted to say the *slipperiness* of the whole endeavor—is that it *is* possible to envisage a systematic, cognitive-science-based program of research on fluency. It is feasible (but no one said it would be easy!) and this feasibility is the second take-home message.

Here, in places in this volume and in the writing of others, fluency is sometimes talked about in metaphorical terms. Fluency is spoken about as fluidity of processing; it is claimed that underlying fluency is the metaphor that "language is motion"; the smooth planning, assembly, and execution of utterances can be likened to the complex choreography required for dance or performance on a musical instrument. These are all metaphorical ways of thinking and they are useful. They channel ideas about fluency away from simple mechanical models of thought and focus attention on how elements of time and coordination enter into the picture. But, as metaphors, they also have their limitations. The "flow" of language is not really like the flow of water, or of traffic, despite some possible superficial similarities. Ultimately, if fluency is to be fully understood, notions like "fluidity," "smoothness," "coordination" will have to be operationalized. This is not an impossible task, but it has not been done yet in a systematic way for the study of L2 fluency. Recognizing the value *and* limitations of metaphorical thinking about L2 fluency, and the need to move beyond it, is the third take-home message.

One of the things that was particularly striking in researching the vast literature on L2 acquisition for information about fluency, was that often the item "fluency" did not even appear in the index sections of books. No doubt, this might sometimes have been because other terms were being used instead (e.g., "oral proficiency"; "language expertise"). But one gets a strong impression that there is also a tendency to shy away from explicitly addressing the topic of fluency because it just seems to be too ill-defined, too slippery a topic to get a handle on satisfactorily, too hard to know what to do with it. It is hoped that the cognitive science framework presented here will help to dispel that worry, and that researchers and theorists from different disciplines will see here instead an opportunity to study a profoundly interesting phenomenon—one with wide-ranging implications for understanding language and language acquisition, the nature of high level skill development, the functioning of complex socio-affective-neurocognitive systems, and the continuity of issues in human development from infancy to adulthood.

Recommended Reading

Breznitz, Z. (2006). *Fluency in reading: Synchronization of processes.* Mahwah, NJ: Lawrence Erlbaum Associates.
Although this volume deals exclusively with L1 reading fluency, it is nevertheless relevant to L2 fluency. The relevance lies in the way the author conceptualizes fluency. Reading fluency is seen to depend on the rate of single word decoding, which itself depends on the speed of processing of the various systems that become active during reading. These different systems function at different speeds. According to Breznitz, for reading to be fluent, there must be *synchronization* of information that is generated from different sources. Fluency is thus understood as reflecting the degree to which there is this synchronization. Breznitz's synchronization perspective, although presented in the contexts of L1 reading and problems of dyslexia, may hold interesting implications for understanding L2 cognitive fluency.

DeKeyser, R. M. (Ed.) (2007). *Practice in a second language: perspectives from applied linguistics and cognitive psychology.* Cambridge, UK: Cambridge University Press.
Because practice is absolutely central to the acquisition of L2 fluency, this volume makes an important contribution to the fluency literature by bringing together for the first time so many perspectives on practice. The 10 chapters by leading authors in the field discuss the concept of practice, the various forms practice can take in different learning settings, and the impact practice has as a function of age and context. The contributors go beyond simply claiming that practice matters by discussing some of the underlying details of the effect of practice on specific aspects of performance.

Dörnyei, Z. (2005). *The psychology of the language learner: Individual differences in second language acquisition.* Mahwah, NJ: Lawrence Erlbaum Associates.
This volume treats the topic of individual differences in L2 acquisition very comprehensively, with a strong emphasis on aptitude, motivation, learning strategies, and social factors—discussions that complement the

present volume. The topic of fluency is not a primary focus of Dörnyei's book, but it is represented implicitly in its discussions of proficiency and competence. The volume is relevant to fluency issues insofar as it discusses sources of individual variability that may lead to differences in fluency attainment.

Dörnyei, Z. (2009). *The psychology of second language acquisition.* Oxford: Oxford University Press.
This volume is perhaps the most complete, single-authored, recent volume on L2 acquisition. It provides an excellent and highly accessible introductory overview of the field as a whole. Fluency issues are well represented in sections dealing with automaticity, chunking, formulaic language, and various approaches to instructed language learning. The reader will obtain a good idea of where fluency is situated in the "big picture" of L2 acquisition.

Dörnyei, Z. (2009). The L2 motivational self system. In Z. Dörnyei & E. Ushioda (Eds.), *Motivation, language identity and the L2 Self* (pp. 9–42). Bristol, UK: Multilingual Matters.
This chapter presents Dörnyei's proposal regarding the L2 motivational self system. Because his ideas are discussed at some length in Chapter 5 of the present book, it is not summarized again here. What deserves to be underscored, however, is that Dörnyei's theory makes an important contribution to a cognitive science approach to L2 fluency by proposing a new way of thinking about the role of motivation that builds on earlier work by Gardner (1985, 2001; Gardner & Lambert, 1972).

Ellis, R. (Ed.) (2005). *Planning and task performance in a second language.* Amsterdam: John Benjamins.
This volume contains 10 contributions on various aspects of how a speaker's planning activities can affect speech production, an important consideration regarding fluency. The chapters consider different types of planning activities, different task contexts in which planning is relevant, and the different kinds of impact that planning can have. The contributors discuss various research paradigms and operational measures, going beyond *whether* planning has general impact on communication to *how* planning affects specific aspects of linguistic accuracy and complexity.

Gullberg, M., & Indefrey, P. (Eds.) (2006). *The cognitive neuroscience of second language acquisition.* Oxford: Blackwell.
This edited volume provides a good overview of issues, of research techniques currently used in the neuroscientific study of bilingualism, and of their limitations. It addresses questions about critical periods for L2 acquisition, individual differences, executive control in bilingual language processing, and L2 proficiency. This book provides useful background

regarding the cognitive neuroscience aspects of a cognitive science perspective on fluency.

Kormos, J. (2006). *Speech production and second language acquisition*. Mahwah, NJ: Lawrence Erlbaum Associates.
This is the most recent and comprehensive book-length treatment of second language speech production and it is also the first volume in the present series focusing on the cognitive sciences and second language acquisition. Her Chapters 7 (problem-solving mechanisms in L2 speech) and 8 (fluency and automaticity) are especially relevant to L2 fluency. Kormos concludes the volume with an update of Levelt's (1999) blueprint of the speaker. Her model differs from Levelt's principally by the addition of a memory store for declarative knowledge of syntactic and phonological rules for L2 production, and by the inclusion of mechanisms for controlling the competition between L1 and L2. The bibliography provides a comprehensive listing of recent research on L2 speech production, focusing primarily on psycholinguistic studies concerned with the cognitive-perceptual systems underlying L2 use.

Kroll, J. F., & de Groot, A. M. B. (Eds.) (2005). *Handbook of bilingualism: Psycholinguistic approaches*. Oxford: Oxford University Press.
This handbook contains many chapters reviewing broad topic areas relevant to L2 fluency issues. Of particular relevance are the following chapters. MacWhinney presents an update to the Competition Model that includes aspects dealing with fluency. Segalowitz and Hulstijn focus on automaticity, a central issue in L2 fluency. Michael and Gollan discuss individual differences, in particular whether factors that underlie differences in L1 fluency also influence individual differences in L2 fluency. Abutalebi et al. review neuroimaging evidence on the bilingual brain, including evidence concerned with L2 fluency.

Levelt, W. J. M. (1989). *Speaking: From intention to articulation*. Cambridge, MA: MIT Press.
Levelt's volume is by now a classic in the literature on speech production. The book provides a detailed discussion of the many cognitive and perceptual processing issues underlying speech production in the L1, in a model described as a blueprint of the speaker (see Levelt, 1999, for an important update). The Levelt blueprint has served as a point of departure for numerous papers in the L2 speech literature. De Bot (1992) and Kormos (2006, Chapter 9) discuss their adaptations of this blueprint to cover issues relevant to the L2 speaker. Although Levelt's blueprint and its variants do not specifically target L2 *fluency* issues as such, they nevertheless touch on foundational issues relevant to L2 fluency.

Luoma, S. (2004). *Assessing speaking*. Cambridge, MA: Cambridge University Press.

This volume reviews the issues and challenges in creating tests for assessing and evaluating L2 speech production, including fluency. The focus is primarily on the nature of the tasks that have been used for language elicitation and on how to assess accuracy and what I have called *utterance fluency*. Luoma discusses important considerations regarding the reliability and validity of such tasks and draws attention to the many contextual issues that need to be kept in mind when designing speech elicitation tasks. The volume contains detailed examples of various scales and tests used for assessing L2 speaking abilities.

McDonough, K., & Trofimovich, P. (2009). *Using priming methods in second language research*. London: Routledge.
The priming task is among the most commonly used method in psycholinguistics to investigate the nature of language processing, including in the L2 user. Priming techniques provide a powerful tool for investigating what I have been calling cognitive fluency. McDonough and Trofimovich present a comprehensive review of the use of priming tasks in the L2 research literature, introducing the reader to the basic priming task and its variants. They discuss auditory, syntactic, and semantic priming, and they provide comments on the design, analysis, and reporting of priming studies for researchers who would like to begin using this technique in their own laboratory. The authors also report findings from studies addressing basic questions such as whether and to what extent a bilingual's L2 mental lexicon is similar to the L1 mental lexicon. They demonstrate how priming tasks can reveal important subtleties involved in answering questions about L2 processing.

Meyer, A. S., Wheeldon, L. R., & Krott, A. (Eds.) (2007). *Automaticity and control in language processing*. New York: Psychology Press.
This edited volume is one of the very few recent books that deals extensively with automaticity in language. Only one chapter deals with automaticity in L2, and that one focuses only on language switching. Nevertheless, the volume is relevant because of its wide treatment of automaticity issues in many different aspects of language processing, including conversational alignment, in multitasking while using language, in avoiding ambiguity, in self-monitoring, in lexical retrieval, and in other aspects of L1 processing. Although the authors in this book do not address automaticity and speech production fluency directly, most of the topics dealt with could be seen to be relevant to fluency issues. Many of the studies presented could be readily adapted for addressing interesting questions regarding automaticity in L2 fluency.

Paradis, M. (2009). *Declarative and procedural determinants of second languages*. Amsterdam: John Benjamins.
This volume provides a thorough and comprehensive review of issues regarding the distinction between declarative and procedural aspects

of processing in the L2. It includes a strong emphasis on the neurocognitive underpinnings of this distinction. Paradis discusses the differences between L1 and L2 in terms of the involvement of implicit versus explicit knowledge, and he makes important claims about the inability of studies that use single-word stimuli to reveal much about processing in implicit knowledge systems. Paradis defends the no-interface view of the relationship between explicit and implicit knowledge (i.e., that explicit or metalinguistic knowledge cannot be converted into forms of implicit knowledge), and this has implications for an understanding of fluency development.

Riggenbach, H. (Ed.) (2000). *Perspectives on fluency*. Ann Arbor: University of Michigan Press.
This volume contains a number of important papers regarding different aspects of both L1 and L2 fluency. Fillmore's 1979 classic paper on fluency is reprinted here. Pawley and Syder have a chapter on their "one-clause-at-a-time" hypothesis. Chapters by Koponen and Riggenbach, and by Brumfit, Lennon, Segalowitz, Oppenheim, and Freed, are also especially relevant to the topics addressed in the present book.

Robinson, P., & Ellis, N. (Eds.) (2008). *Handbook of cognitive linguistics and second language acquisition*. London: Routledge.
This volume is particularly relevant to a cognitive science approach to second language fluency. The chapters provide excellent reviews for L2 acquisition and fluency researchers wanting to learn more about how concepts from cognitive linguistics might apply to SLA. Although the term *fluency* as such is barely mentioned, nevertheless the chapters by Talmy (attention), Langacker (cognitive grammar and instruction), Lieven and Tomasello (usage-based acquisition), Goldberg and Casenhiser (constructions), Bybee (usage-based grammar), MacWhinney (unified model), Ellis (learning), and the concluding chapter by Robinson and Ellis (research issues), are quite relevant in different ways to the topic of L2 fluency. Overall, this volume is a rich source of information for a cognitive sciences approach to L2 acquisition, including L2 fluency.

Wray, A. (2002). *Formulaic language and the lexicon*. Cambridge, UK: Cambridge University Press.
Wray provides a comprehensive overview of issues in formulaic language, including a detailed account of the social communicative functions served by formulaic sequences and fixed expressions in both L1 and L2, devoting four chapters to formulaic language in child and adult L2 acquisition. She develops the theory that the use of formulaic language serves the psychosocial function of promoting the self and at the same time plays an important role in imparting to L2 speech important features of fluency.

References

Abutalebi, J. (2008). Neural aspects of second language representation and language control. *Acta Psychologica, 128,* 466–478.

Abutalebi, J., Cappa, S., & Perani, D. (2001). The bilingual brain as revealed by functional neuroimaging. *Bilingualism: Language and Cognition, 4,* 179–190.

Abutalebi, J., Cappa, S., & Perani, D. (2005). What can functional neuroimaging tell us about the bilingual brain? In J. Kroll & A. De Groot (Eds.), *Handbook of bilingualism: Psycholinguistic approaches* (pp. 497–515). Oxford, UK: Oxford University Press.

Abutalebi, J., & Green, D. (2007). Bilingual language production: The neurocognition of language representation and control. *Journal of Neurolinguistics, 20,* 242–275.

Abutalebi, J., & Green, D. (2008). Control mechanisms in bilingual language production: Neural evidence from language switching studies. *Language and Cognitive Processes, 23,* 557–582.

Ackerman, P. L. (1988). Determinants of individual differences during skill acquisition: Cognitive abilities and information processing. *Journal of Experimental Psychology: General, 177,* 288–318.

Ackerman, P. L. (1989). Individual differences and skill acquisition. In P. L. Ackerman, R. J. Sternberg, & R. Glaser (Eds.), *Learning and individual differences: Advances in theory and research* (pp. 165–217). New York: Freeman.

Akamatsu, N. (2008). The effects of training on automatization of word recognition in English as a foreign language. *Applied Psycholinguistics, 29,* 175–193.

Albert, L. & Obler, L. (1978). *The bilingual brain.* New York: Academic Press.

Allard, F., & Starkes, J. L. (1991). Motor-skill experts in sports, dance, and other domains. In K. A. Ericsson & J. Smith (Eds.), *Toward a general theory of expertise* (pp. 126–152). Cambridge, UK: Cambridge University Press.

Alter, D., & Oppenheimer, D. (2008). Effects of fluency on psychological distance and mental construal (or why New York is a large city, but *New York* is a civilized jungle). *Psychological Science, 19,* 161–167.

Alter, D., & Oppenheimer, D. (2009, manuscript under review). Uniting the tribes of fluency to form a metacognitive nation. *Personality and Social Psychology Review, 13,* 219–235.

Anderson, J. R. (1982). Acquisition of cognitive skill. *Psychological Review, 89,* 369–406.

Anderson, J. R. (1983). *The architecture of cognition.* Cambridge, MA: Harvard University Press.

Anderson, J. R., & Lebiere, C. (1998). *The atomic components of thought.* Mahwah, NJ: Lawrence Erlbaum Associates.

Ardila, A., & Ramos, E. (Eds.) (2007). *Speech and language disorders in bilinguals.* Hauppauge, New York: Nova Science Publishers.

Ascham, R. (1570/1967). *The scholemaster.* New York: AMS Press.

Bachman, L. F. (1988). Problems in examining the validity of the ACTFL Oral Proficiency Interview. *Studies in Second Language Acquisition, 10,* 149–161.

Bachman, L. F. (1990). *Fundamental considerations in language testing.* Oxford, UK: Oxford University Press.

Bachman, L. F., & Palmer, A. S. (1996). *Language testing in practice.* Oxford, UK: Oxford University Press.

Baker, M. (2003). Linguistic difference and language design. *TRENDS in Cognitive Sciences, 7,* 349–353.

Barlow, M. & Kemmer, S. (Eds.). (2000). *Usage based models of language.* Stanford: CSLI Publications.

Barshi, I., & Healy, A. F. (1998). Misunderstandings in voice communication: Effects of fluency in a second language. In A. F. Healy & L. E. Bourne (Eds.), *Foreign language learning: Psycholinguistic studies in training and retention* (pp. 161–192). Mahwah, NJ: Erlbaum.

Beakley, B., & Ludlow, P. (Eds.) (1992). *The philosophy of mind: Classical problems and contemporary issues.* Cambridge, MA: MIT Press.

Bialystok, E., Craik, F. I. M., Grady, C., Chau, W., Ishii, R., Gunji, A., et al. (2005). Effect of bilingualism on cognitive control in the Simon task: Evidence from MEG. *NeuroImage, 24,* 40–49.

Blaxton, T. A. (1989). Investigating dissociations among memory measures: Support for a transfer-appropriate processing framework. *Journal of Experimental Psychology: Learning, Memory, Cognition, 15,* 657–668.

Bornstein, R. F. (1989). Exposure and affect: Overview and meta-analysis of research, 1968–1987. *Psychological Bulletin, 106,* 265–289.

Bourdieu, P. (1991). *Language and symbolic power.* Cambridge, UK: Cambridge University Press.

Bourne, L. E., Jr., Healy, A. F., Parker, J. T., & Rickard, T. C. (1999). The strategic basis of performance in binary classification tasks: Strategy choices and strategy transitions. *Journal of Memory and Language, 41,* 223–252.

Boyd, R. (1993). Metaphor and theory change: What is metaphor a metaphor for? In A. Ortony (Ed.), *Metaphor and thought* (pp. 481–532). Cambridge, UK: Cambridge University Press.

Breiner-Sanders, K., Lowe, P., Miles, J., & Swender, E. (2000). ACTFL proficiency guidelines: Speaking, revised 1999. *Foreign Language Annals, 33,* 13–18.

Breznitz, Z. (2006). *Fluency in reading: Synchronization of processes.* Mahwah, NJ: Lawrence Erlbaum Associates.

Briellmann, R., Saling, M., Connell, A., Waites, A., Abbott, D., & Jackson, G. (2004). A high-field functional MRI study of quadri-lingual subjects. *Brain and Language, 89,* 531–542.

Broeder, P., & Plunkett, K. (1994). Connectionism and second language acquisition. In N. C. Ellis (Ed.), *Implicit and explicit learning of languages* (pp. 421–455). London: Academic Press.

Bybee, J. (2008). Usage-based grammar and second language acquisition. In P. Robinson & N. C. Ellis (Eds.), *Handbook of cognitive linguistics and second language acquisition* (pp. 216–236). New York: Routledge.

Cadierno, T. (2008). Learning to talk about motion in a foreign language. In P. Robinson & N. C. Ellis (Eds.), *Handbook of cognitive linguistics and second language acquisition* (pp. 239–275). New York: Routledge.

Canale, M., & Swain, M. (1980). Theoretical bases of communicative approaches to second language teaching and testing. *Applied Linguistics, 1,* 1–47.

Chalmers, D. (Ed.) (2002). *Philosophy of mind: Classical and contemporary readings.* Oxford, UK: Oxford University Press.

Chambers, F. (1997). What do we mean by fluency? *System, 25,* 535–544.

Chee, M., Hon, N., Lee, H. L., & Soon, C. S. (2001). Relative language proficiency modulates BOLD signal change when bilinguals perform semantic judgments. *NeuroImage, 13,* 1155–1163.

Chemero, A. (2003). An outline of a theory of affordances. *Ecological Psychology, 15,* 181–195.

Cheng, P. (1985). Restructuring versus automaticity: Alternative accounts of skill acquisition. *Psychological Review, 92,* 195–222.

Cherry, E. C. (1953). Some experiments on the recognition of speech, with one and with two ears. *Journal of the Acoustical Society of America, 25,* 975–979.

Chiswick, B., & Miller, P.W. (2007). *The economics of language: International analyses.* London: Routledge.

Chocholle, R. (1940). Variations des temps de réaction auditifs en fonction de l'intensité à diverses fréquences. *L'Année Psychologique, 41,* 65–124.

Chomsky, N. (1965). *Aspects of the theory of syntax.* Cambridge, MA: MIT Press.

Chomsky, N. (1975). *Reflections on languages.* New York: Pantheon Books.

Christensen, H., Dear, K., Anstey, K., Parslow, R., Sachdev, P., & Jorm, A. (2005). Within-occasion intraindividual variability and preclinical diagnostic status: Is intraindividual variability an indicator of mild cognitive impairment? *Neuropsychology, 19,* 309–317.

Clahsen, H. (1987). Natural language development: Acquisitional processes leading to fluency in speech production. In H. W. Dechert & M. Raupach (Eds.), *Psycholinguistic models of production* (pp. 67–75). Norwood, NJ: Ablex Publishing Corporation.

Clark, H. H., & Fox Tree, J. (2002). Using uh and um in spontaneous speaking. *Cognition, 84,* 73–111.

Cohen, J. D., Aston-Jones, G., & Gilzenrat, M. S. (2004). A systems-level perspective on attention and cognitive control. In M. Posner (Ed.), *Cognitive neuroscience of attention* (pp. 71–90). New York: The Guilford Press.

Cohen, J. (1988). *Statistical power analysis for the behavioral sciences.* Mahwah, NJ: Laurence Erlbaum Associates.

Collard, P., Corley, M., MacGregor, L., & Donaldson, D. (2008). Attention orienting effects of hesitations in speech: Evidence from ERPs. *Journal of Experimental Psychology: Learning, Memory and Cognition, 34,* 696–702.

Costa, A. (2005). Lexical access in bilingual production. In J. Kroll & A. M. B. de Groot (Eds.), *Handbook of bilingualism: Psycholinguistic perspectives* (pp. 308–325). New York: Oxford University Press.

Costa, A., & Santesteban, M. (2004). Lexical access in bilingual speech production: Evidence from language switching in highly proficient bilinguals and L2 learners. *Journal of Memory and Language, 50,* 491–511.

Costa, A., & Santesteban, M. (2006) (Guest Eds.). Lexical access in bilingual speech production. Special issue of *Bilingualism: Language and Cognition, 9.*

Council of Europe (2001). *Common European Framework of reference for languages: Learning, teaching assessment.* Cambridge, UK: Cambridge University Press.

Coupland, N., Bishop, H. A., Williams, A., Evans, B., & Garrett, P. (2005). Affiliation, engagement, language use and vitality: Secondary school students' subjective orientations to Welsh and Welshness. *International Journal of Bilingual Education and Bilingualism, 8,* 1–24.

Craik, F. I. M., & Lockhart, R. S. (1972). Levels of processing: A framework for memory research. *Journal of Verbal Learning and Verbal Behavior, 11,* 671–684.

Croft, W., & Cruse, D. A. (2004). *Cognitive linguistics.* Cambridge, UK: Cambridge University Press.

Crossman, E. (1959). A theory of the acquisition of speed skill. *Ergonomics, 2,* 153–156.

Cucchiarini, C., Strik, H., & Boves, L. (2000). Quantitative assessment of second language learners' fluency by means of automatic speech recognition technology. *Journal of the Acoustical Society of America, 107,* 989–999.

Cucchiarini, C., Strik, H., & Boves, L. (2002). Quantitative assessment of second language learners' fluency: Comparisons between read and spontaneous speech. *Journal of the Acoustical Society of America, 111,* 2862–2873.

Cutler, A., & Clifton, C., Jr. (1999). Comprehending spoken language: A blueprint of the listener. In C. Brown and P. Hagoort (Eds.), *The neurocognition of language* (pp. 123–166). Oxford, UK: Oxford University Press.

De Bleser, R., Dupont, P., Postler, J., Bormans, G., Speelman, D., Mortelmans, L., & Debrock, M. (2003). The organization of the bilingual lexicon: A PET study. *Journal of Neurolinguistics, 16,* 439–456.

De Bot, K. (1992). A bilingual production model: Levelt's "Speaking" model adapted. *Applied Linguistics, 13,* 1–24.

De Bot, K., Lowie, W., & Verspoor, M. (2007). A dynamic systems theory approach to second language acquisition. *Bilingualism: Language and Cognition, 10,* 7–21.

De Jong, N. H., Schoonen, R., & Hulstijn, J. (2009). *Fluency in L2 is related to fluency in L1.* Paper presented at the Seventh International Symposium on Bilingualism (ISB7), Utrecht, The Netherlands.

De Jong, N. H., Steinel, M. P., Florijn, A. F., Schoonen, R., & Hulstijn, J. H. (2007). The effect of task complexity on fluency and functional adequacy of speaking performance. In S. Van Daele, A. Housen, M. Pierrard, F. Kuiken, & I. Vedder (Eds.), *Complexity, accuracy and fluency in second language use, learning and teaching* (pp. 53–63). Brussels: Koninklijke Vlaamse Academie van België voor Wetenschappen en Kunsten.

De Jong, N. H., & Wempe, T. (2009). Praat script to detect syllable nuclei and measure speech rate automatically. *Behavior Research Methods, 41,* 385–390.

Dechert, H. W. (1980) Pause and intonation as indicators of verbal planning in second-language speech productions: Two examples from a case study. In H. W. Dechert & M. Raupach (Eds.), *Temporal variables in speech: Studies in honour of Frieda Goldman-Eisler* (pp. 271–285). The Hague: Mouton.

Dechert, H. W. (1984). Second language production: Six hypotheses. In H.W. Dechert, D. Möhle, & M. Raupach (Eds.), *Second language productions* (pp. 211–230). Tübingen, Germany: Gunter Narr Verlag.

Dechert, H. W., Möhle, D., & Raupach, M. (Eds.) (1984). *Second language productions.* Tübingen, Germany: Gunter Narr Verlag.

Dechert, H. W., & Raupach, M. (Eds.) (1987). *Psycholinguistic models of production.* Norwood, NJ: Ablex Publishing Corporation.

DeKeyser, R. M. (1997). Beyond explicit rule learning: Automatizing second language morphosyntax. *Studies in Second Language Acquisition, 19,* 195–222.

DeKeyser, R. M. (2001). Automaticity and automatization. In P. Robinson (Ed.), *Cognition and second language instruction* (pp. 125–151). Cambridge, UK: Cambridge University Press.

DeKeyser, R. M. (2003). Implicit and explicit learning. In C. Doughty & M. Long (Eds.), *Handbook of second language acquisition* (pp. 314–348). Oxford, UK: Blackwell.

DeKeyser, R. M. (Ed.) (2007a). *Practice in a second language: Perspectives from applied linguistics and cognitive psychology.* Cambridge, UK: Cambridge University Press.

DeKeyser, R. M. (2007b). Introduction: Situating the concept of practice. In R. M. DeKeyser (Ed.), *Practice in a second language: Perspectives from applied linguistics and cognitive psychology* (pp. 1–13). Cambridge, UK: Cambridge University Press.

DeKeyser, R. M. (2007c). Conclusion: The future of practice. In R. M. DeKeyser (Ed.), *Practice in a second language: Perspectives from applied linguistics and cognitive psychology* (pp. 287–304). Cambridge, UK: Cambridge University Press.

Derwing, T., Rossiter, M., Munro, M., & Thomson, R. (2004). Second language fluency: Judgments on different tasks. *Language Learning, 54,* 655–679.

Derwing, T., Thomson, R., & Munro, M. (2006). English pronunciation and fluency development in Mandarin and Slavic speakers. *System, 34,* 183–193.

Dewaele, J.-M., Housen, A., & Wei, L. (2003). Introduction and overview. In J.-M. Dewaele, A. Housen, & L. Wei (Eds.), *Bilingualism: Beyond basic principles* (pp. 1–9). Clevedon: Multilingual Matters.

Dijkstra, T., & Van Heuven, W. (1998). The BIA model and bilingual word recognition. In J. Grainger & A. Jacobs (Eds.), *Localist connectionist approaches to human cognition* (pp. 189–225). Mahwah, NJ: Lawrence Erlbaum Associates.

Dijkstra, T., & Van Heuven, W. (2002). The architecture of the bilingual word recognition system: From identification to decision. *Bilingualism: Language and Cognition, 5,* 175–197.

Dil, A. (1972). Introduction. In W. E. Lambert, *Language, psychology and culture: Essays by Wallace E. Lambert.* Stanford, CA: Stanford University Press.

Dörnyei, Z. (2005). *The psychology of the language learner: Individual differences in second language acquisition.* Mahwah, NJ: Lawrence Erlbaum Associates.

Dörnyei, Z. (2009a). *The psychology of second language acquisition.* Oxford, UK: Oxford University Press.

Dörnyei, Z. (2009b). The L2 motivational self system. In Z. Dörnyei & E. Ushioda (Eds.), *Motivation, language identity and the L2 Self* (pp. 9–42). Bristol, UK: Multilingual Matters.

Dörnyei, Z., Csizér, K, & Németh, N. (2006). *Motivation, language attitudes and globalization: A Hungarian perspective.* Clevedon: Multilingual Matters.

Dörnyei, Z., & Kormos, J. (1998). Problem-solving mechanisms in L2 communication: A psycholinguistic perspective. *Studies in Second Language Acquisition, 20,* 349–385.

Dörnyei, Z., & Scott, M.L. (1997). Communication strategies in a second language: Definitions and taxonomies. *Language Learning, 47,* 173–210.

Dörnyei, Z., & Ushioda, E. (Eds.) (2009). *Motivation, language identity and the L2 Self.* Bristol, UK: Multilingual Matters.

Doughty, C. (2001). Cognitive underpinnings of focus on form. In P. Robinson (Ed.), *Cognition and second language instruction* (pp. 206–257). Cambridge, UK: Cambridge University Press.

Doughty, C., & Williams, J. (Eds.) (1998). *Focus on form in classroom second language acquisition.* Cambridge, UK: Cambridge University Press.

Elliott, D., & Lyons, J. (1998). In Jan P. Piek (Ed.), *Motor behavior and human skill: A multidisciplinary approach* (pp. 57–72). Champaign, IL: Human Kinetics.

Elliott, D., Lyons, J., & Dyson, K. (1997). Rescaling an acquired discrete aiming movement: Specific or general motor learning. *Human Movement Science, 16,* 81–96.

Ellinger, B. (2000). The relationship between ethnolinguistic identity and English language achievement for native Russian speakers and native Hebrew speakers in Israel. *Journal of Multilingual and Multicultural Development, 21,* 292–307.

Ellis, N. C. (1994). *Implicit and explicit learning of languages.* New York: Academic Press.

Ellis, N. C. (1998). Emergentism, connectionism and language learning. *Language Learning, 48,* 631–664.

Ellis, N. C. (2002). Frequency effects in language processing: A review with implications for theories of implicit and explicit language acquisition. *Studies in Second Language Acquisition, 24,* 143–188.

Ellis, N. C. (2003). Constructions, chunking, and connectionism: The emergence of second language structure. In C. Doughty & M. Long (Eds.), *Handbook of second language acquisition* (pp. 63–103). Oxford, UK: Blackwell.

Ellis, N. C. (2007). Dynamic systems and SLA: The wood and the trees. *Bilingualism: Language and Cognition, 10,* 23–25.

Ellis, N. C. (2008). Usage-based and form-focused language acquisition: The associative learning of constructions, learned attention, and the limited L2 endstate. In P. Robinson & N. C. Ellis (Eds.), *Handbook of cognitive linguistics and second language acquisition* (pp. 372–405). New York: Routledge.

Ellis, N. C., & Ferreira, Jr., F. (2009). Construction learning as a function of frequency, frequency distribution, and function. *Modern Language Journal, 93,* 370–385.

Ellis, N. C., & Schmidt, R. (1997). Morphology and longer distance dependencies: Laboratory research illuminating the A in SLA. *Studies in Second Language Acquisition, 19,* 145–171.

Ellis, R. (Ed.) (2005). *Planning and task performance in a second language.* Amsterdam: John Benjamins.

Ellis, R., & Barkhuizen, G. (2005). *Analysing learner language.* Oxford, UK: Oxford University Press.

Ellis, R., Loewen, S., Elder, C., Erlam, R., Philp, J., & Reinders, H. (2009). *Implicit and explicit knowledge in second language learning, testing and teaching*. Bristol: Multilingual Matters.

Ellis, R., & Yuan, F. (2005). The effects of careful within-task planning on oral and written task performance. In R. Ellis (Ed.), *Planning and task performance in a second language* (pp. 167–192). Amsterdam: John Benjamins.

Ericsson, K. A., Krampe, R. T., & Tesch-Romer, C. (1993). The role of deliberate practice in the acquisition of expert performance. *Psychological Review, 100*, 363–406.

Evans, V., & Green, M. (2006). *Cognitive linguistics: An introduction*. Mahwah, NJ: Lawrence Erlbaum Associates.

Faisal, A., Selen, L., & Wolpert, D. (2008). Noise in the nervous system. *Nature Reviews Neuroscience, 9*, 292–303.

Fan, J., McCandliss, B., Sommer, T., Raz, A., & Posner, M. (2002). Testing the efficiency and independence of attentional networks. *Journal of Cognitive Neuroscience, 14*, 340–347.

Farris, C., Trofimovich, P., Segalowitz, N., & Gatbonton, E. (2008). Air traffic communication in a second language: Implications of cognitive factors for training and assessment. *TESOL Quarterly, 42*, 397–410.

Fauconnier, G. (1994). *Mental spaces*. Cambridge, UK: Cambridge University Press.

Fauconnier, G. (1997). *Mappings in thought and language*. Cambridge, UK: Cambridge University Press.

Favreau, M., & Segalowitz, N. (1983). Automatic and controlled processes in the first and second language reading of fluent bilinguals. *Memory & Cognition, 11*, 565–574.

Feltovich, P. J., Spiro, R. J., & Coulson, R. L. (1997). Issues of expert flexibility in contexts characterized by complexity and change. In P. J. Feltovich, K. M. Ford, & R. R. Hoffman (Eds.), *Expertise in context* (pp. 125–146). Cambridge, MA: MIT Press.

Ferguson, C. (1975). Towards a characterization of English foreigner talk. *Anthropological Linguistics, 17*, 1–14.

Fillmore, C. (1979). On fluency. In C. Fillmore, D. Kempler, & W. S.-Y. Wang (Eds.) (1979), *Individual differences in language ability and language behavior* (pp. 85–101). New York: Academic Press.

Finkbeiner, M., Almeida, J., Janssen, N., & Caramazza, A. (2006). Lexical selection in bilingual speech production does not involve language suppression. *Journal of Experimental Psychology: Learning, Memory and Cognition, 32*, 1075–1089.

Fischler, I. (1998). Attention and language. In R. Parasuaraman (Ed.), *The attentive brain* (pp. 381–399). Cambridge, MA: MIT Press.

Fishman, J. (1967) Bilingualism with and without diglossia; diglossia with and without bilingualism. *Journal of Social Issues, 23*, 29–38.

Flege, J. E. (1995). Second-language speech learning: Theory, findings, and problems. In W. Strange (Ed.), *Speech perception and linguistic experience: Issues in cross-language research* (pp. 229–273). Timonium, MD: York Press.

Foster, P., Tonkyn, A., & Wigglesworth, G. (2000). Measuring spoken language: A unit for all reasons. *Applied Linguistics, 21*, 354–375.

Fox Tree, J. (2001). Listeners' uses of um and uh in speech comprehension. *Memory and Cognition, 29,* 320–326.

Fox Tree, J. (2002). Interpreting pauses and ums at turn exchanges. *Discourse Processes, 34,* 37–55.

Freed, B. (1995). What makes us think that students who study abroad become fluent? In B. Freed (Ed.), *Second language acquisition in a study abroad context* (pp. 123–148). Amsterdam: John Benjamins.

Freed, B. (2000). Is fluency, like beauty, in the eyes (and ears) of the beholder? In H. Riggenbach (Ed.), *Perspectives on fluency* (pp. 243–265). Ann Arbor: University of Michigan Press.

Freed, B. F., Segalowitz, N., & Dewey, D. (2004). Context of learning and second language fluency in French: Comparing regular classroom, study abroad, and intensive domestic immersion programs. *Studies in Second Language Acquisition, 26,* 275–301.

French, R. M. (1998). A simple recurrent network model of bilingual memory. In M. A. Gernsbacher & S. J. Derry (Eds.), *Proceedings of the 20th Annual Conference of the Cognitive Science Society* (pp. 368–373). Mahwah, NJ: Lawrence Erlbaum Associates.

Fulcher, G. (1996). Does thick description lead to smart tests? A data-based approach to rating scale construction. *Language Testing, 13,* 208–238.

Fulcher, G. (2003). *Testing second language speaking.* London: Longman.

Gallagher, H. L., & Frith, C. (2003). Functional imaging of "theory of mind." *Trends in Cognitive Sciences, 7,* 77–83.

Gardner, R. C. (1985). *Social psychology and second language learning: The role of attitudes and motivation.* London: Edward Arnold.

Gardner, R. C. (2001). Integrative motivation and second language acquisition. In Z. Dörnyei and R. Schmidt (Eds.), *Motivation and second language acquisition* (pp. 1–20). Honolulu: University of Hawaii Press.

Gardner, R. C., & Lambert, W. E. (1972). *Attitudes and motivation in second language learning.* Rowley, MA: Newbury House.

Garrod, S., & Pickering, M. J. (2007). Automaticity of language production in monologue and dialogue. In A. S. Meyer, L. R. Wheeldon, & A. Krott, (Eds.), *Automaticity and control in language processing* (pp. 1–20). New York: Psychology Press.

Gass, S. (1997). *Input, interaction, and the second language learner.* Mahwah, NJ: Lawrence Erlbaum Associates.

Gasser, M. (1990). Connectionism and universals of second language acquisition. *Studies in Second Language Acquisition, 12,* 179–199.

Gatbonton, E. (1978). Patterned phonetic variability in second-language speech: A gradual diffusion model. *Canadian Modern Language Review, 34,* 335–347.

Gatbonton, P. (2009, August 28). Personal communication.

Gatbonton, E., & Segalowitz, N. (1988). Creative automatization: Principles for promoting fluency within a communicative framework. *TESOL Quarterly, 22,* 473–492.

Gatbonton, E., & Segalowitz, N. (2005). Rethinking communicative language teaching: A focus on access to fluency. *Canadian Modern Language Review, 61,* 325–353.

Gatbonton, E., & Trofimovich, P. (2008). The ethnic group affiliation and L2 proficiency link: Empirical evidence. *Language Awareness, 17,* 229–248.

Gatbonton, E., Trofimovich, P., & Magid, M. (2005). Learners' ethnic group affiliation and L2 pronunciation accuracy: A sociolinguistic investigation. *TESOL Quarterly, 39*, 489–511.

Gatbonton, E., Trofimovich, P., & Segalowitz, N. (2007). *Language and identity: Does ethnic group affiliation affect L2 performance?* Paper presented at the Sixth International Symposium on Bilingualism (ISB6). Hamburg, Germany.

Gibson, E. J., & Pick, A. D. (2000). *An ecological approach to perceptual learning and development.* Oxford, UK: Oxford University Press.

Gibson, J. J. (1977). Towards a theory of affordances. In R. Shaw & J. Bransford (Eds.), *Perceiving, acting and knowing* (pp. 67–82). Hillsdale, NJ: Lawrence Erlbaum Associates.

Goldberg, A. (1995). *Constructions: A construction grammar approach to argument structure.* Chicago: University of Chicago Press.

Goldberg, A. (2006). *Constructions at work: The nature of generalization in language.* Oxford, UK: Oxford University Press.

Goldman-Eisler, F. (1951). The measurement of time sequences in conversational behaviour. *British Journal of Psychology, 42*, 355–362.

Goldman-Eisler, F. (1961). Hesitation and information in speech. In C. Cherry (Ed.), *Information theory* (pp. 162–174). London: Butterworths.

Goldman-Eisler, F. (1968). *Psycholinguistics experiments in spontaneous speech.* London: Academic Press.

Goldman-Eisler, F. (1972). Pauses, clauses, sentences. *Language and speech, 15*, 103–113.

Goldschneider, J., & DeKeyser, R. (2001). Explaining the "natural order of L2 morpheme acquisition" in English: A meta-analysis of multiple determinants. *Language Learning, 51*, 1–50.

Golestani, N., Alario, F.-A., Meriaux, S., Le Bihan, D., Dehaene, S., & Pallier, C. (2006). Syntax production in bilinguals. *Neuropsychologia, 44*, 1029–1040.

Green, D. (1998). Mental control of the bilingual lexico-semantic system. *Bilingualism: Language and Cognition, 1*, 67–81.

Green, D. (Guest Ed.) (2001). Special issue: The cognitive neuroscience of bilingualism. *Bilingualism: Language and Cognition, 4*(2).

Greeno, J. G. (1994). Gibson's affordances. *Psychological Review, 101*, 336–342.

Gregg, M., & Hall, C. (2006). Measurement of motivational imagery abilities in sport. *Journal of Sport Sciences, 24*, 961–971.

Grosjean, F. (1980a). Linguistic structures and performance structures: Studies in pause distribution. In H. W. Dechert & M. Raupach, (Eds.), *Temporal variables in speech: Studies in honour of Frieda Goldman-Eisler* (pp. 91–106). The Hague: Mouton.

Grosjean, F. (1980b). Temporal variables within and between languages. In H. W. Dechert & M. Raupach, (Eds.), *Towards a cross-linguistic assessment of speech production* (pp. 39–53). Frankfurt: Lang.

Gullberg, M., & Indefrey, P. (Eds.) (2006). *The cognitive neuroscience of second language acquisition.* Oxford, UK: Blackwell.

Gumperz, J. (1972). Sociolinguistics and communication in small groups. In J. B. Pride & J. Holmes (Eds.), *Sociolinguistics* (pp. 203–224). Middlesex, UK: Penguin Books.

Gumperz, J., & Hymes, D. (Eds.) (1972). *Directions in sociolinguistics: The ethnography of communication.* New York: Holt, Rinehart and Winston.

Haier, R., Siegel, B., MacLachlan, A., Soderling, E., Lottenberg, S., & Buchsbaum, M. (1992). Regional glucose metabolic changes after learning a complex visuospatial/motor task: A positron emission tomographic study. *Brain Research, 570,* 134–143.

Haier, R., Siegel, B., Neuchterlein, K., Hazlett, E., Wu, J., Paek, J., Browning, H., & Muchsbaum, M. (1988). Cortical glucose metabolic rate correlates of abstract reasoning and attention studied with positron emission tomography. *Intelligence, 12,* 199–217.

Halliday, M. A. K. (1973). *Explorations in the functions of language.* London: Edward Arnold.

Healy, A. F., Barshi, I., & Crutcher, R. J., et al. (1998). Toward the improvement of training in foreign languages. In A. F. Healy & L. E. Bourne, Jr. (Eds.), *Foreign language learning* (pp. 3–53). Mahwah, NJ: Lawrence Erlbaum Associates.

Heaton, J.B. (1966/1995). *Composition through pictures.* Essex, UK: Longman.

Heft, H. (2003). Affordances, dynamic experience, and the challenge of reification. *Ecological Psychology, 15,* 149–180.

Henderson, A., Goldman-Eisler, F., & Skarbek, A. (1966). Sequential patterns in spontaneous speech. *Language and Speech, 9,* 207–216.

Herdina, P., & Jessner, U. (2002). *A dynamic model of multilingualism.* Clevedon, UK: Multilingual Matters.

Hernandez, A., Li, P., & MacWhinney, B. (2005). The emergence of competing modules in bilingualism. *TRENDS in Cognitive Sciences, 9,* 220–225.

Hieke, A. (1985). A componential approach to oral fluency evaluation. *Modern Language Journal, 69,* 135–142.

Higgins, E. (1987). Self-discrepancy: A theory relating self and affect. *Psychological Review, 94,* 319–340.

Higgins, E. (1996). The "self-digest": Self-knowledge serving self-regulatory functions. *Journal of Personality and Social Psychology, 71,* 1062–1083.

House, J. (1996). Developing pragmatic fluency in English as a foreign language: Routines and metapragmatic awareness. *Studies in Second Language Acquisition, 18,* 225–252.

Howard, V. A. (2008). *Charm and speed: Virtuosity in the performing arts.* New York: Peter Lang.

Hull, R., & Vaid, J. (2005). Clearing the cobwebs from the study of the bilingual brain: Converging evidence from laterality and electrophysiological research. In J. Kroll & A. De Groot (Eds.), *Handbook of bilingualism: Psycholinguistic approaches* (pp. 480–496). Oxford, UK: Oxford University Press.

Hulstijn, J. H. (2001). Intentional and incidental second-language vocabulary learning: A reappraisal of elaboration, rehearsal and automaticity. In P. Robinson (Ed.), *Cognition and second language instruction* (pp. 258–286). Cambridge, UK: Cambridge University Press.

Hulstijn, J. H. (2005). Theoretical and empirical issues in the study of implicit and explicit second-language learning: Introduction. *Studies in Second Language Acquisition, 27,* 129–140.

Hultsch, D., & MacDonald, S. (2004). Intraindividual variability in performance as a theoretical window onto cognitive aging. In R. Dixon, L. Bäckman, &

L. Nilsson (Eds.), *New frontiers in cognitive aging* (pp. 65–88). Oxford, UK: Oxford University Press.

Hultsch, D., MacDonald, S., & Dixon, R. (2002). Variability in reaction time performance of younger and older adults. *Journal of Gerontology: Psychological Sciences, 57B*, P101–P115.

Hultsch, D., MacDonald, S., Hunter, M., Levy-Bencheton, J., & Strauss, E. (2000). Intraindividual variability in cognitive performance in older adults: Comparison of adults with mild dementia, adults with arthritis, and healthy adults. *Neuropsychology, 14*, 588–598.

Hymes, D. (1967). Models of the interaction of language and social setting. *Journal of Social Issues, 23*, 8–28.

Hymes, D. (1972). On communicative competence. In J. B. Pride & J. Holmes (Eds.), *Sociolinguistics* (pp. 269–293). Harmondsworth, UK: Penguin Books.

International Civil Aviation Organization. (2004a). *Manual on the implementation of ICAO language proficiency requirements.* (Doc 9835 AN/453) Montreal, Quebec, Canada. Available from http://caa.gateway.bg/upload/docs/9835_1_ed.pdf. Downloaded September 5, 2009.

International Civil Aviation Organization. (2004b). *The Second Meeting of the Regional Airspace Safety Monitoring Advisory Group* (RASMAG/2–IP/3–4/10/04). Bangkok, Thailand. Available from http://www.icao.int/icao/en/ro/apac/2004/rasmag2/ip03.pdf. Downloaded September 6, 2009.

Iwashita, N., Brown, A., McNamara, T., & O'Hagan, S. (2008). Assessed levels of second language speaking proficiency: How distinct? *Applied Linguistics, 29*, 24–49.

Iwashita, N., McNamara, T., & Elder, C. (2001). Can we predict task difficulty in an oral proficiency test? Exploring the potential of an information-processing approach to task design. *Language Learning, 51*, 401–436.

James, W. (1890/1950). *The principles of psychology*, Vol. 1. New York: Dover Publications.

Johnson, K. (1996). *Language teaching and skill learning.* Oxford, UK: Blackwell.

Johnson, M., & Tyler, A. (1998). Re-analysing the OPI: How much does it look like natural conversation? In R. Young & A. Weiyun He (Eds.), *Talking and testing: Discourse approaches to the assessment of oral proficiency* (pp. 27–51). Amsterdam: John Benjamins.

Jones, K.S. (2003). What is an affordance? *Ecological Psychology, 15*, 107–114.

Kaponen, M., & Riggenbach, H. (2000). Overview: Varying perspectives on fluency. In H. Riggenbach (Ed.), *Perspectives on fluency* (pp. 5–24). Ann Arbor: University of Michigan Press.

Kasper, G., & Rose, K. (1999). Pragmatics and SLA. *Annual Review of Applied Linguistics, 19*, 81–104.

Kauffman, S. (1993). *The origins of order: Self organization in selection and evolution.* Oxford, UK: Oxford University Press.

Kim, K., Relkin, N., Lee, K., & Hirsch, J. (1997). Distinct cortical areas associated with native and second languages. *Nature, 388*, 171–174.

Kolers, P. (1973). Remembering operations. *Memory & Cognition, 1*, 347–355.

Kolers, P. (1979). A pattern-analyzing basis of recognition. In L. Cermak & F. I. M. Craik (Eds.), *Levels of processing in human memory* (pp. 363–384). Hillsdale, NJ: Lawrence Erlbaum Associates.

Kormos, J. (2000). The role of attention in monitoring second language speech production. *Language Learning, 50, 343–384.*

Kormos, J. (2006). *Speech production and second language acquisition.* Mahwah, NJ: Lawrence Erlbaum Associates.

Kormos, J., & Dénes, M. (2004). Exploring measures and perceptions of fluency in the speech of second language learners. *System, 32,* 145–164.

Kotz, S., & Elston-Gütler, K. (2004). The role of proficiency on processing categorical and associative information in the L2 as revealed by reaction times and event-related brain potentials. *Journal of Neurolinguistics, 17,* 215–235.

Krashen, S. (1985). *The input hypothesis: Issues and implications.* New York: Longman.

Kroll, J. F., & de Groot, A. M. B. (Eds.) (2005). *Handbook of bilingualism: Psycholinguistic approaches.* Oxford, UK: Oxford University Press.

Kroll, J. F., & Stewart, E. (1994). Category interference in translation and picture naming: Evidence for asymmetric connection between bilingual memory representations. *Journal of Memory and Language, 33,* 149–174.

Kroll, J. F., & Tokowicz, N. (2005). Models of bilingual representation and processing: Looking back and to the future. In J. Kroll & A. M. B. de Groot (Eds.), *Handbook of bilingualism: Psycholinguistic perspectives* (pp. 531–553). New York: Oxford University Press.

Kutas, M., & Dale, A. (1997). Electrical and magnetic readings of mental functions. In M. Rugg (Ed.), *Cognitive Neuroscience* (pp. 197–242). Cambridge, MA: MIT Press.

Kutas, M., Federmeier, D., & Sereno, M. (1999). Current approaches to mapping language in electromagnetic space. In C. Brown and P. Hagoort (Eds.), *The neurocognition of language* (pp. 359–392). Oxford, UK: Oxford University Press.

La Heij, W. (2005). Selection processes in monolingual and bilingual lexical access. In J. Kroll & A. M. B. de Groot (Eds.), *Handbook of bilingualism: Psycholinguistic perspectives* (pp. 289–307). New York: Oxford University Press.

LaBerge, D., & Samuels, J. (1974). Toward a theory of automatic information processing in reading. *Cognitive Psychology, 6,* 293–323.

Labov, W. (1970). The study of language in its social context. *Studium Generale, 23,* 30–87. Reprinted in J. B. Pride & J. Holmes, (Eds.) (1972), *Sociolinguistics* (pp. 180–202). Harmondsworth, UK: Penguin.

Lambert, W. E. (1967). A social psychology of bilingualism. *Journal of Social Issues, 23,* 91–103.

Langacker, R. W. (1987). *Foundations of cognitive grammar,* Vol. 1, *Theoretical prerequisites.* Stanford: Stanford University Press.

Langacker, R. W. (1991). *Foundations of cognitive grammar,* Vol. 2, *Descriptive application.* Stanford: Stanford University Press.

Langacker, R.W. (2008). Cognitive grammar as a basis for language instruction. In P. Robinson & N. Ellis (Eds.), *Handbook of cognitive linguistics and second language acquisition* (pp. 66–88). New York: Routledge.

Lantolf, J., & Thorne, S. (2006). *Sociocultural theory and the genesis of second language development.* Oxford, UK: Oxford University Press.

Lantolf, J., & Thorne, S. (2007). Sociocultural theory and second language learning. In B. VanPatten & J. Williams (Eds.), *Theories in second language acquisition* (pp. 201–224). Mahwah, NJ: Lawrence Erlbaum Associates.

Larsen-Freeman, D., & Cameron, L. (2008). *Complex systems and applied linguistics*. Oxford, UK: Oxford University Press.

Laufer, B. (2005). Lexical frequency profiles: From Monte Carlo to the Real World. *Applied Linguistics, 26*, 582–588.

Lennon, P. (1984). Retelling a story in English as a second language. In H. W. Dechert, D. Möhle, & M. Raupach (Eds.), *Second language productions* (pp. 50–68). Tübingen, Germany: Gunter Narr Verlag.

Lennon, P. (1990). Investigating fluency in EFL: A quantitative approach. *Language Learning, 40*, 387–417.

Leow, R. (2007). Input in the L2 classroom: An attentional perspective on respective practice. In R. DeKeyser (Ed.), *Practice in a second language* (pp. 21–50). Cambridge, UK: Cambridge University Press.

Levelt, W. (1989). *Speaking: From intention to articulation*. Cambridge, MA: MIT Press.

Levelt, W. (1999). Producing spoken language: A blueprint of the speaker. In C. Brown and P. Hagoort (Eds.), *The neurocognition of language* (pp. 83–122). Oxford, UK: Oxford University Press.

Levelt, W., Roelofs, A., & Meyer, A. (1999). A theory of lexical access in speech production. *Behavioral and Brain Sciences, 22*, 1–75.

Léwy, N., & Grosjean, F. (1997). A computational model of bilingual lexical access. Manuscript in preparation, Neuchâtel University, Switzerland.

Li, P., & Farkas, I. (2002). A self-organizing connectionist model of bilingual processing. In R. Eherdia & J. Altarriba (Eds.), *Bilingual sentence processing*. Amsterdam: Elsevier.

Lieven, E., & Tomasello, M. (2008). Children's first language acquisition from a usage-based perspective. In P. Robinson & N. C. Ellis (Eds.), *Handbook of cognitive linguistics and second language acquisition* (pp. 168–196). New York: Routledge.

Lightbown, P. (2007). Transfer appropriate processing as a model for classroom second language acquisition. In Z. Han (Ed.), *Understanding second language process* (pp. 27–44). Clevedon: Multilingual Matters.

Lightbown, P., & Spada, N. (2006). *How languages are learned* (3rd edition). Oxford, UK: Oxford University Press.

Logan, G. (1988). Toward an instance theory of automatization. *Psychological Review, 95*, 492–527.

Logan, G. (1992). Shapes of reaction time distributions and shapes of learning curves: A test of instance theory of automaticity. *Journal of Experimental Psychology: Learning, Memory, and Cognition, 18*, 883–914.

Long, M. (1983). Native speaker/non-native speaker conversation and the negotiation of comprehensible input. *Applied Linguistics, 4*, 126–141.

Long, M. (2003). Stabilization and fossilization in interlanguage development. In C. Doughty & M. Long (Eds.), *Handbook of second language acquisition* (pp. 487–435). Oxford, UK: Blackwell.

Long, M., & Robinson, P. (1998). Focus on form: Theory, research, and practice. In C. Doughty & J. Williams (Eds.), *Focus on form in classroom second language acquisition* (pp. 15–41). New York: Cambridge University Press.

Luoma, S. (2004). *Assessing speaking*. Cambridge, MA: Cambridge University Press.

Luria, A.R. (1973). *The making of mind*. Cambridge, MA: Harvard University Press.

Luria, A.R. (1980). *Higher cortical functions in man* (2nd edition) (original Russian version, 1962). New York: Basic Books.

MacKay, D. (1982). The problems of flexibility, fluency, and speed-accuracy trade-off in skilled behavior. *Psychological Review, 89,* 483–506.

Mackey, A. (2007a). Interaction as practice. In R. M. DeKeyser (Ed.), *Practice in a second language* (pp. 85–110). Cambridge, UK: Cambridge University Press.

Mackey, A. (Ed.) (2007b). *Conversational interaction in second language acquisition.* Oxford, UK: Oxford University Press.

MacWhinney, B. (1997). Second language acquisition and the competition model. In A. M. B. de Groot & J. Kroll (Eds.), *Tutorials in bilingualism: Psycholinguistic perspectives* (pp. 113–144). Hillsdale, NJ: Lawrence Erlbaum Associates.

MacWhinney, B. (2008). A unified model. In P. Robinson & N. Ellis (Eds.), *Handbook of cognitive linguistics and second language acquisition* (pp. 341–371). New York: Routledge.

Marian, V., & Spivey, M. (2003). Competing activation in bilingual language processing: Within- and between-language competition. *Bilingualism: Language and Cognition, 6,* 97–115.

Markus, H., & Nurius, P. (1986). Possible selves. *American Psychologist, 41,* 954–969.

Markus, H., & Ruvolo, A. (1989). Possible selves: Personalized representations of goals. In L. A. Pervin (Ed.), *Goal concepts in personality and social psychology* (pp. 211–241). Hillsdale, NJ: Lawrence Erlbaum Associates.

Martin, J. G. (1972). Rhythmic (hierarchical) versus serial structure in speech and other behavior. *Psychological Review, 79,* 487–509.

Mayer, M. (1969). *Frog, where are you?* New York: Dial Press.

McClelland, J. L. (1989). Parallel distributed processing: Implications for cognition and development. In R. G. M. Morris (Ed.), *Parallel distributed processing: Implications for psychology and neurobiology* (pp. 8–45). Oxford, UK: Oxford University Press.

McClelland, J. L., & Patterson, K. (2002). Rules or connections in past-tense inflections: What does the evidence rule out? *Trends in Cognitive Science, 6,* 465–472.

McDonough, K., & Trofimovich, P. (2009). *Using priming methods in second language research.* London: Routledge.

McGlone, M. S., & Tofighbakhsh, J. (2000). Birds of a feather flock conjointly(?): Rhyme as reason in aphorisms. *Psychological Science, 11,* 424–428.

McLaughlin, B., & Cohen, J. (Eds.) (2007). *Contemporary debates in philosophy of mind.* Oxford, UK: Blackwell.

McLaughlin, B., & Heredia, R. (1996). Information-processing approaches to research on second language acquisition and use. In W. C. Ritchie & T. K. Bhatia (Eds.), *Handbook of second language acquisition* (pp. 213–228). New York: Academic Press.

McLaughlin, B. P., Rossman, T., & McLeod, B. (1983). Second language learning: An information processing perspective. *Language Learning, 33,* 135–158.

McNamara, T. (1996). *Measuring second language performance.* London: Longman.

Meara, P. (1993). The bilingual lexicon and the teaching of vocabulary. In R. Schreuder & B. Weltens (Eds.), *The bilingual lexicon* (pp. 279–297). Amsterdam: John Benjamins.

Meara, P. (2004). Modelling vocabulary loss. *Applied Linguistics*, 25, 137–155.

Meara, P. (2006). Emergent properties of multilingual lexicons. *Applied Linguistics*, 27, 620–644.

Meara, P. (2007). Growing a vocabulary. *EUROSLA Yearbook*, 7(1), 49–65. Amsterdam: John Benjamins.

Meara, P. (2009, April 8). Personal communication.

Mehnert, U. (1998). The effects of different lengths of time for planning on second language performance. *Studies in Second Language Acquisition*, 20, 83–108.

Meisel, J. (1987). A note of second language speech production. In H.W. Dechert & M. Raupach (Eds.), *Psycholinguistic models of production* (pp. 83–90). Norwood, NJ: Ablex Publishing Corporation.

Meuter, R. (2005). Language selection in bilinguals: mechanisms and processes. In J. Kroll & A. De Groot (Eds.), *Handbook of bilingualism: Psycholinguistic approaches* (pp. 349–370). Oxford, UK: Oxford University Press.

Meuter, R., & Allport, A. (1999). Bilingual language switching in naming: Asymmetrical costs in language selection. *Journal of Memory and Language*, 40, 25–40.

Meyer, A. S., Wheeldon, L. R., & Krott, A. (Eds.) (2007). *Automaticity and control in language processing*. New York: Psychology Press.

Mezynski, K. (1983). Issues concerning the acquisition of knowledge: Effects of vocabulary training on reading comprehension. *Review of Educational Research*, 53, 253–279.

Michael, E., & Gollan, T. (2005). Being and becoming bilingual: Individual differences and consequences for language production. In J. Kroll & A. De Groot (Eds.), *Handbook of bilingualism: Psycholinguistic approaches* (pp. 389–407). Oxford, UK: Oxford University Press.

Michaels, C. F. (2003). Affordances: Four points of debate. *Ecological Psychology*, 15, 135–148.

Miyake, A., & Friedman, N. P. (1998). Individual differences in second language proficiency: working memory as language aptitude. In A. Healy & L. E. Bourne, Jr. (Eds.), *Foreign language learning: Psycholinguistic studies on training and retention* (pp. 339–364). Mahwah, NJ: Lawrence Erlbaum Associates.

Möhle, D. (1984). A comparison of the second language speech production of different native speakers. In H. W. Dechert, D. Möhle, & M. Raupach (Eds.), *Second language productions* (pp. 26–49). Tübingen, Germany: Gunter Narr Verlag.

Moors, A., & De Houwer, J. (2006). Automaticity: A theoretical and conceptual analysis. *Psychological Bulletin*, 132, 297–326.

Morris, C. D., Bransford, J. D., & Franks, J. J. (1977). Level of processing versus transfer appropriate processing. *Journal of Verbal Learning and Verbal Behavior*, 16, 519–533.

Munro, M. J., & Derwing, T. M. (2001). Modeling perceptions of the accentedness and comprehensibility of L2 speech: The role of speaking rate. *Studies in Second Language Acquisition*, 23, 451–468.

Muranoi, H. (2007). Output practice in the L2 classroom. In R. DeKeyser (Ed.), *Practice in a second language* (pp. 51–84). Cambridge, UK: Cambridge University Press.

Nadasdi, T., Mougeon, R., & Rehner, K. (2005). Learning to speak everyday (Canadian) French. *Canadian Modern Language Review, 61,* 543–563.

Nairne, J. (2002). The myth of the encoding-retrieval match. *Memory, 10,* 389–395.

Nation, P. (1993). Vocabulary size, growth and use. In R. Schreuder & B. Weltens, (Eds.), *The bilingual lexicon* (pp. 115–134). Amsterdam: John Benjamins.

Nattinger, J., & Decarrico, J. (1992). *Lexical phrases and language teaching.* Oxford, UK: Oxford University Press.

Neely, J. (1977). Semantic priming and retrieval from lexical memory: Roles of inhibitionless spreading activation and limited-capacity attention. *Journal of Experimental Psychology: General, 106,* 226–254.

Newell, A., & Rosenbloom, P.S. (1981). Mechanisms of skill acquisition and the law of practice. In J. R. Anderson (Ed.), *Cognitive skills and their acquisition* (pp. 1–55). Hillsdale, NJ: Lawrence Erlbaum Associates.

Neville, H., Mills, D., & Lawson, D. (1992). Fractionating language: Different neural subsystems with different sensitive periods. *Cerebral Cortex, 2,* 244–258.

O'Brien, I., Segalowitz, N., Freed, B., & Collentine, J. (2007). Phonological memory predicts second language oral fluency gains in adults. *Studies in Second Language Acquisition, 29,* 557–582.

O'Grady, W. (2003). The radical middle: nativism without universal grammar. In C. Doughty & M. Long (Eds.), *Handbook of second language acquisition* (pp. 43–62). Oxford, UK: Blackwell.

Ojemann, G., & Whitaker, H. (1978). The bilingual brain. *Archives of Neurology, 35,* 409–412.

Oppenheimer, D. (2006). Consequences of erudite vernacular utilized irrespective of necessity: Problems with using long words needlessly. *Applied Cognitive Psychology, 20,* 139–156.

Ortega, L. (1999). Planning and focus on form in L2 oral performance. *Studies in Second Language Acquisition, 21,* 109–148.

Ortega, L. (2005). What do learners plan: Learner-driven attention to form during pre-task planning. In R. Ellis (Ed.), *Planning and task performance in a second language* (pp. 77–109). Amsterdam: John Benjamins.

Ortega, L. (2007). Meaningful L2 practice in foreign language classrooms: A cognitive-interactionist SLA perspective. In R. M. DeKeyser (Ed.), *Practice in a second language* (pp. 180–207). Cambridge, UK: Cambridge University Press.

Otten, L. J., & Rugg, M. D. (2001). Task-dependency of the neural correlates of episodic encoding as measured by fMRI. *Cerebral Cortex, 11,* 1150–1160.

Oxford, R. L. (2003). Toward a more systematic model of L2 learner autonomy. In D. Palfreyman & R. C. Smith (Eds.), *Learner autonomy across cultures: Language education perspectives* (pp. 75–91). Basingstoke, UK: Palgrave Macmillan.

Paradis, M. (Ed.) (1983). *Readings on aphasia in bilinguals and polyglots.* Montreal: Didier.

Paradis, M. (2004). *A neurolinguistic theory of bilingualism.* Amsterdam: John Benjamins.

Paradis, M. (2009). *Declarative and procedural determinants of second languages.* Amsterdam: John Benjamins.

Pashler, H. (1998). *The psychology of attention.* Cambridge, MA: MIT Press.

Pashler, H., Johnston, J., & Ruthruff, E. (2001). Attention and performance. *Annual Review of Psychology, 52,* 629–651.

Pavlenko, A. (2005). *Emotions and multilingualism.* New York: Cambridge University Press.

Pawley, A., & Syder, F. (1983). Two puzzles for linguistic theory: Nativelike selection and nativelike fluency. In J. Richards & R. Schmidt (Eds.), *Language and communication* (pp. 191–226). London: Longman.

Perani, D., Dehaene, S., Grassi, F., Cohen, L., Cappa, S., Dupoux, E., Fazio, F., & Mehler, J. (1996). Brain processing of native and foreign languages. *NeuroReport, 7,* 2439–2444.

Perani, D., Paulesu, E., Sebastian-Galles, N., Dupoux, E., Dehaene, S., Bettinardi, V., Cappa, S., Fazio, F., & Mehler, J. (1998). The bilingual brain: Proficiency and age of acquisition of the second language. *Brain, 121,*1841–1852.

Perfetti, C.A. (1999). Comprehending written language: a blueprint of the reader. In C. Brown and P. Hagoort (Eds.), *The neurocognition of language* (pp. 167–208). Oxford, UK: Oxford University Press.

Pienemann, M. (1999). *Language processing and second language development: Processability theory.* Amsterdam: John Benjamins.

Phillips, N., Segalowitz, N., O'Brien, I., & Yamasaki, N. (2004). Semantic priming in a first and second language: evidence from reaction time variability and event-related brain potentials. *Journal of Neurolinguistics, 17,* 237–262.

Pinker, S., & Ullman, M. (2002). The past and future of the past tense. *Trends in Cognitive Science, 6,* 456–463.

Pohl, R. (Ed.) (2006). *Cognitive illusions: A handbook on fallacies and biases in thinking, judgment and memory.* New York: Psychology Press.

Polanyi, M. (1962). *Personal knowledge.* Chicago: University of Chicago Press.

Polanyi, M., & Prosch, H. (1975). *Meaning.* Chicago: University of Chicago Press.

Pool, J. (1993). Linguistic exploitation. *International Journal of the Sociology of Language, 103,* 31–55.

Port, R. F. (2007). The problem of speech patterns in time. In M. G. Gaskell (Ed.), *The Oxford handbook of psycholinguistics* (pp. 503–514). Oxford, UK: Oxford University Press.

Port, R. F., & Van Gelder, T. (1995). *Mind as motion: Explorations in the dynamics of cognition.* Cambridge, MA: MIT Press.

Postma, A. (2000). Detection of errors and during speech production: a review of speech monitoring models. *Cognition, 77,* 97–131.

Poulton, E.C. (1957). On prediction in skilled movements. *Psychological Bulletin, 54,* 467–478.

Proctor, R. W., & Dutta, A. (1995). *Skill acquisition and human performance.* London: Sage.

Proteau, L. (1992). On the specificity of learning and the role of visual information for movement control. In L. Proteau & D. Elliott (Eds.), *Vision and motor control* (pp. 67–103). Amsterdam: Elsevier.

Pulvermüller, F., Birbaumer, N., Lutzenberger, W., & Mohr, B. (1997). High frequency brain activity: Its possible role in attention, perception and language processing. *Progress in Neurobiology, 52,* 427–445.

Quinlan, P., van der Maas, H., Jansen, B., Booij, O., & Rendell, M. (2007). Re-thinking stages of cognitive development: An appraisal of connectionist models of the balance scale task. *Cognition, 103*, 413–459.

Raichle, M., Fiez, J., Videen, T., MacLeod, A-M., Pardo, J., Fox, T., & Petersen, S. (1994). Practice-related changes in human brain functional anatomy during nonmotor learning. *Cerebral Cortex, 4*, 8–26.

Ranta, L., & Lyster, R. (2007). A cognitive approach to improving immersion students' oral language abilities: The awareness-practice-feedback sequence. In R. DeKeyser (Ed.), *Practice in a second language* (pp. 141–160). Cambridge, UK: Cambridge University Press.

Reber, R., Winkielman, P., & Schwarz, N. (1998). Effects of perceptual fluency on affective judgments. *Psychological Science, 9*, 45–48.

Rehbein, J. (1987). On fluency in second language speech. In H. W. Dechert & M. Raupach (Eds.), *Psycholinguistic models of production* (pp. 97–105). Norwood, NJ: Ablex Publishing Corporation.

Riggenbach, H. (1991). Toward an understanding of fluency: A microanalysis of non-native speaker conversations. *Discourse Process, 14*, 423–441.

Riggenbach, H. (Ed.) (2000). *Perspectives on fluency.* Ann Arbor: University of Michigan Press.

Roberts, B., & Kirsner, K. (2000). Temporal cycles in speech production. *Language and Cognitive Processes, 15*, 129–157.

Robinson, M. (2002). *Communication and health in a multi-ethnic society.* Bristol, UK: The Policy Press.

Robinson, P. (1995). Attention, memory and the "noticing" hypothesis. *Language Learning, 45*, 283–293.

Robinson, P. (1997). Generalizability and automaticity of second language learning under implicit, incidental, enhanced, and instructed conditions. *Studies in Second Language Acquisition, 19*, 223–247.

Robinson, P. (2001a). Task complexity, task difficulty, and task production: Exploring interactions in a componential framework. *Applied Linguistics, 22*, 27–57.

Robinson, P. (2001b). Task complexity, cognitive resources, and syllabus design: a triadic framework for examining task influences on SLA. In P. Robinson (Ed.), *Cognition and second language instruction* (pp. 287–318). Cambridge, UK: Cambridge University Press.

Robinson, P. (2002a). Learning conditions, aptitude complexes, and SLA: A framework for research and pedagogy. In P. Robinson, (Ed.), *Individual differences and instructed language learning* (pp. 113–133). Amsterdam: John Benjamins.

Robinson, P. (Ed.) (2002b). *Individual differences and instructed language learning.* Amsterdam: John Benjamins.

Robinson, P. (2003). Attention and memory during SLA. In C. Doughty & M. Long (Eds.), *The handbook of second language acquisition* (pp. 631–678). Oxford, UK: Blackwell.

Robinson, P., & Ellis, N. (Eds.) (2008). *Handbook of cognitive linguistics and second language acquisition.* London: Routledge.

Robinson, P., & Ha, M. (1993). Instance theory and second language rule learning under explicit conditions. *Studies in Second Language Acquisition, 15*, 413–438.

Roediger, H. L., Gallo, D. A., & Geraci, L. (2002). Processing approaches to cognition: the impetus from the levels of processing framework. *Memory, 10*, 319–332.

Roediger, H. L., & Guynn, M. J. (1996). Retrieval processes. In E. L. Bjork & R. A. Bjork (Eds.), *Memory* (pp. 197–236). New York: Academic Press.

Rogers, R., & Monsell, S. (1995). Costs of a predictable switch between simple and cognitive tasks. *Journal of Experimental Psychology: General, 124*, 207–231.

Rossiter, M. J., Derwing, T., & Jones, V. (2008). Is a picture worth a thousand words? *TESOL Quarterly, 42*, 325–329.

Rugg, M. D., Johnson, J. D., Park, H., & Uncapher, M. R. (2008). Encoding-retrieval overlap in human episodic memory: a functional neuroimaging perspective. In W. S. Sossin, J.-C. Lacaille, V. F. Castellucci, & S. Belleville (Eds.), *Progress in Brain Research*, Vol. 169 (pp. 339–352). Amsterdam: Elsevier.

Sachdev, I., & Giles, H. (2004). Bilingual accommodation. In W. C. Ritchie & T. K. Bhatia (Eds.), *Handbook of second language acquisition* (pp. 353–378). New York: Academic Press.

Sajavaara, K. (1987). Second language speech production: Factors affecting fluency. In H. W. Dechert & M. Raupach (Eds.), *Psycholinguistic models of production* (pp. 45–65). Norwood, NJ: Ablex Publishing Corporation.

Sanders, A. (1998). *Elements of human performance*. Mahwah, NJ: Lawrence Erlbaum Associates.

Scheffler, I. (1985). *Of human potential: An essay in the philosophy of education*. Boston: Routledge & Kegan Paul.

Schmid, M., Köpke, B., Keijzer, M., & Weilemar, L. (Eds.) (2004). *First language attrition: Interdisciplinary perspectives on methodological issues*. Amsterdam: John Benjamins.

Schmidt, R. (1992). Psychological mechanisms underlying second language fluency. *Studies in Second Language Acquisition, 14*, 357–385.

Schmidt, R. (1995). *Attention and awareness in foreign language learning*. Honolulu: University of Hawaii Press.

Schmidt, R. (2001). Attention. In P. Robinson (Ed.), *Cognition and second language instruction* (pp. 3–32). Cambridge, UK: Cambridge University Press.

Schmidt, R. A., & Lee, T. D. (2005). *Motor control and learning: A behavioral emphasis* (4th edition). Champaign, IL: Human Kinetics.

Schmitt, N. (Ed.) (2004). *Formulaic sequences*. Amsterdam: John Benjamins.

Schneider, W., & Chein, J. (2003). Controlled & automatic processing: behavior, theory, and biological mechanisms. *Cognitive Science, 27*, 525–559.

Schneider, W., Dumais, S., & Shiffrin, R. (1984). Automatic and control processing and attention. In R. Parasuraman (Ed.), *Varieties of attention* (pp. 1–27). New York: Academic Press.

Segalowitz, N. (1976). Communicative incompetence and the non-fluent bilingual. *Canadian Journal of Behavioural Science, 8*, 122–131.

Segalowitz, N. (1997). Individual differences in second language acquisition. In A. M. B. de Groot & J. F. Kroll (Eds.), *Tutorials in bilingualism: Psycholinguistic perspectives* (pp. 85–112). Mahwah, NJ: Lawrence Erlbaum Associates.

Segalowitz, N. (2003). Automaticity and second languages. In C. Doughty & M. Long (Eds.), *The handbook of second language acquisition* (pp. 382–408). Oxford, UK: Blackwell.

Segalowitz, N., & de Almeida, R.G. (2002). Conceptual representation of verbs in bilinguals: Semantic field effects and a second-language performance paradox. *Brain and Language, 81*, 517–531.

Segalowitz, N. & Freed, B.F. (2004). Context, contact and cognition in oral fluency acquisition: Learning Spanish in At Home and Study Abroad contexts. *Studies in Second Language Acquisition, 26*, 173–199.

Segalowitz, N. & Frenkiel-Fishman, S. (2005). Attention control and ability level in a complex cognitive skill: attention-shifting and second language proficiency. *Memory & Cognition, 33*, 644–653.

Segalowitz, N., & Gatbonton, E. (1995). Automaticity and lexical skills in a second language fluency: Implications for computer assisted language learning. *Computer Assisted Language Learning, 8*, 129–149.

Segalowitz, N., Gatbonton, E., & Trofimovich, P. (2009). Links between ethnolinguistic affiliation, self-related motivation and second language fluency: Are they mediated by psycholinguistic variables? In Z. Dörnyei & E. Ushioda (Eds.), *Motivation, language identity and the L2 Self* (pp. 172–192). Bristol, UK: Multilingual Matters.

Segalowitz, N., & Hulstijn, J. (2005). Automaticity in bilingualism and second language learning. In J. Kroll & A. De Groot (Eds.), *Handbook of bilingualism: Psycholinguistic approaches* (pp. 371–388). Oxford, UK: Oxford University Press.

Segalowitz, N., & Lightbown, P. (1999). Psycholinguistic approaches to SLA. *Annual Review of Applied Linguistics, 19*, 43–63.

Segalowitz, N., & Segalowitz, S. (1993). Skilled performance, practice and the differentiation of speed-up from automatization effects: Evidence from second language word recognition. *Applied Psycholinguistics, 14*, 369–385.

Segalowitz, N., Trofimovich, P., Gatbonton, E., & Sokolovskaya, A. (2008). Feeling the emotion of emotion words in a second language: The role of word recognition automaticity and of linguistic interaction with speakers of the target language. *The Mental Lexicon, 3*, 47–71.

Segalowitz, N., Watson, V., & Segalowitz, S. (1995). Vocabulary skill: Single case assessment of automaticity of word recognition in a timed lexical decision task. *Second Language Research, 11*, 121–136.

Segalowitz, S. J., Segalowitz, N., & Wood, A. (1998). Assessing the development of automaticity in second language word recognition. *Applied Psycholinguistics, 19*, 53–67.

Seliger, H. W., & Vago, R. M. (1991). *First language attrition*. Cambridge, UK: Cambridge University Press.

Seyfeddinipur, M., Kita, S., & Indefrey, P. (2008). How speakers interrupt themselves in managing problems in speaking: Evidence from self-repairs. *Cognition, 108*, 837–842.

Simon, J. R. (1969). Reactions towards the source of stimulation. *Journal of Experimental Psychology, 81*, 174–176.

Skehan, P. (1996). A framework for the implementation of task-based instruction. *Applied Linguistics, 17*, 38–62.

Skehan, P. (1998). *A cognitive approach to language learning*. Oxford, UK: Oxford University Press.

Skehan, P. (2003). Task based instruction. *Language Teaching, 36*, 1–14.

Skehan, P., & Foster, P. (2001). Cognition and tasks. In P. Robinson (Ed.), *Cognition and second language instruction* (pp. 183–205). Cambridge, UK: Cambridge University Press.

Skehan, P., & Foster, P. (2005). Strategic and on-line planning: The influence of surprise information and task time on second language performance. In R. Ellis (Ed.), *Planning and task performance in a second language* (pp.193–216). Amsterdam: John Benjamins.

Slifkin, A., & Newell, K. (1998). Is variability in human performance a reflection of system noise? *Current Directions in Psychological Science, 7,* 170–177.

Slobin, D. (1996). From "thought and language" to "thinking for speaking." In J. J. Gumperz & S. C. Levinson (Eds.), *Rethinking linguistic relativity* (pp. 70–96). Cambridge, UK: Cambridge University Press.

Slobin, D. (1997). The origins of grammaticizable notions: Beyond the individual mind. In D. Slobin (ed.), *The crosslinguistic study of language acquisition,* Vol. 5, *Expanding the contexts* (pp. 265–323). Mahwah, NJ: Lawrence Erlbaum Associates.

Song, H. S., & Schwarz, N. (2008). If it's hard to read, it's hard to do: Processing fluency affects effort prediction and motivation. *Psychological Science, 19,* 986–988.

Stainton, R. (2006). Preface. In R. Stainton (Ed.), *Contemporary debates in cognitive science* (pp. xiii–xiv). Oxford, UK: Blackwell.

Stanovich, K. (2000). *Progress in understanding reading.* New York: The Guilford Press.

Stevens, G. (2006). The age-length-onset problem in research on second language acquisition among immigrants. *Language Learning, 56,* 671–692.

Stoffregen, T. A. (2003). Affordances as properties of the animal-environment system. *Ecological Psychology, 15,* 115–134.

Stroop, J. R. (1935). Studies of interference in serial and verbal reactions. *Journal of Experimental Psychology, 18,* 643–662.

Stuss, D., Shallice, T., Alexander, M., & Picton, T. (1995). A multidisciplinary approach to anterior attentional functions. In J. Grafman, K. Holyoak, & F. Boller (Eds.), *Structure and functions of the human prefrontal cortex* (pp. 191–211). New York: New York Academy of Sciences.

Swain, M. (2005). The output hypothesis: Theory and research. In E. Hinkel (Ed.), *Handbook of research in second language teaching and learning* (pp. 471–483). Mahwah, NJ: Lawrence Erlbaum Associates.

Taguchi, T., Magid, M., & Papi, M. (2009). The L2 motivational self system among Japanese, Chinese and Iranian learners of English: A comparative study. In Z. Dörnyei & E. Ushioda (Eds.), *Motivation, language identity and the L2 self* (pp. 66–97). Bristol, UK: Multilingual Matters.

Talmy, L. (2001). *Towards a cognitive semantics,* Vol. 1. Cambridge, MA: MIT Press.

Talmy, L. (2008). Aspects of attention in language. In P. Robinson & N.C. Ellis (Eds.), *Handbook of cognitive linguistics and second language acquisition* (pp. 27–38). New York: Routledge.

Tallon-Baudry, C., & Bertrand, O. (1999). Oscillatory gamma activity in humans and its role in object representation. *Trends in Cognitive Sciences, 3,* 151–162.

Taube-Schiff, M., & Segalowitz, N. (2005a). Linguistic attention control: Attention-shifting governed by grammaticized elements of language. *Journal of Experimental Psychology: Learning, Memory and Cognition, 31*, 508–519.

Taube-Schiff, M., & Segalowitz, N. (2005b). Within-language attention control in second language processing. *Bilingualism: Language and Cognition, 8*, 195–206.

Tavakoli, P., & Foster, P. (2008). Task design and second language performance: the effect of narrative type on learner output. *Language Learning, 58*, 439–473.

Tavakoli, P., & Skehan, P. (2005). Strategic planning, task structure, and performance testing. In R. Ellis (Ed.), *Planning and task performance in a second language* (pp. 239–273). Amsterdam: John Benjamins.

Taylor, D., Meynard, R., & Rhéault, E. (1977). Threat to ethnic identity and second language learning. In H. Giles (Ed.), *Language, ethnicity, and intergroup relations* (pp. 98–118). London: Academic Press.

Thomas, M. (1998). Bilingualism and the single route/dual route debate. In M. A. Gernsbacher & S. J. Derry (Eds.), *Proceedings of the 20th Annual Conference of the Cognitive Science Society* (pp. 1061–1066). Mahwah, NJ: Lawrence Erlbaum Associates.

Thomas, M. (2005). Computational models of bilingual comprehension. In J. Kroll & A. De Groot (Eds.), *Handbook of bilingualism: Psycholinguistic approaches* (pp. 202–225). Oxford, UK: Oxford University Press.

Tomasello, M. (1999). *The cultural origins of human cognition.* Cambridge, MA: Harvard University Press.

Tomasello, M. (2000). First steps toward a usage-based theory of language acquisition. *Cognitive Linguistics, 11*, 61–82.

Tomasello, M. (2003). *Constructing a language.* Cambridge, MA: Harvard University Press.

Tomlin, R., & Villa, V. (1994). Attention in cognitive science and second language acquisition. *Studies in Second Language Acquisition, 16*, 183–203.

Towell, R., & Hawkins, R. (1994). *Approaches to second language acquisition.* Clevedon: Multilingual Matters.

Towell, R., Hawkins, R., & Bazergui, N. (1996). The development of fluency in advanced learners of French. *Applied Linguistics, 17*, 84–119.

Treisman, A.M. (1964). Selective attention in man. *British Medical Bulletin, 20*, 12–16.

Trofimovich, P., Ammar, A., & Gatbonton, E. (2007). How effective are recasts? The role of attention, memory and analytical ability. In A. Mackey (Ed.), *Conversational interaction in second language acquisition: A series of empirical studies* (pp. 171–195). Oxford, UK: Oxford University Press.

Trofimovich, P., & Gatbonton, E. (2006). Repetition and focus on form in L2 Spanish word processing: Implications for pronunciation instruction. *Modern Language Journal, 90*, 519–535.

Trofimovich, P., Gatbonton, E., & Segalowitz, N. (2007). A dynamic look at L2 phonological learning: Investigating effects of cross-language similarity and input frequency. *Studies in Second Language Acquisition, 29*, 407–448.

Tucker, G. R. (1997). Multilingualism and language contact: An introduction. *Annual Review of Applied Linguistics, 17*, 3–10.

Tulving, E. (1983). *Elements of episodic memory*. Oxford, UK: Oxford University Press.

Tulving, E., & Thomson, D. (1973). Encoding specificity and retrieval processes in episodic memory. *Psychological Review, 80*, 352–373.

Turner, M. (1991). *Reading minds*. Princeton: Princeton University Press.

Turvey, M.T. (1992). Affordances and prospective control: An outline of the ontology. *Ecological Psychology, 4*, 173–187.

Tversky, B., & Kahneman, D. (1973). Availability: A heuristic for judging frequency and probability. *Cognitive Psychology, 5*, 207–232.

Tyler, A. (2008). Cognitive linguistics and second language instruction. In P. Robinson & N. Ellis (Eds.), *Handbook of cognitive linguistics and second language acquisition* (pp. 456–488). New York: Routledge.

Tzelgov, J., Henik, A., Sneg, R., & Baruch, O. (1996). Unintentional word reading via the phonological route: The Stroop effect with cross-script homophones. *Journal of Experimental Psychology: Learning, Memory and Cognition, 22*, 336–349.

Ullman, M.T. (2001). The neural basis of lexicon and grammar in first and second language: The declarative/procedural model. *Bilingualism: Language and Cognition, 4*, 105–122.

Underwood, G., Schmitt, N., & Galpin, A. (2004). The eyes have it: An eye-movement study into the processing of formulaic sequences. In N. Schmitt (Ed.), *Formulaic sequences* (pp. 153–172). Amsterdam: John Benjamins.

Van den Bergh, O., Vrana, S., & Eelen, P. (1990). Letters from the heart: Affective categorization of letter combinations in types and nontypists. *Journal of Experimental Psychology: Learning, Memory and Cognition, 16*, 1153–1161.

Van den Branden, K., Bygate, M., & Norris, J. M. (2009). *Task-based language teaching: A reader*. Amsterdam: John Benjamins.

Van Gelder, T. (1998). The dynamical hypothesis in cognitive science. *Behavioral and Brain Sciences, 21*, 615–628.

Van Lier, L. (2000). From input to affordances: Socio-interactive learning from an ecological perspective. In J. Lantolf (Ed.), *Sociocultural theory and second language learning* (pp. 245–259). Oxford, UK: Oxford University Press.

Van Patten, B. (Ed.) (2004). *Processing instruction: Theory, research, and commentary*. Mahwah, NJ: Lawrence Erlbaum Associates.

Vygotsky, L. (1978). *Mind in society: The development of higher psychological processes*. Cambridge, MA: Harvard University Press.

Wagenmakers, E.-J., & Brown, S. (2007). On the linear relation between the mean and the standard deviation of a response time distribution. *Psychological Review, 114*, 830–841.

Wagenmakers, E.-J., Grasman, R., & Molenaar, P. (2005). On the relation between the mean and the variance of a diffusion model response time distribution. *Journal of Mathematical Psychology, 49*, 195–204.

Walters, J. (2005). *Bilingualism: The sociopragmatic-psycholinguistic interface*. Mahwah, NJ: Lawrence Erlbaum Associates.

Ward, L. (2002). *Dynamic cognitive science*. Cambridge, MA: MIT Press.

Warren, W.H. (1984). Perceiving affordances: Visual guidance of stair climbing. *Journal of Experimental Psychology: Human Perception and Performance, 10*, 683–703.

Wascher, E., Schatz, U., Kuder, T., & Verleger, R. (2001). Validity and boundary conditions of automatic response activation in the Simon Task. *Journal of Experimental Psychology: Human Perception and Performance, 27*, 731–751.

Weber-Fox, C., Davis, L., & Cuadrado, E. (2003). Event-related brain potential markers of high-language proficiency in adults. *Brain and Language, 85*, 231–244.

Weber-Fox, C., & Neville, H. (1996). Maturational constraints on functions specializations for language processing: ERP and behavioral evidence in bilingual speakers. *Journal of Cognitive Neuroscience, 8*, 231–256.

Weber-Fox, C., & Neville, H. (2001). Sensitive periods differentiate processing of open- and closed-class words: An ERP study of bilinguals. *Journal of Speech, Language, and Hearing Research, 44*, 1338–1353.

White, L. (1990). Second language acquisition and universal grammar. *Studies in Second Language Acquisition, 12*, 121–133.

White, L. (2003). *Second language acquisition and universal grammar.* Cambridge, UK: Cambridge University Press.

Whittlesea, B., Jacoby, L., & Girard, K. (1990). Illusions of immediate memory: Evidence of an attributional basis for feelings of familiarity and perceptual quality. *Journal of Memory and Language, 29*, 716–732.

Whittlesea, B., & Leboe, J. (2003). Two fluency heuristics (and how to tell them apart). *Journal of Memory and Language, 49*, 62–79.

Whittlesea, B., & Williams, L. (1998). Why do strangers feel familiar, but friends don't? A discrepancy-attribution account of feelings of familiarity. *Acta Psychologica, 98*, 141–165.

Whittlesea, B., & Williams, L. (2000). The source of feelings of familiarity: the discrepancy-attribution hypothesis. *Journal of Experimental Psychology: Learning, Memory and Cognition, 26*, 547–565.

Wilkins, D. P. (2006). Towards an Arrernte grammar of space. In S. C. Levinson and D. P. Wilkins (Eds.), *Grammars of space: Explorations in cognitive diversity* (pp. 24–62). Cambridge, UK: Cambridge University Press.

Wilks, C., & Meara, P. M. (2002). Untangling word webs: graph theory and the notion of density in second language association networks. *Second Language Research, 18*, 303–324.

Wimmer, H., & Perner, J. (1983). Beliefs about beliefs: Representation and constraining function of wrong beliefs in young children's understanding of deception. *Cognition, 13*, 103–128.

Wingfield, A., Goodglass, H., & Lindfield, K. (1997). Separating speed from automaticity in a patient with focal brain atrophy. *Psychological Science, 8*, 247–249.

Wong Fillmore, L. (1979). Individual differences in second language acquisition. In C. J. Fillmore, D. Kempler, & W. S.-Y. Wang (Eds.), *Individual differences in language ability and language behavior* (pp. 203–228). New York: Academic Press.

Wood, D. (2001). In search of fluency: What is it and how can we teach it? *Canadian Modern Language Review, 57*(4), 573–589.

Wray, A. (2000). Formulaic sequences in second language teaching: principles and practice. *Applied Linguistics, 21*, 463–489.

Wray, A. (2002). *Formulaic language and the lexicon*. Cambridge, UK: Cambridge University Press.

Wray, A. (2008). *Formulaic language: Pushing the boundaries*. Oxford, UK: Oxford University Press.

Yang, S., Gallo, D., & Beilock, S. L. (2009). Embodied memory judgments: A case of motor fluency. *Journal of Experiment Psychology: Learning, Memory, and Cognition, 35*, 1359–1365.

Young, R. (1999). Sociolinguistic approaches to SLA. *Annual Review of Applied Linguistics, 19*, 105–132.

Young, R., & He, A. W. (Eds.) (1998). *Talking and testing: Discourse approaches to the assessment of oral proficiency*. Amsterdam: John Benjamins.

Zatorre, R. (1989). On the representation of multiple languages in the brain: Old problems and new directions. *Brain and Language, 36*, 127–147.

Index

Entries in bold refer to Figures and Tables